MW01126127

ADVANCE PRAISE FOR SOCIAL VISION:
The Lubavitcher Rebbe's Transformative Paradigm for the World

During my several visits with Rabbi Menachem M. Schneerson, I experienced firsthand his kindness and his compassion for all humanity. The Rebbe expressed to me his view that we are all children of God, regardless of our race or religion, and we must all work together for the betterment of the entire society. He urged me to join him as we aim to transform the entire world, and especially encourage all children to personally give charity with their own hands. The Rebbe's social vision is a timeless message that should be an inspiration for all people.

David N. Dinkins, 106th Mayor of the City of New York

Contra sociology's view of secular modernity as represented in particular by Max Weber, Philip Wexler has written a remarkable study of Menachem Mendel Schneerson, in which he shows how the mystical and social dimensions of Hasidic teaching are a force towards the resacralization and re-enchantment of the modern world. In this original and innovative study, combining Hasidic and sociological understanding of the well-being of the individual and the flourishing of society, Wexler expounds on the Rebbe's social vision as inclusive, dynamic and modern. In celebrating the freedom made possible through the dialectic of exile and redemption in secular America, Schneerson's social vision also paved the way for a global Jewish renaissance.

Bryan S. Turner, Presidential Professor and Director of the Committee for the Study of Religion, The Graduate Center, City University of New York

A consistently insightful account of how Rabbi Menachem Mendel Schneerson's understanding of Judaism offered a vision to transform the life of the individual and, through the individual, the world. Wexler's wide-ranging knowledge of the sources is apparent but his presentation of even highly scholarly material is always accessible. This book can elevate your mind and your soul.

Joseph Telushkin, author of *Rebbe: The Life and Teachings of Menachem M. Schneerson, the Most Influential Rabbi in Modern History*

Philip Wexler has spent a good portion of his academic career, evinced in his earlier *Mystical Society*, fleshing out the relation between religion and society. Now, along with Eli Rubin and Michael Wexler, he has taken this noble pursuit further by examining in detail the spiritual and social vision of the Lubavitcher Rebbe: Menachem Mendel Schneerson. Banking off the noted Weberian thesis concerning the rise of a disenchanted world and a soulless capitalism, Wexler finds the antidote in the resacralization and reenchantment offered through Rebbe Schneerson's thought and ethos. Valorizing not alienated individuality and selfish hoarding but interdependence, mutuality, reciprocity and communality, this book offers a social vision, touching on matters of importance from individual reformation to education to justice that is the needed prescription for our times. It should be read widely with great care and an openness to heed the call for sorely needed transformative action.

William B. Parsons, Professor of Religion and Culture, Rice University

Through a fresh and compelling reading of the writings of Max Weber, Philip Wexler exposes deep structures of contemporary social reality. Then, in an excitingly bold move, Wexler reads Hasidic teachings as a joyous, love-centered, intensely communal counterpoint for the bleak landscape painted by the early giant of sociology. Seemingly esoteric religious texts are skillfully transformed into manifestoes for 'wholly contemporary' engagement, interwoven with American reality. At the same time, the cosmic and the social converge in a panoramic vision of transformative reciprocity. Indeed, reciprocity may well become the foundation of fresh sociological thought. *Social Vision* is a model for socially meaningful scholarly writing. It heralds the advent of prophetic sociology.

Professor Jonathan Garb, Gershom Scholem Chair in Kabbalah,
The Hebrew University of Jerusalem

In recent years, there has been a steady increase of scholarly books and essays on Menachem Mendel Schneerson, the seventh master in the Habad-Lubavitch dynasty. *Social Vision: The Lubavitcher Rebbe's Transformative Paradigm for the World*, written by Philip Wexler, in collaboration with Eli Rubin and Michael Wexler, presents a unique approach by putting emphasis on the social dimensions of Schneerson's teaching, revealing thereby the theoretical novelty and supreme practicality of his worldview. Avoiding an artificial split between the mystical and the social, Wexler's work offers a cross-disciplinary method that bridges phenomenology and sociology, especially locating Schneerson in social theory discourse beginning with the work of Weber. *Social Vision* is an uncompromisingly sophisticated but eminently accessible study of one of the fascinating religious figures of the twentieth century. This book is a culmination of Wexler's intellectual odyssey, advocating, to some extent against the grain, for understanding religion as a handmaiden of a new sociology. The fruit of many years of study and reflection has produced a book that confirms that there is no conceptual ground to distinguish in Schneerson's mind between social reality and mystical truth. As one well versed in sociology, Wexler has demonstrated that the commonplace distinction between elite and popular forms of religiosity is not a viable paradigm to understand Hasidism, particularly exemplified by the evolution of Habad in America. The social is infused with the mystical and the mystical with the social. Wexler, in partnership with Rubin, has produced a book that amply demonstrates the need to avoid disentangling the ethnographic and phenomenological threads. I am confident that *Social Vision* will not only find a wide readership but that it will significantly advance the author's desideratum to forge a new theoretical framework that reunites religious studies and sociology.

Elliot R. Wolfson, Marsha and Jay Glazer Chair in Jewish Studies,
University of California, Santa Barbara

In their book, *Social Vision: The Lubavitcher Rebbe's Transformative Paradigm for the World*, sociologist Philip Wexler, with Eli Rubin and Michael Wexler, beautifully elucidate and theorize the life-work and underlying core principles of Menachem Mendel Schneerson, the seventh Rebbe of Chabad-Lubavitch (1902-1994). Placing Schneerson's vision for a global social-spiritual transformation, the authors trace the beginnings of Chassidism in eighteenth-century Eastern Europe to its twentieth-century home in Brooklyn, New York, where Schneerson developed his extraordinary loving and joyful vision for a sacralized humanity. Special attention is paid here to the role of women as active social agents both in the home and in the world, and to the intimate social community of the Lubavitcher farbrengen (gatherings), where music becomes a vehicle for devekuth (adherence to God). An extraordinary portrait of a visionary leader whose message continues to be both relevant and imperative for us, today.

Ellen Koskoff, Professor of Ethnomusicology, Emerita,
the University of Rochester's Eastman School of Music,
Author of *Music in Lubavitcher Life*

Against the popular-secularist penchant for seeing the resurgence of religion and its perils, Philip Wexler offers in this book an original, if not provocative thesis, on the mystical-social potential of the Hasidic vision of the late Lubavitcher Rebbe, Rabbi Menachem M. Schneerson. Recognizing Schneerson as a charismatic, even prophetic, social visionary, the book explores Schneerson's writings on the self, family, community, politics and education in order to argue that the late Rebbe, an incisive social thinker, offered us a new social, cultural, mental, and moral order and placed it on the agenda of history. Informed by cutting edge scholarship on Hasidism as well as critical social theory, and avoiding the pitfalls of a messianic reductive analysis, Wexler's artful and engaging study will be of great interest to scholars of religion, spirituality and society and to educated readers alike.

Rachel Werczberger, Professor of Sociology, Ariel University

This ambitious volume sets forth the social vision of Rabbi Menachem M. Schneerson, the Lubavitcher Rebbe, and places it within the context of modern social thought. Well-chosen quotations illuminate the Rebbe's distinctive views on American society, the role of the individual and the community, the purpose of education, and much more. A bracing introduction to the central ideas that shaped Chabad-Lubavitch in America, and that continue to inspire the Rebbe's disciples in their quest to change the world.

Jonathan D. Sarna, Joseph H. & Belle R. Braun Professor
of American Jewish History, Brandeis University,
Author of *American Judaism: A History*

With power and panache, Philip Wexler documents the public pedagogy of Rabbi Schneerson, demonstrating its educational significance: bridging faiths, unifying souls, sacralising the mundane, a civic religiosity animated by joy. This is teaching in service to subjective and social reconstruction, in Wexler's wise words constructing "our redemption out of the world we inhabit in the present." Wexler invokes the great Rabbi's "gatherings," explaining that these "mass events" were also "deeply personal." This book promises to be both.

William F. Pinar, Professor and Canada Research Chair,
University of British Columbia

Social Vision offers readers a compelling way to understand the vast contributions of Rabbi Menachem Mendel Schneerson to world Jewry. Philip Wexler understands the towering, spiritual visionary the "Rebbe" truly was and the lingering and complex impact of his leadership across the globe. Much is to be learned on these pages in re-thinking leadership for an emerging generation.

Erica **Brown**, Director, Mayberg Center for Jewish Education
and Leadership, Associate professor of curriculum and instruction,
The George Washington University

Philip Wexler and companions have written a remarkably bold and challenging book. Its original, insightful thesis proposes that Hasdism presents a radical social movement that provides a paradigmatic alternative for individuals and communities to the Weberian iron cage of capitalism. The Hasidic ethos and socially embodied practices, they contend, offer a new foundation for a sacralised global society. The book will appeal to scholars of Jewish spirituality, and challenge sociologists of religion and social movements with its innovative theoretical model. It will certainly enliven debate on the post-secular turn and invite rich reflection on the vision and teaching of the Lubavitcher Rebbe.

Catherine **Casey**, Professor of Organization and Society,
Loughborough University, UK

Wexler's *Social Vision* is a sweeping and a daring engagement with the Hassidic socio-mystical ethos—as charted, in particular, by Menachem Mendel Schneerson, the seventh Rebbe of Chabad-Lubavitch. Compellingly showing the extent to which Schneerson's Hasidic mysticism is fundamentally social, Wexler's book provides the reader with an insightful and comprehensive account of a critical analysis out of the sources of Jewish mysticism. *Social Vision* is a rich and vibrant examination of how Schneerson's critique of modernity aimed at transgressing the "iron cage" of mechanized petrification and how it entailed a viable universal social vision that provided a new paradigm for individual life, human relations, social institutions, and politics. Wexler presents us once again with an overarching, knowledgeable and ambitious study that challenges the great divide between religion and society, modernity and theology, faith and political action, while breaking new ground for social theory.

Yotam **Hotam**, Faculty of Education, University of Haifa

SOCIAL VISION

SOCIAL VISION

The Lubavitcher Rebbe's Transformative Paradigm for the World

PHILIP WEXLER
with
Eli Rubin & Michael Wexler

A Herder & Herder Book
The Crossroad Publishing Company
New York

A Herder & Herder Book
The Crossroad Publishing Company www.crossroadpublishing.com

© 2019 by Philip Wexler

Crossroad, Herder & Herder, and the crossed C logo/colophon are registered trademarks of The Crossroad Publishing Company.

All rights reserved. No part of this book may be copied, scanned, reproduced in any way, or stored in a retrieval system, or transmitted, in any form or by any means, electronic, mechanical, photocopying, recording, or otherwise, without the written permission of The Crossroad Publishing Company. For permission please write to rights@crossroadpublishing.com.

In continuation of our 200-year tradition of independent publishing, The Crossroad Publishing Company proudly offers a variety of books with strong, original voices and diverse perspectives. The viewpoints expressed in our books are not necessarily those of The Crossroad Publishing Company, any of its imprints, or of its employees, executives, or owners. Although the author and publisher have made every effort to ensure that the information in this book was correct at press time, the author and publisher do not assume and hereby disclaim any liability to any party for any loss, damage, or disruption caused by errors or omissions, whether such errors or omissions result from negligence, accident, or any other cause. No claims are made or responsibility assumed for any health or other benefits.

The text of this book is set in 11.4/14 Janson MT Pro.

Composition by Rachel Reiss
Cover design by Sophie Apel

LIBRARY OF CONGRESS CATALOGING-IN-PUBLICATION DATA
available upon request from the Library of Congress.

ISBN 978-0-8245-5038-7 cloth
ISBN 978-0-8245-5041-7 ePub
ISBN 978-0-8245-5042-4 mobi

Books published by The Crossroad Publishing Company may be purchased at special quantity discount rates for classes and institutional use. For information, please e-mail sales@crossroadpublishing.com.

CONTENTS

᠖᠎᠔

IN SEARCH OF A NEW BEGINNING: AN INTRODUCTORY RETROSPECTIVE

by Philip Wexler

their end contained in their beginning,
their beginning in their end,
like coals and a lambent flame
           —SEFER YETSIRAH, TRANSLATED BY PETER COLE[1]

MAINSTREAM CULTURE, MAINSTREAM politics, and mainstream intellectual discourse all seem increasingly and inexorably commercialized, reduced either to tokenism, or to frivolity, if not to endless futility and to the weighty grind of work, work, work.

Is there a way to repair society?

Alongside the mainstream of contemporary cultural life and academic discourse, there is an alternate and intersecting stream—a kind of counterculture—that is increasingly visible, and which increasingly seems to gather strength and to inspire new forms of engagement. I refer here to an emergent Jewish mystical culture that is not closeted or ghettoized, but seeks to engage the world, to change the world, to intervene on the global stage of history, to advance a universal good. And yet, it is precisely the particularisms, or idiosyncrasies, of this "counterculture"—and its juxtapositional proximity to the contemporary mainstream—that make it such a compelling source of new social ideas.

Might the Jewish mystical alternative provide a new paradigm, a transformative path via which we can extricate ourselves from bureaucratic drudgery and dehumanization?

Some dismiss the Lubavitcher Rebbe (Menachem Mendel Schneerson, 1902-1994) as a mere avatar of popular Jewish spirituality in the post-war era, or even as a failed messiah; a leader only for the deluded. But as Elliot Wolfson has shown in his magisterial *Open Secret*, Schneerson's deeply complex and original reinterpretation of the kabbalistic wisdom traditions cannot be ignored.[2] Schneerson was not only a charismatic religious leader, but also a scholar, mystic, and philosopher. A systematic reading of his transcribed talks and published writings reveals the breadth, depth, and complexity of his learning and of his thought. Wolfson's sweeping study showed that Schneerson's intellectual legacy entails a "mystical revision" that is as radical as it is challenging. It is partly due to its sheer esotericism that the significance and ramifications of Schneerson's contribution still remain to be more widely appreciated.

The work that I undertake in this book is a move from Schneerson's "mystical revision" to what can be termed his "social revision." It is a move that seeks to reveal the supreme practicality, as well as the theoretical novelty, of the Lubavitcher Rebbe's vision for society. Crucially, however, I make this move without leaving the mystical and esoteric dimension behind. As far as possible, the goal is to communicate the fullness of his social ideas, without reducing the cosmic weight of their mystical significance. This is not a purely sociological investigation, but rather a cross-disciplinary intervention that bridges religious studies—particularly the disciplinary bounds of Jewish mysticism and Hasidism—with classical sociology and social theory. On the latter score, the goal is to locate Schneerson in the wider disciplinary discourse, beginning with the paradigmatic work of Max Weber (1864-1920).

In the introductory retrospective that follows I would like to say something about my own scholarly journey over the course of the last twenty years, and how I came to write this book. I would also like to say something about religion as the handmaiden of a new sociology, about the

sociological relevance of Hasidism in the twenty-first century, and about
the fruitfulness of interdisciplinary and intercommunal interaction.

Religion as the Handmaiden of a New Sociology

WEBERIAN CONCEPTS, NOTABLY charisma and authority, are imported
to religious and Jewish studies as a matter of course. Yet the wider system of meaning that generates those specific categories is too often set
aside, even ignored. A corrective to this trend is especially relevant in
the present context because Weber's wider system of analytic meaning
speaks to our times, and can help us to make sense of the still vibrant—
indeed, resurgent—currents of religion in society. But it is even more
relevant if we want to discover a "social revision," an alternate paradigm
for society, a new path that exceeds the normative bounds of secularized progress and scientific bureaucratization. To discover something
different we need to understand what it is different from, and so we
must begin with Weber, who provided us with the clearest conception
of the modern social paradigm of our current habitation.

For Weber the economic motor of modern social life is the translation
of an ascetic Protestantism ("the Protestant ethic") into a secularized
vocationalism ("the spirit of capitalism")—a culture of specialization,
of expertise, of methodical precision and calculation, of bureaucracy,
and, above all, of rationalization. This paradigm displaces an earlier
world of direct personal relations, enforcing in its place the materialistic instrumentalism that now seems all but inescapable.[3]

Yet it was precisely my desire to find a sociological route by which
to escape this paradigm that led me to leave my career in traditional
sociology behind, and to extend the horizons of my research to include
the Jewish mystical tradition. In 2000 I resigned as dean of the Warner
School of Education at the University of Rochester and took up a fellowship at the Shalom Hartman Institute in Jerusalem. This was a turn
to religion, and to Jewish studies, but, as I will soon explain, it was also
a return to the roots of the very tradition from whose bounds I sought
to release myself. I subsequently took up a post at the Hebrew University of Jerusalem, keeping one foot in the world of religious studies and
Jewish mysticism while continuing my work in sociology as chair of the
School of Education.

To me it seems that Émile Durkheim's defense of his own preoccupation with the sociology of religion is well worth appropriating:

> The according of the first rank to this sort of phenomenon has produced some astonishment, but it is these phenomena which are the germ from which all others—or at least almost all others—are derived. Religion contains in itself from the very beginning, even if in indistinct state, all the elements which in dissociating themselves from it, articulating themselves, and combining with one another in a thousand ways, have given rise to the manifestations of collective life...One cannot understand our perception of the world...if one does not know the religious beliefs which are their primordial forms.[4]

In order to find the way toward a new form for "the manifestations of collective life," I reasoned, it was necessary to once again begin taking religion seriously. My purpose was not merely to make religion the subject of my sociological research, but also to make sociology the subject of new disciplinary insights, new theoretical models. Perhaps sacrilegiously, my not-so-secret wish was to make religion the handmaiden of a new sociology. There were two primary issues that called me to seek a new sociological beginning: (1) the need to open a path by which humanity could be extricated from the petrifying straits—what Weber called the "iron cage" or "steel shell"—of the capitalist order, and (2) the need to explain why religion had not only survived the scientific revolution, but was indeed thriving and giving birth to an array of new forms, even as the old institutions of religion increasingly lose their credibility.

My interest in Kabbalah and Hasidism began while I was still in Rochester, where Nehemia Vogel was an early partner in my study of Chabad ideas, and where I first began to consume the relevant academic literature. But in Jerusalem I found myself in the company of the leading academic scholars in the field. With Moshe Idel, Jonathan Garb, and others, I began to enter into the critical, textual, and historical study of an ancient wisdom tradition whose indigenous scholars and practitioners also thrive in their own Jerusalem academies and communities. On the pretext of ethnographic research I entered some of these spaces too, and was especially interested in the pedagogic methods and student experience at the Mayanot Institute of Jewish Studies, a Chabad school that engages students with minimal prior Judaic knowledge in the direct study of classical Jewish legal and mystical texts, while also immersing them in a Jewish communal experience in which everyday life practice is prescribed by the very texts they study. I still have much "uncooked" material from my participating, observing, and interviewing, but for now all that must be left aside. The relevance here is that this provided me with the opportunity to read Chabad texts not only from the outside, but from within the indigenous world of Chabad's own pedagogical tradition.

I was drawn to the pedagogical openness of the Hasidic teachers at Mayanot, which I later discerned to be innate to Chabad's ethos of education and communication. Moreover, the pertinence of the ideas and practices of Hasidism to contemporary social issues and social analytical problems led me to agitate for a deeper meeting between Hasidism and sociology, a meeting that would work through and beyond the crises of contemporary Western culture and of academic social science. I was also drawn more and more to the mystery of the man who inspired the Chabad teachers I encountered and studied with, the man they called "the Rebbe."

Who was Menachem Mendel Schneerson?

At that time, there was not a single scholarly monograph that tried to answer this question. Even now there is only one that does so with any seriousness, but its orientation is fundamentally phenomenological, rather than sociological (here I refer again to Wolfson's *Open Secret*). In recent years we have also seen several important articles from scholars such as Ada Rapoport-Albert, Naftali Loewenthal, and Don Seeman, which are likewise not merely concerned with Chabad in a general way—as either a mystical movement or a social movement—but which indeed begin to cast light on Schneerson's mystical vision *of* society, and *for* society.[5]

It is this deeper meeting between Hasidism and sociology—and more particularly, between Schneerson and critical social theory—that drove me and drew me into the world of Hasidism, Chabad, and the Lubavitcher Rebbe. I sensed the promise of a new system, a social path that has so far been taken up only outside of the mainstream of contemporary life. To borrow a Weberian turn of phrase, it has only been taken up "pianissimo."[6] As the religion scholar Jeffrey Kripal has argued, the mainstream of society relegates all that is perceived as "mystical" and "paranormal" to the realm of pop culture, a domain that ostensibly lies outside the critical reach of science and the rational assumptions by which society is governed.[7]

The pioneering scholars of Hasidic mysticism, Martin Buber (1878-1965) and Gershom Scholem (1897-1982), agreed that Hasidism is "Kabbalah become ethos."[8] This means that while it is rooted in esoteric mysticism it nevertheless becomes a this-worldly social form, a way of being in the world, a way of building an everyday communal practice that pulsates with transcendent meaning—or in Weber's language, with something "that corresponds to the prophetic pneuma."[9] In other words, Hasidism does not bifurcate the paranormal from ordinary life in the world, but rather integrates the paranormal within the normal.

I do not wish to make do with a "pianissimo" account of one aspect or another of Hasidism's social theories and practices. Rather I take on the larger task of describing the fuller possibility of a global "risorgimento," a global resurgence of the mystical in a form that will not shatter the world but repair it. Menachem Mendel Schneerson, I will argue, was more than the herald of such a resurgence. Through his own activist teaching he provided a complete blueprint for a new mode of being in the world, and set the ripples of resurgence in motion. His own pedagogical method, which will be described at some length below, did not merely translate Kabbalah into ethos, but took the additional step of translating Kabbalah into activism. To be clear, this was not a reductive shift *from* Kabbalah *to* activism. He never left Chabad's deeply contemplative approach to the mystical tradition behind. Instead he implanted its contemplative beginning in its activist end, and its activist end in its contemplative beginning. Schneerson's oft-repeated motto, "action is the main thing," emphasized that his kabbalistic theorizations of Torah law and lore were themselves a form of activism.[10]

Schneerson was not only a religious leader and theorist, but also an engineer of social change, engagement, and participation. He was a brilliant tactician who re-created and galvanized a transformative social movement. The purpose of this book is to get "under the hood" and understand not only the theoretical and practical axioms of his tactical agenda, but also the full extent of his vision for society. In his own view at least, Schneerson's theoretical and practical agenda was to provide a new basis for social repair, for the restoration of both interpersonal

meaning and individual significance, on a scale that starts with the local and extends to the global. This book takes Schneerson at his own
word, critically engaging his social ideas and exposing them to scrutiny.

Was Schneerson concerned only with the Jewish people, with narrow interests of religion and peoplehood, or did he also have a broader
agenda for humanity, an agenda with universal application? Clearly
Schneerson wanted to change the world, but what is the nature of the
change that he envisioned? How would it come about? What sets him
apart from other changemakers, from other social theorists and cultural critics? In a word, we ask the question: what did Schneerson want?

The Sociological Relevance of Hasidism
in the Twenty-First Century

HERE AND THERE Weber himself briefly entertained the possibility of
the socio-mystical alternative that I perceive in Hasidism. According
to Weber, the Protestant ethic is an example of a religious typology
dubbed "inner-worldly asceticism," juxtaposed with "other-worldly asceticism," "other-worldly mysticism," and "inner-worldly mysticism."
He devotes the least attention to the last of these typologies.[11] In his
view, even an inner-worldly mystic—that is, a mystic who does not seek
to escape the world entirely—is unlikely to intervene in society, and
he only grudgingly admits the phenomenon of mystical communities:

> A typical mystic is never a man of conspicuous social activity,
> nor is he at all prone to accomplish any rational transforma-
> tion of the mundane order on the basis of a methodical pattern
> of life directed toward external success. Wherever genuine
> mysticism did give rise to communal action, such action was
> characterized by the acosmism of the mystical feeling of love.
> Mysticism may exert this kind of psychological effect, thus
> tending—despite the apparent demands of logic—to favor
> the creation of communities.[12]

It was this conception of mysticism that Rivka Schatz-Uffenheimer
echoed in the title of her book, *Hasidism as Mysticism*. It is little wonder that she felt the need to argue that Chabad was an anti-spiritualist

aberration in the mystical, "quietistic" pantheon of Hasidism.[13] The fact that she never mentions Weber by name only underscores the degree to which his categories of religious typology have become axiomatic in scholarly literature, and indeed to all our collective cultural assumptions. The same reductive equation—according to which mysticism is synonymous with acosmistic indifference to the world—has often led outsiders, including some scholars, to regard Hasidism with suspicion and disdain. If the Hasidism were "genuine" mystics, why are Hasidic doctrine and culture sometimes seen to embrace the world in all its crass materiality? Why and how did Hasidism build such vibrant social institutions and evolve into a multi-stranded social movement? Weber did not regard the inner-worldly mystics as charlatans, as did some opponents of Hasidism.[14] But he did insist that their tendency to favor the creation of communities was an affront to "the apparent demands of logic."

On this score I disagree with Weber. Perhaps due to the strictures of history and geography, Weber failed to support his characterization of "inner-worldly mysticism" with empirical examples. But we are not so impoverished. We have before us the example of Hasidism, and more particularly that of the Lubavitcher Rebbe, with an abundance of source material that can be mined for new social concepts and for new social practices. Weber's reductive characterization needs to be cast aside, and a new understanding of "inner-worldly mysticism" needs to be adduced from within the indigenous teachings of the Hasidic tradition. My view is that this alternative religious type—which Weber identified but marginalized—actually has the capacity to replace the dominant paradigm of "inner-worldly asceticism" (the Protestant ethic) as the foundation of a new culture, as a new beginning for our broken society.

I first gave voice to my disagreement with Weber, and first pointed to the example of Hasidism, in a book titled *The Mystical Society: An Emerging Social Vision*, published in 2000.[15] A few years later Randall Collins pointed to an additional example of what he prefers to term "mysticism in-the-world," in which he suggested that the Franciscan friars, inspired by St. Francis of Assisi, constituted "the first radical left-wing social movement."[16] The Franciscans constituted a "social movement in religious guise, but with the social-humanitarian ends, and the reaching out to a hitherto ignored constituency that pointed the way toward modern altruistic social movements." His theorization is worth citing more fully:

A mystic inside the monastery is necessarily limited in what he or she can see; implicitly their community is that of the elite world of the monks and nuns surrounding them. A mystic-in-the-world, however, sees God everywhere; that means to see society everywhere, community everywhere. The universalism of humanitarian social movements is born at that moment.[17]

Collins goes on to suggest that "the humanitarianism and pantheism of Green environmentalists" can be seen as a contemporary instantiation of a semi-secularized "mysticism-in-the-world."[18] In a more recent paper, two younger scholars followed Collins' lead, using more contemporary examples to argue that "mystical practices can create meaningful social change," that "inner-worldly mysticism holds the potential to generate solidarity across traditional power and status divides," and that "the number of small groups committed to carrying out inner-worldly mystical practices can grow until such groups spread across communities and beyond."[19]

In broad terms I concur with these analyses, which are aligned with my own.[20] Yet, in my estimation, Hasidism is both more developed and more relevant as an example of how transformative inner-worldly mysticism can be; while the Franciscan movement arose in the Middle Ages, the Hasidic movement arose in the modern era. This distinction is all the more acute in the case of Schneerson, a Hasidic leader who sought to address some of the most pressing social and political problems of our own age, including criminal justice reform, education reform, and the intersecting problems of geopolitics, human rights, and renewable energy. Significantly, he addressed these issues from an explicitly Hasidic and mystical perspective, and did not simply assent to agendas emanating from sources external to his own tradition. Moreover, by taking up the example of Hasidism and transcending the bounds of Christian hegemony, we have the further advantage of entertaining a much starker set of alternative concepts and practices. The combination of Chabad's radical alterity to the reigning paradigm, together with its juxtapositional visibility on the periphery of contemporary American culture, makes the transformative potential of Schneerson's social vision all the more intriguing.

Mystical Interactions: Sociology, Jewish Mysticism, and Education was published in 2007.[21] That book represents the development of my intuitions into a coherent methodological approach, working out the sociological basis for a mystical sociology, and applying it in practice as a tool of social analysis. The traditions of classical sociology and kabbalistic theory, I argued, need to be brought into collaborative interaction in order to describe and explain social phenomena and social possibilities in ways that go beyond normative disciplinary bounds. Sociologists were increasingly recognizing that the assumed unilinear tendency toward secularization has been usurped by a salient movement toward resacralization. This is an empirical historical phenomenon, and I argued that it calls for a corresponding change in the principles of the sociological discipline itself, in its governing concepts and explanatory language. Grace Davie, a well known British sociologist, would subsequently express a similar conclusion:

> [The phenomenon of resacralization] demands in fact a fundamental rethinking not only of the paradigms of the sociology of religion, but of social science as a whole, in order to take on board the abiding significance of religion in the modern world. Religion continues to influence almost every aspect of human society—economic, political, social and cultural. No longer can it be relegated to the past or to the edge of social scientific analysis. Hence the challenge for the economic and social sciences: to rediscover the place of religion in both the empirical realities of the twenty-first century and the paradigms that are deployed to understand this. In short, social science itself, just as much as its subject matter, must respond to the demands of re-sacralization.[22]

The kabbalistic system is observed to have its own internal logic, its own system of anthropological concepts for describing and explaining the cosmic interaction between God and humanity. Moreover, the Hasidic masters already recognized that this system also provides a way to understand human psychology and human interactions, and thereby also to restore the sacred core of embodied social action. As a sociologist I already had a set of interpretive tools through which to offer a new reading of Jewish mystical texts, concepts, and practices, and I hoped that my intervention in *Mystical Interactions* would spur scholars of Jewish mysticism to incorporate similar interdisciplinarity into their own work. Correspondingly, I used a series of close comparative readings to show that society too could be read and interpreted differently—reimagined—using conceptual tools borrowed from the world of Kabbalah and Hasidism.

To put it more straightforwardly, I see the great kabbalists and Hasidic masters as sociologists—and certainly as social psychologists and social thinkers—in their own rights. Sociology cannot simply explain Jewish mysticism using tools and categories imposed from the outside. But a sensitive sociological lens can filter out the social concepts that inhere in the Jewish mystical tradition itself, identifying them and translating them into a more universally appreciable idiom.

In *Mystical Interactions* I took a closer look at Chabad's social psychological theory of the soul, its practices of self-repair through sacralized social interaction, and Schneerson's mass redistribution of messianic boundlessness for the revitalization of each individual encompassed in the collective. Drawing on Rachel Werczberger's case study of Habad study groups for newly religious women, as well as on my own fieldwork, I argued that Chabad shows us how education can be at once social and critical, but also religious, spiritual, and mystical, producing enhanced measures of agency and social connectedness.[23] I argued that Chabad should not be assessed from a modernist vantage point, but rather from a postmodernist one, and further that Chabad is an example of a prophetic social movement in the sense that it does not react to history but rather anticipates history.

This intellectual journey continued and expanded in 2008 and 2009 through a year-long research group on "the sociology and anthropology of Jewish mysticism in comparative perspective," which I led together with Jonathan Garb at the Institute for Advanced Studies at the Hebrew University in Jerusalem. This galvanized an international field of collaboration that went far beyond my particular concerns, and beyond the field of Jewish studies, to include perspectives from the religious traditions of the East as well as of the West.[24]

For my part, I was emboldened to write *Mystical Sociology: Toward Cosmic Social Theory*, published in 2013.[25] There I described the temporal and intellectual limits that are inherent to modern disciplinary categories, offered a fully developed critique of the reigning assumption that the mystical and the social only relate to each other dialectically, and also began the work of crafting and imagining what a mystical sociology would look like. In a word, a mystical sociology does not merely deal with external relations that extend horizontally between individual members of society; a mystical sociology also takes into account the vertical dimension that anchors self and society in a larger cosmic structure, in the kind of transcendent sensibility that non-scientists equate with the divine. A mystical sociology is not circumscribed by the materialistic assumptions that are the hallmarks of secularized modernity, and it certainly allows for other forms of modernity that are marked by the arch of resacralization. More so, it also allows for forms of explanation that likewise transcend the materialistic categories that reinforce the secular norms of sociology itself.

Interdisciplinary and Intercommunal Interaction

AT SOME POINT, it seems, my work began to be noticed outside of the scholarly community as well. In 2012 I was asked by Menachem Schmidt, who among other things is president of Chabad on Campus International, to help organize a conference at the University of Pennsylvania, focusing on the theory and practice of education in Chabad. The idea was to enlarge the conversation to include scholars and practitioners from within Chabad, thus building a dialogical bridge between indigenous and academic perspectives. This was the first of several similar meetings, and it was there that I was initially introduced to a young Chabad scholar by the name of Eli Rubin. I didn't know it at the time, but within a couple of years he would become a close partner in my effort to catalyze deeper interaction, not only at the interdisciplinary level but at the intercommunal level as well.

In 2015, after stints as a visiting professor at Brandeis University and then at the University of Wuppertal in Germany, I was persuaded by Schmidt to relocate to Philadelphia, and to pursue the creation of a new institutional home for the type of boundary-crossing scholarship that he and I both wanted to engage in and encourage. From the Chabad side Rubin would assist me in the administration of the Institute of Jewish Spirituality and Society and its activities, but also in navigating new social and—more importantly—intellectual territory. Rubin was already becoming known among academic scholars of Hasidism for his work on the history and phenomenology of Chabad, and I took it upon myself to attune him to the sociological dimensions of the movement's mystical ideas and practices as well. Together we read William James alongside the writings of Shalom DovBer Schneersohn, the fifth rebbe of Chabad, and the writings of Weber and Durkheim alongside Schneur Zalman of Liadi's *Tanya*, and alongside the writings and talks of the seventh rebbe, Menachem Mendel Schneerson, who is the subject of the present book.

It is hard to say at what point exactly the idea for the present book emerged. Certainly, many of its threads were spun during the leisurely walks Rubin and I took between the Van Pelt Library at the University of Pennsylvania and the on-campus "Lubavitch House." Through Schmidt I was given the opportunity to see something of Chabad's internal function, and I became increasingly inclined to explore the revitalization of Chabad in its new American context, and its move from catastrophe to renaissance in the aftermath of the Holocaust. It appeared to me that Schneerson was an American rebbe, and not simply a Hasidic rebbe in America, though of course he spent the first four decades of his life in Eastern and Western Europe.

Things began to take a more coherent shape in the aftermath of the Institute of Jewish Spirituality and Society's inaugural conference, held in the summer of 2017 at a retreat center in Briarcliff Manor, New York. As I worked on producing an edited volume of the conference proceedings, titled *Jewish Spirituality and Social Transformation*,[26] I also took up the task of systematically researching and theorizing the social ideas of the Lubavitcher Rebbe. This involved going back to old notes that I had amassed over many years. But it also required a new look at the totality of his output, which not only includes upward of a hundred volumes of transcripts, edited talks, and letters, but also hundreds of hours of video and audio recordings. A near-comprehensive index of Schneerson's talks (though not of his letters and formal discourses) by the Chabad scholar Michael Seligson was especially helpful in this regard. But even more integral was the close collaboration of Eli Rubin, who became my partner in researching and writing this book, and whose familiarity with Schneerson's corpus has been indispensable.

Our third partner in the writing of this book—brought on board at a later stage—is my son, Michael Wexler. Neither a scholar of Jewish mysticism nor a sociologist, he is a writer and a creator both by training and by vocation. His fiction is particularly notable for its cosmological and existential concerns, and he has also taught writing at the University of Missouri–Kansas City. Michael helped us to craft the narrative arc that structures our scholarly arguments and findings. Due to his good efforts we hope that this book has been made more readable for non-specialists and specialists alike.

An exploration of Hasidism's socio-mystical ethos can go a long way to illuminating many aspects of the movement's social, historical, and intellectual trajectories, whose apparent contradictions have always rendered scholars fascinated, perplexed, and—in some cases—repulsed. Schneerson's own social ideas and practices do not simply provide a window into the motivations and goals of the contemporary Chabad Hasidic movement. More importantly, they provide a mirror that can be held up as a tool for a critical reappraisal of the secularized mainstream of American society, and the sharp fissures of both domestic politics and international geopolitics. This is especially the case when we take stock of his theoretical and activist engagement with a host of policy questions of the sort that have only grown more controversial and divisive as the twentieth century has spilled over into the twenty-first.

There have been two general approaches among scholars of Jewish mysticism and Hasidism: the way of heaven and the way of earth. The way of heaven emphasizes metaphysics and phenomenology, theology and the existentialism of the soul. The way of earth emphasizes ritual and magic, everyday life, social change, and embodied practice. But Schneerson sought to bring heaven and earth together in a dynamic encounter. Does Schneerson point the way toward the new beginning that we seek? Perhaps. What I hope to have demonstrated in this book is that Schneerson's socio-mystical vision illuminates a path by which we, as individuals and as a collective, can release ourselves from the "mechanized petrification" that Weber so presciently described. Against the overwhelming pessimism, even cynicism, of mainstream discourse, Schneerson deserves to be seen not merely as a starry-eyed messianic herald, but also as a clear-eyed engineer of social revitalization and repair.

Philip Wexler
March 2019, Penn Yan, NY

xxv

Notes

1. Peter Cole, *The Poetry of Kabbalah: Mystical Verse from the Jewish Tradition* (New Haven: Yale University Press, 2011), 44.

2. Elliot R. Wolfson, *Open Secret: Postmessianic Messianism and the Mystical Revision of Menachem Mendel Schneerson* (New York: Columbia University Press, 2009).

3. Max Weber, *The Protestant Ethic and the Spirit of Capitalism,* translated by Talcott Parsons (New York and London: Charles Scribner's Sons / George Allen & Unwin Ltd., 1950).

4. Émile Durkheim, "Préface," *Année sociologique,* Vol. II, as translated in K. H. Wolff, *Émile Durkheim (1858-1917): A Collection of Essays, with Translations and a Bibliography* (Columbus: Ohio State University Press, 1960), 350-351.

5. For another important contribution, which also provides a critical evaluation of the only scholarly attempt to provide a biography of Schneerson, see Nehemia Polen, review of *The Rebbe: The Life and Afterlife of Menachem Mendel Schneerson,* by Samuel C. Heilman and Menachem M. Friedman, *Modern Judaism* 34, no. 1 (February, 2014): 123–134.

6. Max Weber, "Science as a Vocation," in *Essays in Sociology,* trans. H.H. Gerth and C. Wright Mills (New York: Oxford University Press, 1946), 155.

7. See Jeffrey J. Kripal, *Mutants and Mystics: Science Fiction, Superhero Comics, and the Paranormal* (Chicago: University of Chicago Press, 2011).

8. Martin Buber, *The Origin and Meaning of Hasidism,* edited and translated by Maurice Friedman (New York: Harper Torchbooks, 1960), 253-254; Gershom Scholem, *Major Trends in Jewish Mysticism* (New York: Schocken Books, 1941), 342.

9. Weber, "Science as a Vocation," 155.

10. See the relevant discussion and citations in Wolfson, *Open Secret,* 186, where this slogan of Schneerson's is rendered "action is the mainstay." Hundreds more citations of Schneerson's use of this phrase could be listed. It is an abridgment of a rabbinic aphorism found in the *Mishnah,* Avot, 1:17.

11. For a fuller discussion see Erika Summers-Effler and Hyunjin Deborah Kwak, "Weber's Missing Mystics: Inner-Worldly Mystical Practices and the Micro Potential for Social Change," *Theory and Society* 44 (May, 2015): 251-282.

12. Max Weber, *Economy and Society,* edited by Guenther Roth and Claus Wittich (Berkeley: University of California Press, 1978), 550.

13. See Rivka Schatz-Uffenheimer, *Hasidism as Mysticism: Quietistic Elements in Eighteenth-Century Hasidic Thought* (Princeton, NJ: Princeton University Press, 1993), 255-289.

14. On this accusation and on the "enlightened" opposition to Hasidism, see Marcin Wodziński, *Haskalah and Hasidism in the Kingdom of Poland: A History of Conflict* (Oxford: Littman Library of Jewish Civilization, 2005); Glenn Dynner, *Men of Silk: The Hasidic Conquest of Polish Jewish Society* (Oxford: Oxford University Press, 2006), esp. 137-195; Jonatan Meir, "Reform Hasidism: The Image of Habad in Haskalah Literature," *Modern Judaism* 37, no. 3 (October, 2017): 297-315.

15. Philip Wexler, *The Mystical Society: An Emerging Social Vision* (Boulder, CO: Westview Press, 2000), esp., 8, 35-38, and 128-130.

16. Randall Collins, "The Four M's of Religion: Magic, Membership, Morality and Mysticism," *Review of Religious Research* 50, no. 1 (Sep., 2008): 5-15.

17. *Ibid.*, 13.

18. *Ibid.*, 14.

19. Summers-Effler and Kwak, "Weber's Missing Mystics," 251-282.

20. As I put it in Wexler, *The Mystical Society*: "[the] religious, innerworldly ascetic foundation of modern culture is transmuting to an innerworldly, ecstatic, contemplative, or mystical orientation" (page 43), and "in the United States, the New Age movement may be seen as part of the present reconstitution of the 'American Religion,'" as a "transformative, innerworldly mysticism that offers the conditions for a new social ethic of being as the basis for social criticism" (page 68).

21. Philip Wexler, *Mystical Interactions: Sociology, Jewish Mysticism and Education* (Los Angeles, CA: Cherub Press, 2007).

22. See Grace Davie, "Resacralization," in *The New Blackwell Companion to the Sociology of Religion*, edited by Bryan S. Turner (Chichester, UK: Wiley-Blackwell, 2010), 175.

23. Rachel Werczberger, *Feminine Messianism and Messianic Femininity: An Ethnography of Women's Shiur in Chabad* (MA thesis, Hebrew University, 2003) [in Hebrew].

24. See Philip Wexler and Jonathan Garb (eds.), *After Spirituality: Studies in Jewish Mystical Traditions* (New York: Peter Lang, 2012). Also see Garb's subsequent monograph, *Shamanic Trance in Modern Kabbalah* (Chicago: University of Chicago Press, 2011). There we find a textually and historically grounded theorization of modern Jewish mystical experience and practice that is greatly enriched by the fundamental integration of deep readings in relevant social scientific literature, especially anthropology.

25. Philip Wexler, *Mystical Sociology: Toward Cosmic Social Theory* (New York: Peter Lang, 2013).

26. Philip Wexler (ed.), *Jewish Spirituality and Social Transformation: Hasidism and Society* (New York: Crossroad, 2019).

CHAPTER 1

⌖

SHATTERING THE IRON CAGE: FROM THE PROTESTANT ETHIC TO THE HASIDIC ETHOS

1.1—Protestantism, Petrification, and the Possibility of Hasidism

ONE OF THE most enduringly influential works in the modern field of sociology is Max Weber's 1905 publication, *The Protestant Ethic and the Spirit of Capitalism*. Weber argued that society is fundamentally shaped by ideas, rather than merely by technological developments. Even more fundamentally, he claimed that beneath the secular facade of modern economics and culture lays a particular set of Christian beliefs.[1]

This may seem a strange way to begin a book about a Jewish spiritual and social visionary. But in order to fully appreciate the new dawn heralded by our protagonist it must be set against the prevailing paradigm of Western modernity, the prevailing paradigm within which he acted, and which he countered. It is Weber's compelling contention that this prevailing paradigm is very much a product of a religious worldview that took Western Europe by storm from the 16th century and on. Our argument in the present book is fundamentally Weberian in its orientation; religious ideas are foregrounded as seminal actors in the continuing formation of social history, in the 20th century, in

1

the 21st century, and beyond. In this we reject the reductive theorization of modernity as secularization, and instead embrace the emerging
consensus that we are now witnessing growing instances of resacralization throughout the world.[2] In this vein, however, the paradigm
described by Weber is one that this book seeks to displace, identifying
and describing the alternative paradigm embodied by the ascendant
Hasidic movement. Hasidism—especially as advanced in postwar
America by Menachem Mendel Schneerson, the seventh rebbe of
Chabad-Lubavitch (1902–1994)—can provide an alternate social model,
an alternate vision of what society can be. It is therefore with *The Protestant Ethic* that we must begin.

Weber's argument is often seen as a polemical attack on the philosophy of the 19th-century philosopher Karl Marx, who famously claimed
that "religion is the opiate of the masses," and that religion should ultimately be viewed as a product of history rather than as an active shaper
of history.[3] The origins of modern society, according to Marx, are to
be found primarily in the invention of technologies of mass production,
which led to the industrial revolution in the 18th and 19th centuries. In
contrast to this materialistic view, Weber argues that modern society is
governed—at least on "one side of the causal chain"[4]—by a spirit, or an
ethic, that can be traced all the way back to the founder of Protestant
Christianity, Martin Luther, and which came to full development in
the theologies of various Puritan sects.

At the heart of the so-called Protestant ethic, per Weber, is the de-
terministic doctrine that "only a small proportion of men are chosen
for eternal grace." "To assume that human merit or guilt play a part in
determining this destiny would be to think of God's absolutely free
decrees, which have been settled from eternity, as subject to change
by human influence, an impossible contradiction." Belief in these doctrines, says Weber, must have imposed a profound sense of loneliness
and helplessness; "everything of the flesh is separated from God by an
unbridgeable gulf," and whether you are saved or not is preordained as
"a dark mystery…impossible to pierce and presumptuous to question."[5]

For Weber these beliefs are synonymous with "the elimination of
magic from the world." By this term—"magic"—he means the ability
for humankind to enter into an interactive relationship with God, the
ability for humankind to shape God's will and thereby to intervene in
the natural, ordained course of events. Protestantism, in its Puritan

form, eliminated the interactive bond between God and humanity, and also between the saved individual and the rest of humanity: "This consciousness of divine grace of the elect and holy was accompanied by an attitude towards the sin of one's neighbour...of hatred and contempt for him as an enemy of God bearing the signs of eternal damnation."[6]

Herein lies the first exemplary counterpoint to the Hasidic ethos, which places a great deal of emphasis on both union with God (*devekut*) and interpersonal love and fellowship. Moshe Idel, one of today's most influential scholars of Kabbalah, has written a book whose title is instructive: *Hasidism: Between Ecstasy and Magic.*[7] This, however, emphasizes only the dynamic relationship between man and God. Even more important is the question of interpersonal relations. Weber concluded that Puritanism "renounced the universalism of love."[8] By contrast, Hasidism's mystical embrace of God is a font for interpersonal love, a point that will be demonstrated and further elaborated below, especially in Chapter 4.[9]

What are the broader psychological, sociological, and cultural repercussions of the above described Protestant doctrines? What kind of character, what kind of ethic, what kind of spirit, do such beliefs produce?

The pious Puritans of yore needed to have faith and confidence that they were among the elect. Without such confidence, Weber tells us, they would fall prey to doubt and to the temptations of the devil. Yet this would have been a faith without any basis; there would have been no assurance at all that they were not indeed doomed to eternal purgatory rather than eternal grace. An individual without the self-confidence to believe that he or she is among the elect would be left to face the void of doom.

Such an ethic produces a psychological state of unshakable anxiety, an anxiety that all the piety in the world can never be enough. Consequently the need arises to fabricate a firm basis upon which a staunch self-confidence in one's own election can be supported. Self-confidence is a rather charitable term, but what this ultimately produces is pride, and Weber is explicit in juxtaposing it with humility.[10] This provides us with a second example of the way in which the Hasidic ethos, with its emphasis on effacement (*bitul*) of the self and the world, stands in stark contrast to the Protestant ethic.[11]

What is most central to Weber's thesis, however, is that the only basis upon which such a conviction can be built is "a type of Christian

conduct which served to increase the glory of God…[the] sanctifica-
tion of his whole life, to augment the glory of God by real, and not
merely apparent, good works…Thus the Calvinist…himself creates
his own salvation, or, as would be more correct, the conviction of it…in
a systematic self-control which at every moment stands before the inexorable alternative, chosen or damned." Or put differently, "in order
to attain that self-confidence intense worldly activity is recommended
as the most suitable means…not of purchasing salvation, but of getting
rid of the fear of damnation."[12]

Herein lies a third counterpoint to the Hasidic ethos according to
which God should be served out of love and joy, rather than fear and
anxiety. Schneur Zalman of Liadi, the founder of Chabad Hasidism,
dedicated several chapters of his foundational work, *Tanya*, to a forceful
manifesto against all forms of anxiety, and to a practical path of cognitive therapy by which to replace anxiety with joy. It is "impossible,"
he wrote, to successfully serve God, "except with alacrity drawn from
joy, and openness of heart, and its purity from every trace of worry and
anxiety in the world."[13] He also wrote that fear of God should rightly
be construed as a facet of love and the consequential desire "not to be
separated" from God's all-encompassing embrace.[14]

The driving anxiety of the Protestant ethic results in an inexorable
urge to accumulate and hoard good works, not because they have any
inherent religious value, but because they are empty signs of one's election. Thereby the entire dynamic of religious life is transformed, robbed
of passion, of spontaneity, of the ebb and flow of reciprocal relationship,
of enchantment. Religion is thereby reduced to an empty praxis, an ascetic and methodological regime by which the individual accumulates
as much evidence for their elected status as they can. This is the one
and only means that one can sustain an ever shaky relief to the insatia-
ble fear that one might be predestined to damnation. It is this theology
that leads to the ethic of worldly asceticism, such that "labour came to
be considered in itself the end of life."[15] The labors of the individual,
and the products of those labors, come to be seen as the only measure
of self-worth. Thereby religion does not only become disenchanted and
secularized, it is also reduced to a personal quest to accumulate wealth.
It is not so difficult to see how the secularized Protestantism of modern
capitalism became fertile ground for the rise of the prosperity gospel
that has been so successful in the United States.[16]

Here again it is worth pausing to take note of the divergence of the Hasidic ethos from the Protestant ethic. As the scholar Marcin Wodziński has noted, many Hasidim—contrary to their popular image—were in fact prosperous or even wealthy, and some Hasidic masters invoked the Talmudic maxim that wealth was a sign of spiritual merit.[17] At the same time, however, Wodziński sharply distinguishes the strongly individualistic significance of wealth in Protestantism to the collective conception of wealth found in Hasidism:

> The Hasidim regarded wealth as belonging to the people of Israel as a whole rather than to individuals, and as a gift from God conditional upon the practice of charity. On the one hand this idea encouraged charity, thus a very traditional way of relieving social inequality, but on the other it annulled the tensions resulting from the existence of this inequality and sanctioned wealth as a just reward for a pious life... The Hasidic ideal and ethos of charity thus might have had economic implications contrary to the accepted knowledge on charity as a destabilizing factor. It was not only a means of curbing the excesses of economic inequality, but also a powerful tool of economic mobilization and empowerment, at least for some Hasidim... It was also Hasidic charity and solidarity, as both religious ideals and the practical ethos of Hasidic groups, which might have contributed to their relative prosperity.[18]

For the Hasidim, wealth was certainly a sign of divine grace. But lack thereof was not cause for spiritual anxiety. Nor was wealth to be hoarded as a sign of personal election. It was instead seen as a collective possession, a gift to be shared charitably as part of a socio-mystical dynamic that will described in more detail in Chapter 3. Moreover, Wodziński argues that Hasidic prosperity was an "indirect" result of its spiritual and social aspirational attractions.[19] Thus Hasidism's economic profile cannot be seen as any kind of prelude to modern capitalism, but should rather be seen as a model for a potential alternative.

This brings us to the essence of Weber's argument. Simply stated: The modern obsession with the personal accumulation of capital and material goods, which drives the vast systems of finance in whose thrall we all toil, has a distinctly religious history. Prior to the advent of Protestantism, worldly work was seen as necessary only "for the maintenance of the individual and the community," and as a calling "that does not apply to anyone who can live without labour." Likewise, contemplation and prayer once took precedence as forms of "spiritual action in the Kingdom of God." But the Protestant ethic turns that precedence on its head, requiring that "even the wealthy shall not eat without working...[because] for everyone without exception God's providence has prepared a calling...in which he should labour."[20]

Originally, Weber explains, this ethic "was directed solely toward a transcendental end, salvation," or the proof thereof. Thus the purpose of worldly labor was "dominated entirely by the aim to add to the glory of God on earth."[21] Worldly labor and its products were never to be enjoyed or indulged in, only to be accumulated. But as time went on, vocation was increasingly emptied of any transcendental or religious meaning. Ultimately, "the treatment of labour as a calling became as characteristic of the modern worker as the corresponding attitude toward acquisition of the modern business man" and "did its part in building the tremendous cosmos of the modern economic order...which today determines the lives of all the individuals who are born into this mechanism."[22]

In one of the most memorable and oft-quoted lines of *The Protestant Ethic* Weber bemoans the sad twist of history: This religious calling was originally intended to reduce concern for material goods to "a light cloak, which can be thrown aside at any moment." Yet "fate decreed that the cloak should become an iron cage."[23]

The power and enduring resonance of Weber's thesis, despite all the criticisms it has sustained, is to be found in his unflinching diagnosis of the intense feelings of loneliness and helplessness, of anxiety and entrapment, that plague modern individuals. Capitalism's many successes are stalked by a sense of meaninglessness, and increasingly by mounting inequalities and injustices that arise from the concentration of massive amounts of wealth in the hands of a tiny proportion of the population. In an especially prescient passage, and one from which the present book derives its title, Weber speculates about where the Protestant ethic might lead:

> In the field of its highest development, in the United States,
> the pursuit of wealth, stripped of its religious and ethical

meaning, tends to become associated with purely mundane passions, which often actually give it the character of sport. No one knows who will live in this cage in the future, or whether at the end of this tremendous development entirely new prophets will arise, or there will be a great rebirth of old ideas and ideals, or, if neither, mechanized petrification, embellished with a sort of convulsive self-importance.[24]

Convulsive self-importance, held in check only by its fragility, certainly seems to be one of the conditions of our age. But here we raise the possibility that contemporaneous to the emergence and development of capitalism, new prophets have indeed arisen—a long line of Hasidic masters who trace their original inspiration to Israel of Mezhbizh, known as the Baal Shem Tov.[25] A kabbalist and a folk healer, the Baal Shem Tov was active in mid-18th-century Ukraine, and ultimately inspired a socio-mystical movement centered today in the United States and in Israel. Though scholars initially regarded the Hasidic movement as a relic of the past, it has now been recognized as belonging to the modern era, even if it oft appears to be at odds with Western social norms.[26]

The argument of this book is that Hasidism's mystical and social dimensions—in particular as charted by Menachem Mendel Schneerson in the latter part of the 20th century—actually make it an ascendant force for the resacralization and reenchantment of Weber's disenchanted world. Moreover, the "new prophets" of Hasidism, together with the "old ideas and ideals" that Hasidism revives, may provide a formula by which society at large can shatter the iron cage and extricate itself from mechanized petrification.

In his foreword to *The Protestant Ethic*, the English historian R. H. Tawney wrote of the clarity that hindsight brings. "All revolutions are declared to be natural and inevitable, once they are successful." Capitalism, as the cultural and economic system "prevailing in Western Europe and America," accordingly stands as an apparently inevitable result of history, a "triumphant fact." (Albeit one that is increasingly subject to question.) But in illuminating capitalism's roots in the Protestant ethic Weber has shown us, per Tawney's caution, that "in its youth [it] was a pretender, and it was only after centuries of struggle that its title was established."[27] The new paradigmatic pretender, we propose, is the Hasidic ethos. This may seem a bold claim, but it was once considered a bold claim that Hasidism could survive the Holocaust. As we prepare to enter the third decade of the 21st century, it survives—and indeed thrives—as a powerful example of the new processes of resacralization, and the resurgence of religion in the postmodern era. Who is to say what the future might bring?

1.2—The Possibility of Prophecy in Society and in Sociology

THE QUESTION OF what the future might bring draws the question of prophecy and its meaning into clearer focus. Here we need to consider prophecy as a social phenomenon and as a category of sociological analysis, but also as a function of the sociological discipline itself. Weber, of course, has much to say about what is distinctive about prophecy as a social phenomenon. Here we will highlight what seem to be the two most salient elements of his analysis. The first relates to the prophetic personage, the second to the prophetic message.

For Weber the prophet is "a purely personal carrier of charisma, whose power of his mission is revealed by a religious teaching or a divine command."[28] What Weber means by this is that the power of the prophet's message is not derived principally from a position of pre-existing, "traditional" authority that he occupies, such as that of a priest or a legislator. Rather the prophet has a purely personal authority, deriving from the transcendent and revolutionary ("religious" and "divine") character of his vision. The prophet is not a product of the flow of history, but interrupts history, intervenes in history, in order to change its course and chart a new future.

When it comes to the character of the prophetic message, Weber tells us that along with the practices of "divination…magical healing and counseling," the Hebrew prophets focused especially on "social reform." But what defines the prophetic message is that it "involves…a unified view of the world derived from a consciously integrated and meaningful attitude toward life."[29] This unified view, moreover, is cosmic in scope:

> To the prophet, both the life of man and the world, both social and cosmic events, have a certain systematic and coherent

meaning. To this meaning the conduct of mankind must be oriented if it is to bring salvation...Moreover, it [prophecy] always
contains the important religious conception of the world as a
cosmos which is challenged to produce somehow a "meaningful," ordered totality, the particular manifestations of which are
to be measured and evaluated according to this requirement.[30]

In his analysis of the role that prophecy could play in modern times
Weber was far less explicit, and far more ambivalent. We have already
seen his hopeful allusion to the rise of "new prophets" at the end of *The
Protestant Ethic.* But in his lecture, "Science as a Vocation," and elsewhere,
he seems more pessimistic, dismissing the "lectern-prophets" of his own
day for their lack of intellectual integrity, for their "public bluster," and
above all for the fanaticism they encourage. They are products of history,
and thus their narrow political agitations cannot save Europe from the
petrification that results from disenchantment.[31] At the same time he invokes an authentic prophet, Isaiah, who warns that "even if the morning
cometh, it is still night: if ye inquire already, ye will come again and inquire once more."[32] He seems to be appropriating the prophetic voice to
predict that there will be a long night before a new prophetic dawn arises, and that for now salvation lies in the vocation of science alone. This
can be read as a suggestion that science is itself the new oracle—the
"daemon" or spirit—through which sociologists can themselves wear the
mantle of prophecy; the social scientist can apparently step outside the
value judgments imposed by history, and can thereby follow Weber's
call to "go about our work and meet the 'challenges of the day'—both in
our human relations and our vocation."[33]

Consciously or unconsciously, prophecy has indeed become a function of sociology as a discipline. Sociologists do not merely describe
and analyze, they also predict, and thereby they prescribe and pro-
scribe. The present book does not merely take a modern prophet as its
subject, but is also a link in the chain of the sociological tradition and
therefore a further iteration of that scientific form of modern prophecy.

A powerful practitioner of the modern prophetic discipline—once
widely read, but often the subject of criticism in his own time, and rarely cited by contemporary scholars—is Pitirim A. Sorokin.[34] Born in
1889 to an itinerant artisan in the Komi region of northern Russia, Sorokin studied at the Saint Petersburg Imperial University. During the

Russian Revolution he was a secretary to Kerensky, the Prime Minister of the Provisional Government. Subsequent to the rise of the Bolsheviks he was forced to leave Russia, and eventually moved to the United States, finishing his career at Harvard University. In his four-volume opus *Social and Cultural Dynamics*, and in other shorter works, he tried to make sense of the massive upheavals that he witnessed in the first three decades of the 20th century and beyond. He saw the revolutions and wars, even the financial crisis of 1929, as symptoms of an epochal crisis of cultural transition from a "sensate" value system, which was formally the prevailing Euro-American paradigm, to an "ideational" one. He also predicted that more crises were still to come. The outbreak of World War Two revealed that—at least in this—he was not wrong.

From the end of the Middle Ages, according to Sorokin, the arc of history began to increasingly turn toward the senses as the primary measure of reality. In its purest form, which is a mere hypothetical, he tells us that "the sensate mentality…does not seek or believe in any supersensory reality; at the most, in its diluted form, it assumes an agnostic attitude toward the entire world beyond the senses…Its needs and aims are mainly physical…The method of realizing them is not that of a modification within the human individuals composing the culture, but of a modification or exploitation of the external world." In sharp contrast stands the "ideational" mentality, according to which "reality is perceived as nonsense and nonmaterial, everlasting Being (*Sein*)." Likewise "needs and ends are mainly spiritual, and they are met either through "self-imposed minimization or elimination of most of the physical needs" or "through the transformation of the sensate world, and especially the socio-cultural world, in such a way as to reform it along the lines of the spiritual reality."[35]

Sorokin argued that the crises of the 20th century extended to every area of cultural life—including the arts, law, politics, moral values, philosophy, etc.—and they were all symptoms of an epochal shift that would replace the dominant sensate culture with a new ideational one. Echoing Weber's well-known statement that the last stage of capitalism will be marked by the rise of "specialists without spirit,"[36] Sorokin tells that in the first stage of this transition the "Galileos, Newtons, Liebnitzes,…Descarteses, Lockes, Kants, and Humes" will be replaced with "mediocre" scientists and philosophers, and with "study of 'the more and more about less and less.'" This signals the demise of the great era of sensate creativity in the areas of science and philosophy. The new geniuses in these areas, by contrast, "will be creating the values of ideational and idealistic types," and likewise "the potential great social thinkers will again increasingly shift to ideational and idealistic social theories.[37] But this transition doesn't come easily; it is marked by increasing polarization between sensates and ideationalists:

> The chasm between these will grow and society in its soul and members will be split more and more into these two extreme types, until the extreme hedonism of the *Carpe diem* dies out.[38]

Within this chaotic struggle, Sorokin predicted, new ideational values would emerge, first as "superindividual and even supergroup systems of meanings, norms and values for making their inner and external lives coherent...meaningful...creative and valuable." Eventually "the reign of rude force will be greatly limited and subjugated to the new values and norms. Might once again will give the way to right. Social relationships will be reshaped into a new form, less coercive and more noble than in the preceding period of transition. New social, cultural, mental, and moral order will be on the *agenda* of history..."[39]

The rise and fall of Nazism and Communism, the new oligarchic turn, and the current political polarization—in which the apparent ascendance of progressive norms is met with aggressive conservatism and a hard nationalistic backlash—can all be seen as symptoms of this great transitional crisis. Though we have seen the rise of the American counterculture, and also new-age religious movements, much of the current discourse still turns on the old sensate value system; our needs, or rights, are still mostly debated in material terms. We likewise see a cynical turn of the type that Sorokin predicted; "real standards" are replaced by "counterfeit criteria," culture by "cultural chewing gum," and "the competent arbiters by the qualified ignoramuses." In the latest stages of sensate culture, he wrote, a "'machinery of selection' will be picking up mainly pseudo-values and neglecting real values."[40] It almost seems as if he knew that soon the most seminal cultural forces would be the machine-like algorithms of Facebook and Google, all but determining what we choose to buy, who we socialize with, and even who we vote for.

It is within this context that the example of Hasidism presents us with an alternate path, one that breaks out of the transitional cycle

of inauthenticity and polarization to offer something fresh, something new. In Sorokin's terms Hasidism can be described as "idealistic"
or "integral," meaning that it achieves, or at least has the capacity to
achieve, "a more or less balanced unification of Ideational and Sensate,
with, however, a predominance of the Ideational elements." For an idealistic and integral cultural form, Sorokin says, "reality is many-sided,
with the aspects of everlasting Being and ever-changing Becoming of
the spiritual and the material..."[41]

Hasidism can indeed be traced back to one "superindividual," and to
a cluster of individuals associated with him. In Hasidism's 18th-century
origins we find the figure of Israel Baal Shem Tov (d. 1760),[42] and if
there is one definitive teaching that can be attributed to him it is that
all the many-sided facets of spiritual and material reality must be co-
hesively integrated and united with the fundamental being of God.[43]
Similarly, when we look more specifically at the leader of Chabad
Hasidism in the latter part of the 20th century, we again find a "superindividual" who was at once of his time and yet not subject to its
wrenching polarizations, and whose vision is the central subject of the
present volume. Tradition and progress, the advance of religion and
of science, the particular mission of the Jewish nation and the universal one of humankind, the individual and the collective, transcendent
spirituality and material being; he embraced all of these as meaningful—integral—elements of a single system, of a single divine vision.
His is an intellectual and practical path by which the spiritual and material elements of the cosmos can become attuned to the singular Being
that is the singular essence of everything.

These seminal actors—"superindividuals" in Sorokin's term, "prophets" in Weber's, "tsadikim" in the Hasidic locution—created whole
constellations of communities, "supergroups" that proliferated outward
in precisely the manner described by Sorokin. Hasidism is a new socio-
cultural form, complete with new "systems of meanings, norms and values
for making...inner and external lives coherent...meaningful...creative
and valuable." In particular, Menachem Mendel Schneerson articulated "a new social, cultural, mental, and moral order" and placed it "on the
agenda of history." This new social form, this new agenda, is worthy of a
more attentive analysis and of a deeper sociological theorization.

Following the models laid out by Weber and Sorokin, it is our suggestion that Schneerson can be cast as a "new prophet" of the type that

the former seems to have hoped would one day "come again." Though he was seventh in the Chabad dynasty of tsadikim, most agree that he would never have inherited the office of traditional authority if not for the powerful personal charisma that was entirely his own. Indeed, from a purely "bureaucratic" and "traditional" perspective—as opposed to a "prophetic" and "charismatic" one—Schneerson's older brother-in-law, Shmaryahu Gourarie, might have been the presumptive heir to the office held by their father-in-law.[44] But in Hasidism the role of the tsadik is a fundamentally charismatic one. It is not simply an office to be filled by a qualified candidate. It is a calling that a prophet must be impelled to undertake. As Iliah Luriah has pointed out, in Hasidism there are almost no instances in which a tsadik explicitly appointed a successor to take the leadership role after his passing. This is because the office needs to be filled by an individual who is seen by the community to be called, to be personally inspired with a sense of divine mission and with a new vision for a new generation.[45] Weber tells us that "it is recognition on the part of those subject to authority which is decisive for the validity of charisma."[46] This means that authentic charismatic continuity, as opposed to the routinization of charisma (which is normally invoked by scholars in relation to Hasidism), can only be secured by its own disruption. The new leader must be a "new prophet," else he cannot legitimately secure the dynastic seat.[47]

In Schneerson's case the particular crisis of the moment made the need for a revolutionary leader, a charismatic visionary, all the more acute. His father-in-law passed away in January 1950, when the Jewish nation was still reeling from the Holocaust. Hasidism had been entirely uprooted, and largely decimated, in its Eastern European heartland, and had not yet laid firm roots either in America or in the fledgling state of Israel. Secular Zionism, to which the Hasidim had been firmly opposed, seemed to hold the only promise of a Jewish national and cultural future. Without the emergence of a new tsadik endowed with the charismatic power to inspire a new age of Hasidism there would indeed be no continuity.

Weber has this to say about the relationship between crisis and charisma:

> Charisma is the great revolutionary force...Charisma...may
> effect a subjective or internal reorientation born out of

suffering, conflicts, or enthusiasm. It may then result in a radical alteration of the central attitudes and directions of action with a completely new orientation of all attitudes toward the different problems of the "world."[48]

This describes Schneerson's rise, and his emergence as a globally significant Jewish leader, with precision: Out of the immense suffering of the Holocaust; out of the immense conflicts between tradition and modernity, as well as between nations; out of the new enthusiasms for assimilation, on the one hand, and secular nationalism on the other; out of all these arose a revolutionary charismatic force, a prophetic visionary who created an international network with the goal of effecting "a radical alteration" of attitudes and an alternate path of action "with a completely new orientation" toward the manifold problems of the world.

1.3—The Hasidic Ethos and the Reenchantment of the World

WHAT IS THE Hasidic ethos? What is the new orientation with which Hasidism faces the manifold problems of the world? One way to answer this question, or at least to begin to answer it, is through a close reading of what can be legitimately seen as the founding teaching of the movement. This teaching is found in the text of a letter addressed by Israel Baal Shem Tov to his brother-in-law, Gershon of Kuty. Published in print in 1781, this letter also exists in several manuscript copies.[49] Intense debates about the different versions of the letter and their relationships with one another abound, but in a comprehensive and critical review of these debates the scholar Elly Moseson concluded that the version published in 1781 is likely a direct copy of the original letter that was written or dictated by the Baal Shem Tov himself. More than anything else, the many citations and discussions of this letter, both in internal Hasidic texts and in scholarly studies of Hasidism, testify to the immense spiritual and historical importance attached to it from the earliest stages of Hasidism's proliferation.[50]

Despite these many discussions, the fundamentally social nature of the mystical experience described by the author—and likewise the social intimations of the teaching he transmitted to the reader—have yet to be noted by scholars. In the relevant section of the letter we read as follows:

> On Rosh Hashanah in the year 1746 I practised an ajuration, an ascent of the soul, as you know, and I saw wondrous things in a vision, which I had till now never seen the like from the day when I attained knowledge... I saw many souls, alive and dead, both known to me and unknown to me... running and returning, to ascend from realm to realm... with immense and great joy... Also, many evildoers returned in reconciliation and their sins were forgiven... and among them too there was very immense joy... All of them as one requested and pleaded with me to the point of embarrassment, saying..., "God has bestowed upon you extraordinary understanding, to grasp and to know in these matters, ascend with us and be for us a help and a support." And due to the great joy that I saw among them I decided to go with them...
>
> I ascended, one plane following another, till I entered the hall of the messiah, there the messiah learns Torah with all the sages and tsadikim... There I saw an exceedingly great joy... and I thought that this joy was due to my passing from this world, and they made known to me that I had not yet passed away for it is pleasurable to them above when I unite unions below by means of their holy Torah... I asked before the messiah, "When will you come Sir?" and he answered me, "By this sign you will know; when your teaching becomes famous and revealed in the world, and your wellsprings— which I taught you and you grasped—will be disseminated outside, and they too will be able to practice unifications and ascents like you, and then... it will be a time of [divine] will and salvation."
>
> I was amazed by this, and I was much pained over the immense length of time that it would take for this to be accomplished. However, while I was there I learned three things... and three divine names... and I thought that perhaps thereby also people of my age could come to a station and plane like mine... And they did not give me permission

to reveal them all the days of my life...I am sworn to stand by this. Yet the following I make known to you, and God shall be at your aid...While you pray and study, and in every single word and utterance of your lips, have intent to unify the name [of God]. For in every single letter there are worlds, and souls, and divinity, and they ascend, bond, and unite with one another...uniting in true singularity with divinity, and you shall encompass your soul together with them...and all the worlds unite as one and ascend, making great joy and pleasure without measure...

Much has been said about the implications of this passage for questions regarding the role of messianism, and likewise regarding the significance of speech, in early Hasidism.[51] Naftali Loewenthal has paid particular attention to Chabad's theorization of the messianic mission to disseminate the Baal Shem Tov's "wellsprings" to the "outside."[52] A brief, but extremely important remark by Elliot Wolfson is especially noteworthy: "the messianic dimension of Beshtian hasidism" is "connected especially with the social need to communicate esoteric truths."[53]

The social element mentioned by Wolfson isn't merely one dimension of the Hasidic vision that can be adduced from this text, but is rather the central and defining feature of this text. Indeed, the most striking and obvious thing about the mystical experience it records is that when the Baal Shem Tov ascends he is not alone. The heavenly realms he enters are teeming with souls, of the living as well as of the dead, running and returning. The Baal Shem Tov does not merely observe the tumult, but is a part of it, in dynamic dialogue and interaction with the souls that he encounters. The first principle of the Hasidic ethos, we accordingly suggest, is that the religious and mystical spheres are inherently social rather than individualistic.[54]

A second remarkable feature of the Baal Shem Tov's ascent is that wherever he turns he encounters a joy so immense that he can't fully comprehend its nature. In the hall of the messiah he learns that the ultimate telos of history is that all people should similarly be able to unify "worlds, souls and divinity," and thereby ascend into states of celestial union, "making joy and pleasure without measure." Here we have a second principle of the Hasidic ethos; mystical ascent and union with the divine is inherently joyous.[55]

The Baal Shem Tov is also told that special joy is derived above from his own work to "unite unions" in the physical world below. This explicates a cosmic dynamic according to which this physical world (along with its individual inhabitants) isn't merely the recipient of celestial impetus, judgment, or blessing, but actually contributes something of supreme value in return. To borrow the Weberian phraseology cited earlier, the celestial realm is not separated from everything of flesh by an unbridgeable gulf, but actually appears to be on one continuum with the realm in which our souls inhabit bodies. Indeed, the Baal Shem Tov himself is a bridge by which events above are made known to his fleshy readers below. He notes that he agreed to accompany other souls he encountered to aid them in their ascent, and in other sections of the letter we also see him acting as an intercessor attempting to avert a celestial decree.[56] These elements bring us to a third principle of the Hasidic ethos: Corporeal embodiment is not an iron cage within which the soul is reduced to a passive recipient of an ordained fate. The embodied soul is actually engaged in a cosmic drama, a dynamic interchange of unification, communication, and—yes—joy.[57]

The possibility of divine and human transformation is underscored in more positive terms by the phenomenon of reconciliation (teshuvah) to God that the Baal Shem Tov witnesses: "Many evildoers returned in reconciliation and their sins were forgiven…and among them too there was very immense joy." We should remember that this ascent of the soul occurred on Rosh Hashanah, which is not only the Jewish New Year but also the beginning of the "ten days of reconciliation" that culminate with Yom Kippur, the Day of Atonement. It is likely that the ascent occurred in the Synagogue, which would have been packed with men, women, and children.[58] In other words, this is a moment of heightened devotion and emotion for the entire community. What is different about the Baal Shem Tov's experience of this is that his vision transcends that which mere eyes of flesh can see. He sees not only what is occurring within the physical confines of his synagogue, but also what is happening in the celestial realms where the phenomena of the soul are foregrounded, rather than those of the body. He beholds the excitement of the souls; such an outpouring of rapture that even evildoers transform themselves, reconcile themselves to God, and receive the gift of forgiveness, not with shame and with weeping, but with joy. The notion of teshuvah brings us to a fourth principle of the Hasidic

ethos: Nobody is irrevocably damned. There is always room for transformation and reconciliation, and this itself is cause for joy. What the
Baal Shem Tov describes is a social cosmos, one that embraces the "impossible contradiction," as Weber put it, that "God's absolutely free
decrees" are indeed "subject to change by human influence."[59]

Also significant is the revelation that the messianic advent will occur
when the Baal Shem Tov's own teaching "becomes famous and revealed
in the world...and they too will be able to practice unifications and ascents like you." Here we have the radical notion, at the very outset of
Hasidic history, that the function of the tsadik as a bridge between
heaven and earth must ultimately be democratized; the practice of
"uniting unities" cannot remain only within the purview of the mystical
elite, but must somehow be made accessible to all. The fifth principle
of the Hasidic ethos, accordingly, is its fundamentally egalitarian aspiration.[60] However, we cannot avoid the fact that for the Baal Shem
Tov this is sobering news. He is dismayed by the length of time that
will pass before a socio-mystical project of such ambition is completed.
This is all the more sobering since he is forbidden from revealing the
specific techniques that he thinks can make unifications and ascents
more universally accessible. On the other hand, he does impart one
very specific practice that apparently does not demand extraordinary
esoteric knowledge or mystical expertise. It is worth paying closer attention to this instruction in particular:

> While you pray and study, and in every single word and utter-
> ance of your lips, have intent to unify the name [of God]. For
> in every single letter there are worlds, and souls, and divinity,
> and they ascend, bond, and unite with one another...uniting
> in true singularity with divinity, and you shall encompass your
> soul together with them...and all the worlds unite as one and
> ascend, making great joy and pleasure without measure...

As far as practice goes there are two central elements here, intent
and speech. The intent of speech is to unify; not merely to unify the
speaker with God, but to unify the self with other souls and worlds as
well. This goes far beyond the normative phenomenon that scholars of
religion term *unio mystica*, in that it includes social and cosmic dimensions as well. Moreover, all these elements—"worlds, and souls, and

divinity"—are present not only within words of prayer and Torah, but "in every single word and utterance of your lips." Intentional speech, accordingly, can transformatively sacralize even the most mundane, or secular, utterance. You may be talking about a business transaction or running through a list of household chores, and yet you are uniting unions. Your speech act is a cosmic communication, a socio-mystical incantation, a disclosure of the divine light that inheres even within the crass darkness of our physical habitation.

Thus far we have adduced five characteristics of the Hasidic ethos: 1) In its mystical core we find the social, 2) it is fundamentally joyous, 3) it endows the embodied soul with cosmic significance, 4) it celebrates the possibility of self-transformation and reconciliation even for evildoers, and 5) an egalitarian impulse is central to its aspirational orientation— mystical practices are for everyone. The Baal Shem Tov's teaching about intentional speech amplifies many of these themes, and also explicates a sixth principle of the Hasidic ethos, namely that divinity is immanent within the mundane. While this notion is only mentioned in passing here, other sources make it clear that this was a theological fundamental of Hasidism, and one that was particularly offensive to the rabbinic critics of the fledgling movement.[61] Here it is already clear, however, that this doctrine of divine immanence is especially linked to very specific conceptions of speech and of unification.[62]

To these six characteristics we can add some that were mentioned earlier in this chapter: 7) A phenomenological emphasis on effacement (*bitul*) of the self and the world, and 8) a conception of wealth as belonging to the people of Israel as a whole rather than to individuals, and as a divine gift conditional upon its charitable redistribution. While there are certainly additional elements of the Hasidic ethos, this provides a complete enough picture to form the basis of the broader argument of this book, which relates to the development of Chabad-Lubavitch Hasidism in particular. In Chabad, beginning with Schneur Zalman of Liadi's *Tanya*, the relationship between divine immanence, speech, and unification is given special attention. In a passage that is directly continuous with the above-cited teaching of the Baal Shem Tov, Schneur Zalman writes:

> It is written, "Lord, your word stands eternally in heaven," (Psalms, 119:89) and the Baal Shem Tov explained [that this

means as follows]: the words that You spoke, "let there be a
firmament..." (Genesis, 1:6) these words and letters are up-
standing eternally within the firmament of the heaven...This
is what the Arizal taught that even within that which is literally inanimate, such as stones, and dirt, and water, there is a
soul and a spiritual vitality, that is the vestment of the letters
of divine speech...that vitalize and create the inanimate in
order that its existence shall emerge from the nothingness
and nullity that preceded the six days of creation...[63]

Simply put: The ground of all existence, including inanimate
physicality, is nothing more and nothing less than the word of God.
Elsewhere Schneur Zalman goes so far as to equate "the revelation of
light and vitality from His blessed self to create the worlds and vitalize
them...which are the ten statements with which the world was created" with "the rest of Torah, Prophets, and Scriptures entirely, which
the prophets grasped in their prophetic visions."[64] The physical world
itself, like the visions of the prophets recorded in the Bible, is nothing
less than the revelation of the word of God, and therefore nothing other
than a manifestation of God's own self. This is the unifying principle
by which all the diverse elements of reality, as we experience it, are
reconfigured as the multifarious modes of divine speech. The work of
unification, accordingly, is the work of aligning our own consciousness
and our own speech with its fundamental essence, the consciousness
and speech of the one God.

Against the processes of secularization and disenchantment described by Weber, the Baal Shem Tov and his successors had a vision
for resacralization and reenchantment of the world. Every utterance
was to be transfigured into a divine incantation—indeed, a prophecy—
that would shatter the iron cage of physical corporeality, and thereby
release the infinite light of the soul from its fleshy encasement. Moreover, against the "inner-worldly asceticism" of the Protestant ethic, the
Hasidic ethos offers a model of "inner-worldly mysticism" according to
which the fleshy body can itself be transformed into a beacon of transcendent light.[65] Against the irrevocable petrification of our social and
cultural institutions—of life itself—the new ethos of Hasidism offers
the joyous possibility of transformation and rehabilitation, reconciliation and revitalization.

1.4—Chabad Hasidism and the Social Vision of the Lubavitcher Rebbe

WHILE SOME SCHOLARS today are in doubt as to whether or not the Baal Shem Tov saw himself as the leader of a new movement, it is clear that within three decades of his death Hasidism had indeed become a movement.[66] Marcin Wodziński's innovative cartographic survey, his *Historical Atlas of Hasidism*, demonstrates the movement's spread across Eastern Europe, and ultimately to Israel and the United States, with strikingly vivid detail. In a double-page map depicting the global network of Chabad outposts we can see that it is clearly this stream of Hasidism that is most dedicated to the mandate—charted by the messiah—to disseminate the Baal Shem Tov's teachings to the "outside."[67] From the late 1920s and on Chabad has also made the publication of Hasidic texts, and their translations in multiple languages, a central plank of its activist agenda.[68]

In a talk delivered in 1980, the Lubavitcher Rebbe reflected on Chabad's mission not only to preserve and publish Hasidic texts, but also to translate them into the "seventy languages" of the world. While this was a project that was initiated by his predecessor, he himself was deeply invested in its advancement. Here we get a sense of his expansive conception of the universal relevance of Hasidic teachings:

> The dissemination of the wellsprings that on the part of my father-in-law, the Rebbe, was such that it reached into the ultimate "outside," even into the "outside" that has no "outside" beyond it. For he translated aspects of the wellsprings, secrets and secrets-of-secrets of the Torah, into the seventy languages. And he translated in such a form that the full understanding and comprehension that is in the interiority of Torah should be there, this being the objective of Chabad Hasidic teaching, that it should be drawn down into understanding and comprehension, in the literal sense...to the degree that even a non-Jew, in the literal sense, can understand it.[69]

To disseminate the fountains of the Baal Shem Tov to the outside is to communicate these teachings universally and to transform the

secular into the sacred. In its earlier phases, however, the scope of
Hasidism's transformative project remained constrained to the Jewish communities in Eastern Europe. The Baal Shem Tov's teachings
proliferated only among Jews, only in the sacred and semi-sacred
languages of the Jews, Hebrew and Yiddish. But the catastrophic
upheavals of the first half of the 20th century dispersed Hasidism
throughout Europe and ultimately throughout the world. This created the necessity and the opportunity to extend the sacralization
of mundane speech to the inherently secular languages of all the
world's nations. In other words, this passage provides us with a theorization of the universal realization of the Baal Shem Tov's vision
through the unfolding of history.

This conception of opportunity born of necessity is worth dwelling on, because it goes to the core of Schneerson's understanding of
the role of history in the transformation of society. In the historical
memory of the Jews, the last two thousand years constitute an exile
that has dragged on for all-too-long, but which is believed to precede
the final redemption with the advent of the messiah. The current
epoch of exile began with the destruction of the Second Temple in
Jerusalem by the Roman general (and later emperor) Titus, and it is
traditionally understood as a withdrawal of divine revelation from
the world.[70] In other words, exile is the kind of phenomenon that Weber termed disenchantment; God's presence in the world is no longer
apparent. In Schneerson's thought, however, exile and redemption
are placed in a dialectical relationship according to which the very
first moment of exile already heralds the even greater revelation that
is to come with the final redemption. This is a notion that he developed on many different occasions and through readings of various
rabbinic texts. In the *Talmud yerushalmi*, for example, we find an anecdote according to which the messiah was already born on the very
day that the Temple was destroyed.[71] For Schneerson this meant that
even the moment of destruction was itself a step toward the ultimate
redemption:

> Not only must we look at the good outcome…that will
> result from this [destruction], but more-so, the loftier at-
> tainment of the redemption should not be seen [merely] as
> something achieved through a secondary (not-good) event.

Rather these [the destruction and the redemption] are a single phenomenon.[72]

One prophecy predicting and depicting the ruin of the Temple and the onset of exile is particularly suggestive: "Zion shall be a plowed field" (Micah, 3:12). To plow a field is not a destructive act but a constructive step that prepares the ground for new growth. Accordingly, Schneerson explained, this aptly captures the dialectic between exile and redemption: "The ruin itself has the advantage of a plowed field; it is destined for sowing and growth."[73]

Practically speaking, this means that every form of adversity, no matter how painful and catastrophic, harbors within it a positive telos. The two thousand years of deep and dark adversity experienced by the Jewish people were also a period of great achievements and progress, not only for the Jews and for Judaism, but for the world at large as well. On one occasion Schneerson explained that if the advent of the messianic age would have occurred ahead of its allocated time, various facets of the Torah would never have been fully disclosed, because they "can be revealed only over the span of many generations."[74] This is not to say that Schneerson was cavalier when confronted with the awful physical and spiritual sufferings of the Jews throughout this long exilic epoch, culminating with the Holocaust. On the contrary, he openly expressed deep pain, frustration, and even astonishment at the continued suffering and the continued impositions of exile. But at the same time he harbored a deep faith that it was out of this pain, out of this destruction, out of this darkness, that the ultimate delight and light of a new utopia would be built.[75]

Notably, Schneerson framed the emergence of democracy and social progress in the same terms. In its early stages, he argued, the French Revolution was a violent eruption with extremely negative and destructive dimensions. But over the course of time it has emerged as one of the founding moments of a new form of progressive government, which aspires to allow for cultural flourishing and religious freedom in equal measure.[76] This relatively new system is still in development, and it has yet to be perfected. Its vulnerabilities have been made clear to us by the ugly forms of totalitarianism that it has birthed and struggled with, as in the cases of Nazi Germany and Communist Russia. Even in the 21st century it continues to encounter new crises—some of them great, some of them small. And yet we can hope that through these very crises it will also continue to progress and improve.

An interesting parallel to Schneerson's understanding of the dialectical unfolding of the ultimate redemption through the painful processes of exile can be found in the work of the sociologist Philip Slater. Following the lead of biologist and futurist Elisabet Sahtouris, Slater theorizes that significant cultural change occurs in a manner that isn't so different from the transformation of a caterpillar into a butterfly:

> Tiny new cells—what scientists call imaginal cells—begin to appear in the caterpillar's body, and start to multiply. The caterpillar's immune system reacts to these new cells as foreign...and quickly attacks them and tries to destroy them...Finally, the caterpillar's immune system is overwhelmed and the caterpillar is liquefied. The imaginal cells then recycle the liquefied mass into a new entity—the butterfly.[77]

Slater invokes this as an illustration of the way in which old cultural forms are transformed from within, with "upholders of tradition" attacking those who seek to advance the emergence of new paradigms. This echoes Sorokin's conception of crisis as a sign of the protracted process of significant social transition. But the image of the chrysalis that the caterpillar both produces and reacts against, and is ultimately encased within, is also reminiscent of Weber's notion of a social paradigm becoming an iron cage within which humanity is ultimately imprisoned. The difference is that Weber did not see the way out of the iron cage, while Slater proposes that the way out is precisely through the cultural process of petrification, or liquefaction: "When the budding culture replaces the previous one, it doesn't create a new way of being out of nothing, but merely rearranges old patterns to make the new ones. Just as the caterpillar has held the blueprint for the butterfly all along."[78]

Arguably, this is a conception of cultural change that Schneerson would concur with. It is specifically through undergoing and overcoming the painful struggles of exile that the beautiful butterfly of the messianic future will be constituted. We cannot simply wait for the messiah with our arms folded, but must instead construct our redemption out of the world we inhabit in the present. In a line that Schneerson would often quote, Schneur Zalman of Liadi made the point clearly and definitively:

> The ultimate completion of the Messianic era…, which is the revelation of the light of the infinite, is dependent on our work and toil throughout the era of exile…[79]

Schneur Zalman goes on to invoke the kabbalistic parallel to Slater's image of the chrysalis, namely, *klipah*, "the shell." At present, he tells us, the divinity that inheres within the world finds itself "under the governance of the *klipah*," which inhibits its revelation. The work of the exilic epoch, therefore, is to redeem these sacred sparks through the sacralization of all our activities—in the three realms of thought, speech, and action—thereby sacralizing the world and "transforming darkness into light" to the point that "this physical world specifically will be filled with the glory of God, and all flesh will perceive it together."[80]

In line with this theorization of the dialectic between exile and redemption, Schneerson argued that it was precisely as a result of the catastrophic upheavals of the modern era that the Jewish people in general, and the Hasidic movement in particular, were now afforded the opportunity to broadcast a universal message. In America especially, but also in other democratic societies, they were not only free to practice their own faith, but also had the right to bring their own perspective onto the stage of public discourse.[81] That right has increasingly given way to real possibility, and through such visually prominent initiatives as the public menorah campaign Chabad has succeeded in making at least a superficial impression on wider cultural consciousness, in America and elsewhere too.[82]

But Schneerson was much more ambitious than that. He was fundamentally a man of ideas as well as of action, and he was not merely interested in making a superficial dent in the dominant culture. Enfusing Jewish life with the transformative culture of Hasidism was a first step toward a more universal vision; he wanted non-Jews too to consciously participate in the cosmic union of worlds, souls, and divinity. He wanted the Hasidic ethos to become the new foundation for a sacralized global society, providing an entirely new paradigm for individual life and communal life, for social institutions and for political norms.

As we have already seen, the first step in this process of Hasidic universalization was translation. Beyond translation, however, Schneerson would explicitly articulate an expansive worldview, addressing himself to the wider world as well as to his Hasidim. His public talks, personal letters, and Hasidic discourses are marked by a clear emphasis both on social ideas and on practical social issues, often with direct reference to policy debates that are still current today. Questions relating to education and its purposes, to law enforcement and the indignities of incarceration, to geopolitics and diplomacy, to energy and stewardship of the world, were often on his agenda. This is an emphasis that has hardly been noted by other scholars, including those who have sought to study Chabad through a sociological lens. Yet a comprehensive survey of his oeuvre reveals that he was as incisive a social thinker as he was a successful social leader.

Schneur Zalman of Liadi, Chabad's first rebbe, was noted for his systematic psychological approach as presented in his enduringly popular work, *Likutei amarim tanya*.[83] That work has important sections relating to social psychology as well, and elsewhere in the Chabad corpus we find additional texts that are noteworthy for their theorizations of social interaction and communitas.[84] What Schneur Zalman was most concerned with, however, was the personal battle that each individual must wage to overcome bodily inclinations toward selfishness rather than service, and to the sensuous rather than the spiritual. The divinely ordained imposition of embodiment upon the soul, and indeed the very construction of the physical world, makes the work of divine union a formidable challenge. Recognizing that challenge, Schneur Zalman provided a toolkit of contemplative practices that enable individuals to achieve self-mastery and to transform all aspects of embodied life into a vehicle for the revelation and realization of God's unified wisdom and will. In other words, he was preoccupied with meeting the psychological and intellectual challenges that stand in the way of the implementation of the Baal Shem Tov's teachings on the personal level.[85]

Menachem Mendel Schneerson shifted Chabad's central focus not from intellectualism to activism—as some have assumed—but from the psychological to the sociological. As should already be clear, Hasidism's ethos was always socio-mystical in its fundamental constitution, and it should likewise be clear that Schneerson did not leave Chabad's psychological and phenomenological approach entirely behind. But what is so strikingly novel here is an emphasis on social questions and social theorizations that is so expansive and far-reaching as to amount to a full system of social thought. Moreover, this is not a purely theoretical system, but one that he also embodied and implemented in practice. He did not merely speak and write, he also acted and inspired others to act.

Resting on a firm foundation in the classical texts of Hasidism, Kabbalah, and rabbinic Judaism, the sociological edifice Schneerson erected is nevertheless wholly contemporary in its orientation. He did not engage only with the particular challenges facing the Hasidic community or the Jewish community, but sought to apply the Hasidic ethos to the challenges faced by human society collectively. Though he never composed a comprehensive and systematic sociological opus analogous to Schneur Zalman's *Tanya*, he did speak and write voluminously over the span of more than forty years. The project of this book is to sift through that material, extracting, organizing, analyzing, elaborating, and contextualizing the various and multifarious elements of his social vision. The point is not merely to apply existing sociological tools in an attempt to understand Schneerson from without, but rather to excavate his own social concepts from within.

Notes

1. Max Weber, *The Protestant Ethic and the Spirit of Capitalism*, translated by Talcott Parsons (New York and London: Charles Scribner's Sons / George Allen & Unwin Ltd., 1950). For more on the weight given to religious ideas by the founders of modern sociology see Philip Wexler, "Social Psychology, the Hasidic Ethos and the Spirit of the New Age," *Kabbalah: Journal for the Study of Jewish Mystical Texts* 7 (2002): 11–15.

2. On the general phenomenon of resacralization and its implications see Grace Davie, "Resacralization," in Bryan S. Turner (ed.) *The New Blackwell Companion to The Sociology of Religion* (Chichester, UK: Wiley, 2010), 160-177; Philip Wexler, *Mystical Sociology: Toward Cosmic Social Theory* (New York: Peter Lang, 2013), 19-26. On resacralization in the mystical vision of the Lubavitcher Rebbe see *ibid.*, 44-6; Eli Rubin, "Divine Zeitgeist—The Rebbe's Appreciative Critique of Modernity," *Chabad.org* <chabad.org/2973252> (accessed April 8, 2018). Also see David Sorkin, "Between Messianism and Survival: Secularization and Sacralization in Modern Judaism," *Journal of Modern Jewish Studies*, 3, no. 1 (2004): 73-86.

3. For a more nuanced presentation see John Raines (ed.), *Marx on Religion* (Philadelphia: Temple University Press, 2002). Also see Michael Löwy, "Weber Against

Marx? The Polemic with Historical Materialism in the Protestant Ethic," *Science & Society* 53, no. 1 (Spring, 1989): 71-83.

4. Weber, *The Protestant Ethic*, 27.

5. *Ibid.*, 103-4.

6. *Ibid.*, 105 and 122.

7. Moshe Idel, *Hasidism: Between Ecstasy and Magic* (Albany: SUNY Press, 1995).

8. Weber, *Essays in Sociology*, trans. H.H. Gerth and C. Wright Mills (New York: Oxford University Press, 1946), 332.

9. See Wexler, "Social Psychology," 19-28.

10. Weber, *The Protestant Ethic*, 110-115.

11. See Wexler, *Mystical Sociology: Toward Cosmic Social Theory* (New York: Peter Lang, 2013), 34, 55-59. On *bittul* as effacement see Elliot Wolfson, *Open Secret: Postmessianic Messianism and the Mystical Revision of Menachem Mendel Schneerson* (New York: Columbia University Press, 2009), 90.

12. Weber, *The Protestant Ethic*, 111-115.

13. Schneur Zalman of Liadi, *Likutei amarim tanya*, Chapter 26. For a fuller overview of this "manifesto" see Naftali Loewenthal, "The Ethics of Joy: Chabad Perspectives on Happiness," *Chabad.org*, <chabad.org/2219688>.

14. Schneur Zalman of Liadi, *Likutei amarim tany*, Chapter 25.

15. Weber, *The Protestant Ethic*, 159.

16. See Kate Bowler, *Blessed: A History of the American Prosperity Gospel* (Oxford: Oxford University Press, 2013), 227: "Modern prosperity believers are not unlike Max Weber's early Puritans, whose religious insecurity about their postmortem fate transmuted into capitalist virtues. It was the Protestant work ethic resurrected for a breathless nation of multitaskers and entrepreneurs and customer service professionals."

17. Marcin Wodziński, "The Socio-Economic Profile of a Religious Movement: The Case of Hasidism," *European History Quarterly*, no. 4 (September, 2016): 684; Glenn Dynner, *Men of Silk: The Hasidic Conquest of Polish Jewish Society* (Oxford, UK: Oxford University Press, 2008).

18. Wodziński, "Socio-Economic Profile of a Religious Movement," 674 and 687.

19. *Ibid.*, 686.

20. Weber, *The Protestant Ethic*, 159-160.

21. *Ibid.*, 118.

22. *Ibid.*, 179-181.

23. *Ibid.*, 181.

24. *Ibid.*, 182.

25. See Moshe Rosman, *Founder of Hasidism: The Quest for the Historical Ba'al Shem Tov* (Liverpool: The Littman Library of Jewish Civilization, 2013), and Immanuel Etkes, *The Besht: Magician, Mystic, and Leader* (Waltham, MA: Brandeis University Press, 2005).

26. For the most complete survey of current research on Hasidism see David Biale, et al., *Hasidism: A New History* (Princeton, NJ: Princeton University Press, 2018). The introduction to this work presents a historical survey of scholarly literature on Hasidism and ultimately argues that the movement's success over the last two centuries should be viewed as a form of "modernization without secularization." Also see Ada Rapoport-Albert (ed.), *Hasidism Reappraised* (Oxford: The Littman Library of Jewish Civilization, 1996); Ada Rapoport-Albert, *Hasidic Studies: Essays in History and Gender* (Liverpool: The Littman Library of Jewish Civilization, 2018); and Marcin Wodziński, *Historical Atlas of Hasidism* (Princeton, NJ: Princeton University Press, 2018). Despite the increasing interest in Hasidism, and the many important publications in recent decades, there are still large swaths of the movement's intellectual and social strata that remain to be researched, analyzed, and understood.

27. H. R. Tawney, "Foreword" to Weber, *The Protestant Ethic*, 1(c).

28. Here we use the translation provided in Christopher Adair-Toteff, "Max Weber's Charismatic Prophets," *History of the Human Sciences* 27, no. 1 (February 2014): 6. Cf. Max Weber, *The Sociology of Religion*, trans. Talcott Parsons (London: Methuen and Co., Ltd, 1965), 46.

29. Weber, *Sociology of Religion*, 47, 50, and 58-59.

30. *Ibid.*, 59.

31. Max Weber, "Science as Vocation," in David Owen and Tracy B. Strong (eds.), *Max Weber: The Vocation Lectures*, trans. Rodney Livingstone (Indianapolis: Hackett Publishing Company, 2004), 30. See the discussion in Adair-Toteff, "Max Weber's Charismatic Prophets," 12-14.

32. Weber, "Science as Vocation," 31, following Isaiah, 21:11-12.

33. *Ibid.*

34. On Sorokin's life and career see Barry V. Johnston, "Pitirim A. Sorokin (1889-1968): Pioneer and Pariah," *International Sociology* 11, no. 2 (June, 1996): 229-238. For a more sociological analysis of his career and reception see Lawrence T. Nichols, "Deviance and Social Science: The Instructive Historical Case of Pitirim Sorokin," *Journal of the History of the Social Sciences* 25 (October 1989): 335-355. Also see Philip J. Allen (ed.), *Pitirim A. Sorokin in Review* (Durham, NC: Duke University Press, 1963).

35. Pitirim A. Sorokin, *Social and Cultural Dynamics*, Vol. 1 (London: George Allen & Unwin Ltd., 1937), 72-73.

36. Weber, *The Protestant Ethic*, 182.

37. Pitirim A. Sorokin, *The Crisis of Our Age: The Social and Cultural Outlook* (New York: E.P. Dutton & Co., Inc., 1941), 300-301.

38. *Ibid.*, 302.

39. *Ibid.*, 306-307.

40. *Ibid.*, 303.

41. *Social and Cultural Dynamics*, Vol. 1, 75.

42. Rosman, *Founder of Hasidism*; Etkes, *The Besht*.

43. Here we refer to the teaching transmitted by the Baal Shem Tov in a letter addressed to his brother-in-law, Gershon of Kuty, which has already received a

huge amount of attention in scholarly literature. For a comprehensive overview
of these discussions, as well as a critical investigation of the various versions of
this letter that exist in manuscript and print, see Chaim Elly Moseson, *From Spoken Word to the Discourse of the Academy: Reading the Sources for the Teachings of the Besht*
(PhD thesis, Boston University, 2017), 35-116. The particular details of this teaching will be presented and analyzed below.

44. The specific circumstances of Schneerson's rise to the leadership are beyond the
scope of this study, but since they have been the subject of heated polemics we
cannot pass them by without any comment at all. In Biale's *Hasidism: A New History*, which aims to provide a canonical account under the rubric of broad scholarly
consensus, we read that Schneerson "staged a swift and successful campaign to ascend to the throne of Chabad" (695). The weight of the evidence, however, shows
that the campaign was not waged by Schneerson, but by the leading Hasidic elders
in the Chabad communities of Israel, Europe, and the United States, who sought
to persuade him to accept the leadership. For nearly a year Schneerson responded to their entreaties with unyielding resistance, finally acquiescing on the first
anniversary of his father-in-law's passing. To cite but one source attesting to this
struggle, the following is from a letter penned by the Hasid Shmuel Zalmanov
in New York to his uncle in Israel, and appears after a lengthy testimony to the
charisma, piety and leadership suitability of Schneerson: "he refuses to accept
the leadership despite all the pleas and urging of the Hasidim here…[however]
it must be brought to fruition…for our sake and the sake of our children…that
they shall be educated in the light of the truth bequeathed to us by our rebbes."
For a facsimile of this letter see Yosef Yitshak Greenberg and Eliezer Zaklikovsky
(eds.), *Yemai beresihit: yoman metekufat kabalat hanesiut* (Brooklyn, NY: Kehot Publication Society, 1993), 173. For a blow-by-blow account of the events and controversy
surrounding the succession that is well rooted in primary sources see "Appendix
2—The Ten Lost Years (1941-1951)," in Chaim Rapoport, *The Afterlife of Scholarship* (Oporto Press, 2011), 133-186. As Elliot Wolfson has noted in a preface to that
work, "despite the overtly polemical tone, Rapoport's criticisms are never offered
ad hominem. On the contrary, he painstakingly documents every point of contention…Rapoport's volume provides an invaluable treasure-trove of scholarship on
the seventh Rebbe of Habad Lubavitch."

45. Ilia Lurie, *Edah umedinah: Chasidut Chabad be'impariyah harusit 5588-5643* (Jerusalem:
Magnes Press, 2006), 104.

46. Max Weber, *Economy and Society*, edited by Guenther Roth and Claus Wittich
(Berkeley, CA: University of California Press, 1978), 242.

47. Though this point is tangential to our main argument here, our theorization of
Hasidic succession departs from that favored by most historians and sociologists,
with the slight exception of Lurie, who have paid attention to this phenomenon.
Rather than reduce this process to the question of the routinization of charisma,
and to the purely mechanistic and materialistic processes of politics, bureaucracy and finance, a deeper ethnographic and sociological investigation yields
a paradoxical social and psychological dynamic by which the office of the charismatic prophet or tsadik can only be filled by a successor who can disruptively
continue the legacy of their predecessor. A fuller examination of this disrup-
tive—or "revolutionary"—element could go a long way to explaining some of

the conflicts that have been noted and partially described by scholars. Cf. Samuel Heilman, *Who Will Lead Us? The Story of Five Hasidic Dynasties in America* (Oakland, CA: University of California Press, 2017); Avrum Ehrlich, *Leadership in the HaBaD Movement: A Critical Evaluation of HaBaD Leadership, History, and Succession* (New Jersey: Jason Aronson Publishers, 2000).

48. Weber, *Economy and Society*, 245.

49. For the original published version see *Ben porat yosef* (Koretz, 1781), 100a.

50. See the extensive discussion in Moseson, *From Spoken Word to the Discourse of the Academy*, 35-116. For a list of studies touching on textual issues relating to this letter see *ibid.*, 35, n. 78. For Moseson's conclusion regarding the Koretz version of the text see *ibid.*, 115.

51. Regarding messianism see the discussion and citations in Jonathan Dauber, "The Baal Shem Tov and the messiah: A Reappraisal of the Baal Shem Tov's Letter to R. Gershon of Kutov" *Jewish Studies Quarterly* 15 (2008): 210-241. Regarding speech see the relevant discussion and citations in Ariel Evan Mayse, *Beyond the Letters: The Question of Language in the Teachings of Rabbi Dov Baer of Mezritch* (PhD thesis, Harvard University, 2015), 166-168. For a more recent and more comprehensive analysis of this topic, taking a wider range of sources and disciplinary considerations into account, see Moshe Idel, *Vocal Rites and Broken Theologies: Cleaving to Vocables in R. Israel Ba'al Shem Tov's Mysticism* (New York: Herder and Herder, 2019).

52. Naftali Loewenthal, "The Baal Shem Tov's 'Iggeret ha-Kodesh' and Contemporary Habad 'Outreach,'" in *"Let the Old Make Way for the New,"* Vol. 1, edited by David Assaf and Ada Rapoport-Albert (Jerusalem: The Zalman Shazar Center for Jewish History, 2009), 69-101.

53. Elliot R. Wolfson, "Walking as a Sacred Duty: Theological Dimensions of Social Reality in Early Hasidism," in *Hasidism Reappraised*, edited by Ada Rapoport-Albert (Oxford: The Littman Library of Jewish Civilization, 1996), 184, n. 10.

54. For earlier iterations of this argument, which will be further developed later in this book, see Philip Wexler, *Mystical Sociology*, 52-53; Eli Rubin, "Habad Hasidism and the Mystical Reconstruction of Society," in *Jewish Spirituality and Social Transformation*, edited by Philip Wexler (New York: Herder and Herder, 2018), 59-78.

55. Despite the fact that joy is popularly associated with Hasidism—or perhaps due to that fact—the importance of joy in Hasidism has yet to receive comprehensive scholarly attention. For an overview of some Hasidic sources that emphasize the importance of joy see Feigue Berman, *Hasidic Dance: A Historical and Theological Analysis* (PhD thesis, New York University, 1999), 169-175. Also see Michael Fishbane, "To Jump for Joy," *Journal of Jewish Thought & Philosophy* 6, no. 2 (1997): 371-387; Naftali Loewenthal. "The Ethics of Joy: Chabad Perspectives on Happiness," *Chabad.org*, <chabad.org/2219688>.

56. "I saw a great accusation, to the extent that the Satan was almost given permission to destroy whole regions and communities. I committed my very soul and prayed, 'let us fall into the hand of God and not fall into the hands of man.'" For discussions of this section of the letter see Moshe Roseman, *Founder of Hasidism: A Quest for the Historical Ba'al Shem Tov* (Oxford: Littman Library of Jewish Civilization, 2013), 110-111; Etkes, *The Besht*, 87-91.

57. For more on anti-asceticism and worship through embodiment in early Hasidism, see Louis Jacobs, "Eating as an Act of Worship in Hasidic Thought," in *Studies in Jewish Religious and Intellectual History Presented to Alexander Altmann on the Occasion of His Seventieth Birthday*, edited by Siegfried Stein and Raphael Loewe (Tuscaloosa, AL: University of Alabama Press, 1979), 157-166; Tsippi Kauffman, *In All Your Ways Know Him: The Concept of God and Avodah be-Gashmiyut in the Early Stages of Hasidism* (Ramat-Gan: Bar Ilan University Press, 2009).

58. Roseman, *Founder*, 109-110.

59. Weber, *The Protestant Ethic*, 103-104. On the dynamic of teshuvah in the Baal Shem Tov's teachings see Naftali Loewenthal, *Communicating the Infinite: The Emergence of the Habad School* (Chicago: University of Chicago Press, 1990), 16 and 25-26. The significance of teshuvah in Hasidism is another topic that awaits comprehensive scholarly treatment.

60. On Hasidism's egalitarian dimensions see Marcin Wodziński, *Hasidism: Key Questions* (Oxford: Oxford University Press, 2018), esp. 9-10, 30; Naftali Loewenthal, "Is Socialism Kosher? Proto-Socialist Resonances in Chassidic Thought," *Chabad.org*, <chabad.org/2703778>. On the question of the extension of this impulse to include women see Nehemia Polen, "Miriam's Dance: Radical Egalitarianism in Hasidic Thought," *Modern Judaism* 12, no. 1 (Feb., 1992): 1-21; Ada Rapoport-Albert, *Hasidic Studies: Essays in History and Gender* (Liverpool: Littman Library of Jewish Civilization, 2018). More will be said about this question below.

61. See the relevant discussion and citations in Biale, *Hasidism*, 161-163, and in Immanuel Etkes, *Rabbi Shneur Zalman of Liady: The Origins of Chabad Hasidism* (Waltham, MA: Brandeis University Press, 2015), 132-133 and 147-148.

62. Ariel Evan Mayse, *Beyond the Letters*, 166-168.

63. *Tanya*, Shaar hayichud veha'emunah, Chapter 1, 76b [152].

64. *Likutei amarim tanya*, Chapter 21, 26b [52].

65. On these two "inner-worldly" typologies see Weber, *Essays in Sociology*, 325-326.

66. See Ada Rapoport-Albert, "Hasidism after 1772: Structural Continuity and Change," in *Hasidism Reappraised*, edited by Ada Rapoport-Albert (Oxford: The Littman Library of Jewish Civilization, 1996); Biale, *Hasidism*, 43-57.

67. Marcin Wodziński, Historical Atlas of Hasidism (Princeton, NJ: Princeton University Press, 2018), 218-219.

68. See Eli Rubin, "A Linguistic Bridge Between Alienation and Intimacy: Habad's Theorization of Yiddish in Historical and Cultural Perspective," Part 2, *In Geveb: A Journal of Yiddish Studies*, Special Issue on Religious Thought (January, 2019).

69. Menachem Mendel Schneerson, *Sichot Kodesh 5740*, Vol. 1 (Brooklyn, NY: Vaad Hanachot Hatemimim, 1986), 804.

70. For an example of this conception as expressed by Schneerson see Menachem Mendel Schneerson, *Torat menachem—hitvaduyot*, Vol. 27 [5720, I] (Brooklyn, NY: Kehot Publication Society, 2004), 408-409: "In the time when the Holy Temple was standing divinity was seen, as the sages say…'ten miracles occurred for our forefathers in the Holy Temple,' (Avot, 5:5) which were even perceived by eyes of flesh. Whereas after the destruction of the Holy Temple,

behold 'we did not see our signs' (Psalms, 74:9), meaning that there are still miracles, but...the one to whom the miracle occurs does not recognize his miracle (Cf. *Talmud bavli,* Nidah, 31a)."

71. *Talmud yerushalmi,* Brakhot, 2:4 (17b). Cf. *Eikha rabbah,* 1:51. For just two examples of Schneerson's many citations of such sources see Menachem Mendel Schneerson, *Torat menachem—hitvaduyot,* Vol. 33 [5722, II] (Brooklyn, NY: Kehot Publication Society, 2006), 331; *idem., Torat menachem—hitvaduyot 5749,* Vol. 4 (Brooklyn, NY: Kehot Publication Society, 1992), 48, n. 24.

72. Menachem Mendel Schneerson, *Likutei sichot,* Vol. 19 (Brooklyn, NY: Kehot Publication Society, 2000), 77.

73. *Ibid.*

74. Schneerson, *Torat menachem—hitvaduyot,* Vol. 33, 331.

75. For one instance in which Schneerson struck an uncharacteristically autobiographical note, explicating the extent to which exilic pain and redemptive faith preoccupied him in equal measure, see his 1966 letter to then president of Israel, Yitzhak Ben-Zvi, in Menachem Mendel Schneerson, *Igrot kodesh,* Vol. 12 (Brooklyn, NY: Kehot Publication Society, 1989), 412: "From the day I first went to school (cheder), and even before then, an image of the future redemption began to form in my mind...such a redemption in such a manner that thereby the suffering of exile, the decrees and the massacres, would become understood...all in a manner that with a whole heart and with complete understanding...'on that day you shall say: I thank you God, that you were wroth with me' (Isaiah, 12:1)." Schneerson himself lost close family members in the Holocaust, including his brother Berel. His wife lost her sister Sheina.

76. See Menachem Mendel Schneerson, *Torat menachem—hitvaduyot 5749,* Vol. 4 (Brooklyn, NY: Kehot Publication Society, 1992), 10-11; *Torat menachem—hitvaduyot 5752,* Vol. 1 (Brooklyn, NY: Kehot Publication Society, 1994), 402-404.

77. Philip Slater, *The Chrysalis Effect: The Metamorphosis of Global Culture* (Eastborne, UK: Sussex University Press, 2009), 1.

78. *Ibid.*

79. *Likutei amarim tanya,* Chapter 37, 46b [92].

80. *Ibid.,* 46b-49b [92-98]. Cf. Numbers, 14:21; Isaiah, 40:5.

81. See the subtitled video of a talk delivered by Schneerson on December 25, 1983 (19 Kislev, 5744), "Light Unto the Nations: Part 2: Greater Opportunity, Greater Responsibility," *Chabad.org,* <chabad.org/1023094>.

82. See Dianne Ashton, *Hanukkah in America: A History* (New York: New York University Press, 2013), 242-249. The cover of this book shows the Chabad-installed "national menorah" in front of the White House in Washington D.C. Also see the Jewish Educational Media documentary, "Menorahs around the World," *YouTube,* <https://www.youtube.com/watch?v=TAGqrYpTBfg>.

83. See Ariel Mayse, "The Sacred Writ," 109-156.

84. See esp. *Likutei amarim tanya,* Chapter 32, 41a-b [81-82]. This text and others have already been discussed in Philip Wexler, *Mystical Sociology,* 67–69; Eli Rubin, "'The Pen Shall Be Your Friend': Intertextuality, Intersociality, and the

Cosmos—Examples of the Tzemach Tzedek's Way in the Development of Chabad Chassidic Thought," Chabad.org, <chabad.org/3286179>; *idem.*, "Purging Divisiveness, Embracing Difference: Rabbi Shalom DovBer Schneersohn's Manifesto against Self-Righteousness in Interpersonal Discourse," *Chabad.org,* <chabad.org/3800391>.

85. On the psychological orientation of Chabad, and of Hasidism more generally, see Gershom Scholem, *Major Trends in Jewish Mysticism* (New York: Schocken Books, 1941), 340-341; Norman Lamm, *The Religious Thought of Hasidism: Text and Commentary* (Hoboken, NJ: Yeshiva University Press, 1999), 60, n. 16; Jonathan Garb, *Yearnings of the Soul: Psychological Thought in Modern Kabbalah* (Chicago: University of Chicago Press, 2015), esp. 11, 59-65.

⚬〰〰〰⚬

CHAPTER 2

FROM CATASTROPHE TO RENAISSANCE: THE REBBE AND HASIDISM IN AMERICA

2.1—Exile and Refuge

IT WAS AS a refugee that Menachem Mendel Schneerson arrived in America, in the Summer of 1941.[1] Ten years later, following the passing of his father-in-law, he would become the new rebbe of the Chabad-Lubavitch stream of Hasidism, seventh in a dynastic line beginning with Schneur Zalman of Liadi. It was in the postwar context of the United States that he came to prominence, and from the iconic building at 770 Eastern Parkway, in Brooklyn, New York, that he broadcast his vision for a global Jewish renaissance. It is with Schneerson's leadership and social vision that this book is most concerned, rather than the fuller story of his life, thought, teachings, and legacy. Yet it is important to understand something of the context from which he emerged, and thereby the prism through which he viewed the social and political upheavals of the 20th century, along with the catastrophes suffered by the Jewish people in particular.

Throughout the quarter century between 1916 and 1941 the entire Chabad-Lubavitch movement was in a perpetual state of displacement, wandering, and exile. In 1916 the movement's fifth leader had left his

historic seat in the town of Lubavitch (Lyubavichi), five hundred ki-
lometers west of Moscow, ahead of the German advance into Russia.
Playing on a rabbinic saying that "the divine presence underwent ten
exiles" (*Talmud bavli*, Rosh Hashanah, 31a) Schneerson would later comment that Chabad-Lubavitch likewise underwent a succession of ten
exiles: "From Lubavitch to Rostov, from Rostov to Petersburg, from
Petersburg to Latvia, and afterwards to Poland, culminating with the
exile to America…"[2] Schneerson himself had been forced into hiding
and then into exile as Stalin cemented his hold on the Soviet Union. In
the late 1920s and early 1930s he shuttled between Riga, Latvia, where
his father-in-law was based, and Berlin, where he attended the lectures
of such scientific luminaries as Erwin Schrödinger and Walther Nernst
at the city's Humboldt University.[3] He left Berlin for Paris following
Hitler's rise to power in 1933, and a few short years later was forced to
flee again as the Nazis occupied France.[4]

Schneerson was unequivocal that even in "the land of the free"—and
as he termed the United States, "a nation of benevolence"—the Jewish
people were still very much in exile. (He was equally unequivocal that
Jews in Israel remained in exile too.)[5] Yet he also saw America as a place
whose rich spiritual and material resources could serve as a foundation
for a new epoch, an epoch in which Hasidism could flourish internationally. This chapter is concerned not only with his vision of America as the
new center for a global Jewish renaissance, but also with his vision of the
American nation as an exporter of charity and justice on a global scale.

This idea of America, and of its role in the family of nations, did
not emerge out of nowhere. Schneerson's arrival in "the new world" has
previously been portrayed as a moment of personal reinvention; it is
imagined that he transformed himself overnight from an aspiring engineer cum bourgeois Parisian into an aspiring mystic and Hasidic rebbe.[6]
Such a farcical thesis depends on a willful disregard of the primary sources that grant direct access to Schneerson's intellectual preoccupations
during the years he spent in Europe, namely his personal journals and
his correspondence—with his own father, the kabbalist Levi Yitzchak
Schneersohn of Ekaterinoslav; with his father-in-law, Yosef Yitzchak
Schneersohn of Lubavitch; and with the Talmudic genius Yosef Rosen
of Rogachov.[7] These sources have hardly received any scholarly attention, yet in many respects they foreshadow ideas that he would develop
in much fuller form during his tenure as rebbe and leader of Chabad.

Here we will focus first on a selection of journal entries that Schneerson penned as the Nazis were still extending their chokehold across Europe. Through a plethora of rabbinic, kabbalistic, and Hasidic texts they reflect on the sort of existential questions that become especially pressing when the specter of evil threatens to engulf the world. The fundamentals of his worldview, it is clear, were fully formed long before the responsibilities of public leadership were thrust upon him. Later in this chapter we will turn to an earlier correspondence between Schneerson and his father-in-law. In this case too, a preoccupation with the kabbalistic and Hasidic significance of America offers a clear preview of the unique geopolitical conception that is repeatedly elaborated and applied in his letters, interviews, and talks from the 1950s and onward.

Taken together, these earlier examples of Schneerson's writings and correspondence serve as a fitting introduction to the fuller theorization of his social ideas as unfolded in the subsequent pages of this book.

2.2—Between Nihilism and Messianism in the Face of Fascism

SCHNEERSON'S VISION, AS reflected in his wartime journal entries, is thrown into stark relief when we note the striking symmetries and asymmetries between Schneerson's path from Berlin, and that of the Jewish philosopher, cultural critic, and essayist Walter Benjamin.

In the wake of Hitler's rise to power both men had moved from Berlin to Paris. Following the invasion of France in 1940 they each fled south, obtained permission to enter the United States, and successfully crossed the Pyrenees mountains into Spain. But here the path of Benjamin was brought to a tragic end. Schneerson, on the other hand, was able to make a safe passage from Lisbon to New York City, where he would forge a new beginning. This is not a merely superficial comparison. It is rather one that extends into the inner movements of the mind, into the parallel struggles of Schneerson and Benjamin to make sense of Europe's unraveling, to confront the deathly march of fascism, and to salvage the enduring hope for messianic redemption.[8]

In this period of flight following desperate flight, Benjamin penned his final fragmentary essay, *Theses on the Philosophy of History*.[9] This is

a text that has received a great deal of scholarly attention; its arguments are cryptic, its implications encrypted, and yet it can be said
with certainty that its preoccupation is with the messiah as fascism's
only antidote. Most will not be surprised that this verdict is implicit
in Schneerson's contemporaneous journal entries as well.[10] But what
makes the comparison of these two figures a fruitful endeavor are the
points of departure that set the resonances apart.

An obvious point of departure is one of background and language.
Benjamin had little direct knowledge of Judaism, and he articulates
himself in the language of European political theory and cultural criticism; he only arrives secondarily at the Jewish concept of messiah.[11]
Schneersohn, on the other hand, was first and foremost a practitioner
of Rabbinic and Hasidic life, and only secondarily a theorist and scholar steeped in texts; his is the language of the Bible, the Talmud and
the Zohar, of Moses, Shimon bar Yochai, and Schneur Zalman of Liadi. Benjamin once said that "the messianic kingdom is always present."
Gershom Scholem, who recorded this remark, at once affirmed this
statement and rebutted it: "This perspective is very true—but only in
a sphere that I believe no one has reached since the prophets."[12] A close
reading of Schneerson's personal journal indicates that he was the kind
of prophet who lived this truth. He did not merely glimpse it despair-
ingly from afar.

On the eve of Schneerson's departure from Lisbon to New York, in
the summer of 1941, he penned a short meditation on the meaning of
an enigmatic Talmudic dictum: "The [messiah] Son of David shall not
come until fish is sought for an invalid and not found."[13] Per Schneerson's reading, this can refer to what he terms "two messianic poles,"
the first resulting from spiritual bankruptcy and the second from spiritual success:

> Amongst the names by which the messiah is called…the
> least of his monikers is "Son of David," which indicates that
> his merit is only due to his forebears…[14] Hence, whenev-
> er it speaks of the ignobility and suffering of the messianic
> era the moniker Son of David is used… *Invalid* refers to one
> who has sinned…and therefore requires healing…[15] Now,
> the possibility of sin arises when one momentarily forgets
> that one is not an autonomous entity, that it is the word of

> God that sustains you etc., and as explained at length in *Sefer shel beinonim*...[16] Therefore the antidote for the invalid is *fish*, which are constantly enveloped in the water that is their lifesource...[17] and when it is *not found* this is a sign that the entire generation is [irredeemably] culpable, and then the Son of David comes.[18]

On this first reading the messianic salvation is initiated when humanity has become utterly desensitized to, and utterly detached from, the divine source of all. But so long as there is fish to be found, so long as there are people who yet remember that they swim in the divine sea, God can stay his hand. There is yet hope for a superior messianic model, for the emergence of a generation that is not sick with sin, but is rather lovesick with longing for utter union with God. When that model materializes, the Talmudic dictum can be interpreted differently:

> *Invalid* refers to one who lacks [only] the fiftieth gate [of wisdom], and therefore is lovesick...He seeks *fish*, which, as mentioned above, are constantly enveloped in the water that is their lifesource. But it is *not found*...for the quest is for utter effacement [in God], which [even] fish does not embody...This is a generation that is entirely meritorious,[19] and then the Son of David comes.[20]

Schneerson observes that the most lofty of messianic scenarios is likewise consummated by the arrival of one who bears the inferior moniker "Son of David," an indication that

> He is of the temperament and standing of David, [who says] "I am a worm rather than a man" (Psalms, 22:)...meaning that he embodies effacement, utter commitment of soul (*mesirat nefesh*)...Commitment of soul and acceptance of the burden reach ever upwards to the apex of all supernal stations.[21]

As Schneerson sailed for America, these are his parting words: "Commitment of soul and acceptance of the burden reach ever upwards to the apex of all supernal stations." They read as a strong declaration of personal commitment to realize the tenuous viability of spiritual success for all humanity, even in the face of debilitating sickness of the worst possible sort. They also convey a sober recognition of the immense personal burden, the utter dedication to the divine mission, that such success must entail.

At this point the comparison between Menachem Mendel Schneerson and Walter Benjamin falls apart. Benjamin concludes his *Theses* with the claim that "the Jews were prohibited from investigating the future," that they instead "stripped the future of its magic." His messianic hope, accordingly, lies only in the foregone present. His final line reads as a retrospective on the messianic opportunity that has already passed: "every second *was* the strait gate through which the messiah might enter."[22] By now, it seems, the past is beyond redemption. Benjamin is like the helpless angel of history that he so famously described in "Theses IX": "His face is turned towards the past…he sees one single catastrophe which keeps piling wreckage upon wreckage and hurls it in front of his feet…This storm irresistibly propels him into the future to which his back is turned…"[23]

There is a nihilism at play in Benjamin's text, and it derives from a forfeiture of individual agency.[24] He tells us that "at a moment when the politicians in whom the opponents of Fascism had placed their hopes are prostate and confirm their defeat," he is developing his thoughts in written form in imitation of the "monastic discipline assigned to friars…designed to turn them away from the world and its affairs."[25] This foreclosure of personal agency in the global arena, and against the forces of fascism most pressingly, leads to the historic foreclosure of a messianic future, and to the personal foreclosure of life.

Having crossed the Pyrenees into Spain, Benjamin and his party were told that the border was closed and that they would have to return to France on the following day. That night he ended his own life. The next day the border was reopened and the rest of his party were able to continue to freedom.[26] In "Theses VI" he had declared that "even the dead will not be safe from the enemy if he wins." In his own death Benjamin embraced the nihilistic determination that follows: "this enemy has not ceased to be victorious."[27]

While still in Vichy, under the thrall of the Nazi collaborators, Schneerson penned a journal entry reflecting on the biblical laws regarding the severe form of ritual contamination contracted through contact with death:

The Midrash Rabbah states that for all forms of contamination the purification was made explicable to Moses, and when he reached the passage *emor el hakohanim*[28]—which speaks of the contamination of death—his face paled and he asked, "with what shall it be purified?"[29]...Why did he have such difficulty with this contamination specifically?[30]

Schneerson's answer turns on his fundamental understanding of the nature of life itself:

True life is the essence and being of God—and as in the dictum [of Maimonides] at the outset of *Yesodei hatorah*, that His being is from His self, and all things "do not exist except by the truth of His being..."[31]—all that cleave to Him are also truly alive.

Now even the...ungodly elements were created in the world. Only that they were not created for their own sake, but in order that there shall be freedom of choice, [and hence] reward and punishment etc. (*Sefer shel beinonim* [*Tanya*], ch. 22)...When its purpose expires so does its life. As our sages say ([*Talmud bavli*,] Shabbat, 77b), "He created no single thing in this world in vain." This explains why Moses was bewildered specifically by the contamination of death, for death is a sign that its subject has no purpose and telos at all, and how shall such contamination as this be rendered pure?[32]

The biblically prescribed antidote to the contamination of death is a complicated and paradoxical ritual that involves the burning of a cow that is "completely red" outside of the Temple, and (among other things) the sprinkling of its blood opposite the Temple's innermost sanctuary, the Holy of Holies.[33] Schneerson accentuates the paradoxes inherent to the ritual as coincidences of opposites that indicate the enduring capacity to elevate even that which is most antithetical to the divine source of life, transforming it and revitalizing it. "To repair the blight of death, the most severe contamination of all...one must descend to its place in order to raise it up; measure-for-measure, the resulting ascent likewise reaches to the ultimate extremity."[34] Accordingly, even death can become a springboard for true life, and for a greater affirmation of life than ever; the loss of divine purpose can become a springboard to cleave to God more deeply and powerfully than before.

"This cleaving," Schneerson crucially concludes, "is through the Torah and its mitzvot specifically, and as implied in the word *mitsvah* (commandment), [meaning] *tsavta* (bond)."[35] The ability to overcome the contamination of death will only be attained fully in the messianic era, when the ritual of the red cow will be restored. In the meantime, however, there is still much Torah to learn and many precepts to act upon; the personal and collective work of cleaving to divine life must be undertaken in the concrete present.

There are many other passages in Schneerson's journals that demonstrate his purposeful determination in the face of extreme adversity. Perhaps most striking is the following, excerpted from an undated entry that reads like a personal manifesto, even a personal covenant with God:

> All of man's actions, and all that happens to him, are in order that he shall fulfill what he is commanded, or to serve that goal. There is no thing or event that is excluded from this category, for the "all" is divided into three: 1) prohibited 2) commanded 3) permitted, and man must transform the permitted portion into the commanded portion, which is possible by means of [the dictums], "in all your ways know Him,"[36] "all your actions shall be for the sake of Heaven"[37]—
>
> Accordingly, in every moment of a person's life and every situation in which he is found, of all things he can possibly do in the next moment, and of all the paths upon which it is possible for him to travel in the instant of time that follows the instant of the present, only one path and one activity will be correct..."even if it is requisite for the body and its sustenance, but his intention is not for the sake of heaven etc., it is rooted and drawn from...the ungodly etc." (*Tanya*, Chs. 7 and 8.)[38]

In contrast to Benjamin's circumscription of the messianic to "a cessation of happening"[39]—to "the presence of the now,"[40] "in which time stands still and has come to a stop"[41]—Schneerson identifies "the instant of the present" as an occurrence in which the individual is passively found. It is in "the instant of time that follows the instant of the present" that the individual is given the agency—indeed the awesome

responsibility—to exceed the present, to act on the opportunity to construct a godly future. This is the messianic dynamic that Schneerson
carves out between himself, the world, and God. Within this dynamic
the sea crossing to America was not simply a reflexive dash for safety,
but rather a deliberative step beyond the catastrophic present, a deliberative step toward the construction of a messianic future. To paraphrase
Benjamin's remark to Scholem, for Schneerson the messianic kingdom
is always present—as the redemptive step beyond the present.[42]

2.3—America, the New Center

HASIDISM'S AMERICAN FUTURE echoes presciently in a letter addressed
to Schneerson in the spring of 1933 by his father-in-law—and predecessor as the leader of Chabad—Rabbi Yosef Yitzchak Schneersohn of
Lubavitch (1880-1951), who is often referred to by the acronym "Rayats."[43]
During this period Rayats would sometimes use letters to his son-in-
law as a pretext to give expression to his reflections; as he put it in
a contemporaneous letter to his daughter, "I wanted to inscribe this
for myself and choose him as the addressee."[44] The form of the letter is notable because it gives the sense that Rayats is thinking aloud,
expressing his inner musings to an intimate confidant or protégé. Its
content is notable because it investigates the meaning and veracity of a
Hasidic aphorism attributed to Schneur Zalman of Liadi, the founder
of Chabad: "the Giving of the Torah did not occur in America."[45]

On its face, this seems like a redundant statement of the obvious. But this
statement is not concerned with the geographical location of God's covenantal revelation of the Decalogue following the exodus of the Israelites
from Egypt. What is at stake here is whether or not the cosmic revolution embodied by "the Giving of the Torah" (*matan torah*)—conceived as
a meeting of heaven and earth[46]—extended to America, or whether it is
only the "upper half of the globe" that was thereby transformed.

Rayats locates the source of this aphorism in a discourse by Schneur
Zalman of Liadi, then still in manuscript but now published, which offers a kabbalistic explanation of the phenomenon that Newton ascribed
to the gravitational force of the globe, and which Einstein ascribed to
the curvature of spacetime around the earth.[47] Namely, why do things
always fall back to earth wherever they are on the planet? As Schneur

Zalman puts it, "since the world is a globe, round like an apple, why is it that the people who dwell on its other side, in America, don't fall?...Are their heads not pointing downward, and their feet upward?"[48]

Chronologically situated after the death of Newton but before the birth of Einstein, Schneur Zalman's explanation is more redolent of the latter's theorization. It relies on a distinction made by the 16th-century kabbalist, Isaac Luria (known as the "Ari"—"Lion"), between two co-existent cosmic systems. The normative system, termed *yosher* ("straight"), is linear and hierarchical; up is up, higher is higher, down is down, lower is lower. We might say that it is mathematically euclidean. But there is also a system of *igulim* ("circles") according to which the cosmos operates on a circular and non-hierarchical basis, which might correspond to the non-Euclidean curvature of spacetime described by Einstein.[49]

Fundamentally, Schneur Zalman explains, God encompasses the cosmos curvaceously, in a non-hierarchical manner: "He encircles all realms with a single equivalence, and there is no up and down at all...For this reason those people who are opposite us below don't fall...and the earth there is below relative to the sky above it."[50] The form of cosmic space curves, conforming to the circular, non-hierarchical, presence of God (*igulim*) rather than to the linear hierarchy assumed by our intuitions (*yosher*). The latter system, however, is the one that is manifest on the level of empirical experience. Hence, Schneur Zalman concludes, "our location is upper because here divinity has been revealed more; the Holy Land and its ten degrees of holiness, as well as the Holy Temple and the reception of the Torah, are here."[51] This matters, even though it is not an entirely accurate reflection of reality, because the ultimate purpose of existence is that the realm of human activity and perception should be made *manifestly* holy.

Indeed, it is on this last point that Rayats dwells in his letter to his son-in-law, commenting that the distinction between the systems of *igulim* and *yosher* is similar to the distinction made in *Tanya* between this physical world and the supernal realms: Although the latter "are immeasurably more spiritual in comparison to this physical earth of ours, nevertheless the telos lies in this lowly world specifically."[52] Significantly, Rayats' reference is to the locus classicus of a Chabad doctrine that would prove to be especially central in the thought of his chosen addressee, namely, that the telos of creation derives from the divine desire for "a dwelling in the lower realms (*dirah betachtonim*)."[53] In other words, human purpose is not to be realized in some transcendent spiritual realm, but rather in the sacralization of the mundane realm of our present habitation. Accordingly, the demarcation of America as "the lower half of the globe" implies not that it is of lesser importance, but on the contrary, that its sacralization is of ultimate importance, carrying more teleological weight than that of the "upper half" in which the Holy Land is located, and in which the Torah was given.

Rayats penned this letter in the aftermath of his ten-month visit to the United States, from September 1929 to July 1930, when he met with President Herbert Hoover at the White House.[54] Chabad already had a presence in America, and he was feted by the large Jewish communities in cities like New York, Chicago, and St. Louis.[55] Though he did consider moving to the United States on a permanent basis, he ultimately decided to return to Europe and establish Chabad's new center in Warsaw, Poland.[56] In a related letter he wrote that "the giving of the Torah was in the form of a revelation from above," but "the revelation of the Torah in the second half of the globe will be through a different manner of service with a greater degree of power…[and] specifically through service out of utter dedication of soul."[57]

Here we might discern the paradoxical ambivalence of his vision of America. America was an entirely new horizon, not only geographically, but spiritually as well. The opportunity it presented was a uniquely challenging one, and in the first instance Rayats decided that Chabad's American era had not yet arrived. Within the decade, however, the winds of history would return him to New York, where he immediately set out to build a network of schools with the aim of ensuring that Judaism in America would be "no different" than it had been in Chabad's traditional seat in the Belarusian town of Lubavitch. It hardly seems coincidental that on the eve before Schneerson set out across the Atlantic to join his father-in-law he penned the above-cited credo: "Dedication of soul and acceptance of the burden reach ever upwards to the apex of all supernal stations."[58]

In 1948 Schneerson published Rayats' letter on America's cosmic significance as "the lower half of the globe," and he would invoke its themes and elaborate them throughout the decades of his leadership. The following excerpt, from a 1986 talk delivered on the forty-fifth anniversary of his arrival in the United States, provides a good example of how he more fully theorized Rayats' musings:

According to the well known principle of "descent for the
sake of ascent," since the migration to the lower half of the
globe, "the exile to America," constituted a very great descent...it is understood that the intention and telos therein
is the ascent that it thereby achieved, culminating in incom-
parable ascent...to the point that the lower half of the globe
has become the source for the dissemination of Torah and of
Judaism, and the dissemination of the [Hasidic] wellsprings
to the outside, throughout the entire world, including the
upper half of the globe.[59]

On the one hand, the migration to America is described as an exile; it
was not undertaken willingly, but was orchestrated and imposed by God.
On the other hand, it is understood that commensurate to the difficulty
of exile is the stature of its elevated telos. Most significantly, however,
this elevation is not understood merely in local terms, but rather extends to the upper half of the globe as well. This reflects Schneerson's
conception, articulated elsewhere, that the work of creating "a dwelling
in the lower realms" (*dirah betachtonim*) brings all the supernal realms to
their divine culmination as well.[60] In this regard, he would sometimes
invoke a simple image of profound practicality: When using a lever to
raise a load, the lever must be placed beneath the lowest point, and then
the upper portion of the load is raised up as well.[61]

In 1951, just a few months after officially succeeding his father-in-
law as the new leader and rebbe of Chabad-Lubavitch, Schneerson
gave an interview to the Jewish educator and sociologist Dr. Gershon
Kranzler.[62] Here his vision of America is transposed from the realm
of kabbalistic theory into the realm of socio-historical analysis. In response to a question about the implications of demographic dispersion
for the future of Judaism, the new rebbe responded:

It is a mistake if we conceive of the worldwide dispersion of the
Jewish people in exile as a catastrophe. As a matter of fact, this
very lack of concentration of the remnants of our nation was the
source of our salvation throughout the centuries of persecution
and pogroms. Hitler was the greatest threat to our national survival because the largest concentration of the masses of Eastern
and Central European Jewry had come into his evil grasp. On

the other hand, however, concentration of large groups of our people in one country has been the means of creating the spiritual centers from which the rest of the Jewish colonies could draw their inspiration, leadership and material replenishment.

Our history in exile is an unbroken chain of the emergence and disappearance of such centers in country after country, and from one corner of the earth to the next. As the Jewish sun set in one land, it had already begun to rise in another...Now that the great centers of Eastern Europe have been destroyed by Fascism and Communism, America has become the focus and fountainhead of Jewish survival. Providence has prepared a new home for Torah and Yiddishkeit in this country, while the flames devoured the bastions of the strongest and most impregnable Jewish fortresses on the other side of the ocean.

[*With earnest emphasis*] American Jewry must recognize this sacred, historical mission which Divine Providence has entrusted to it at this critical moment of our struggle for survival... We must lead the smaller Jewish communities in other countries and continents, even in the Land of Israel, which must lean heavily on American support for its economic and spiritual survival. The very shape which Jewry and Judaism of tomorrow will present, depends on the active leadership of each and every Jew in this country.[63]

Right from the onset of his leadership Schneerson had a clear conception of America as the new center for a global renaissance. This is particularly remarkable when we take note of the context. In the aftermath of the Holocaust most Jews came to see the newly established State of Israel as the foundation upon which a Jewish future could be built, and as the bastion that would secure a flourishing Jewish future. As Mordecai Kaplan put it in a contemporaneous book:

From the viewpoint of the future of the Jewish People, almost as important as having called into being the State of Israel, is for Zionism to call into being the social instrument that would arrive at a new status or classification for the Jewish People as a transnational people with its core in Eretz Yisrael.[64]

Schneerson, by contrast, provided a nuanced counter to the various attempts to carve out a new form of American Zionist ideology in the aftermath of the successful establishment of the State.[65] While he encouraged some of his constituents to settle in Israel, he encouraged others to move to the United States, Canada, or Australia, or even to remain in Europe.[66] Indeed, he was wary that Zionism could replace religious life and practice as the defining feature of Jewish identity, that it could become a means by which individuals could avoid the personal obligations of being a practicing Jew. In a letter to the officers and crew of the Israeli Navy frigate *Misgav*, upon their visit to the United States in the Spring of 1951, Schneerson wrote:

> It is self understood that one of the purposes of the visit…is to acquire honor and praise on behalf of the community in our Holy Land…by presenting to all the best qualities of our people…And what is our significance and nobility in the eyes of all the nations?
>
> From the time that the Israelite people became a nation, meaning from the time of the giving of our Torah…the Israelite people were the fewest of all the nations, fewest in number. But…served as an example and guide for the entire globe in the qualitative, spiritual arena, disseminating the idea of monotheism, and the preservation of God's path to act with charity and justice etc.
>
> …The secret of our nation's survival is not dependent on quantity but on quality. Not by the might of arms but by the eternal spiritual qualities that our people have absorbed and become one with. As the Torah puts it: "You who cleave to the Lord your God are all alive today." (Deuteronomy 4:4)
>
> And the same applies to the purpose of your visit to the place that you have come…[67]

Fascinatingly, even audaciously, Schneerson seeks to co-opt the representatives of the new Israeli Navy to his own global campaign. He seeks to persuade them that the inner content of their nationalistic ideology should transcend the secular conception of nationhood, that their mission is universal and spiritual rather than particular and material. In Schneerson's view, it was through the flourishing of Judaism's divine spirit in daily life and practice, and in a multiplicity of centers around the world, that a secure future could be ensured.[68] Elsewhere he argued that it was America in particular, rather than Israel, that provided the most fertile resources with which to craft a viable model for postwar Jewish life on a global scale. The new Judaism on the American horizon would not flow downward from the pinnacle of the spiritual hierarchy, but would instead be built from the bottom up.

2.4—A Countercultural Strategy for Jewish Renaissance

AT THE CORE of Schneerson's vision for the transformation of American Judaism, and for a global Jewish renaissance, stands the principle of individual agency, which—as we have already seen—was fundamental to his worldview. In his interview with Kranzler, however, this principle is developed in explicit contrast to American individualism, and thereby constitutes an implicit critique of the Protestant ethic and its encroachment within the American Jewish community:

> America's great genius has been in the development of the individual, of the pioneering and self-made man type. Although this helped in developing our potentialities by demanding every last ounce of ingenuity and perseverance, it has on the other hand focused too much attention on egoistic aims and interests. Personal goals have dominated. Only in our spare and leisure time, after we have carved our groove in terms of economic or social success, have we dedicated some time and effort to philanthropic and communal affairs. We have been social workers on an amateur, after-working-hours basis. This pattern of life has been no less characteristic of American Jews than of other Americans.
>
> But it is at this point that there must be a change of basic outlook and concomitant redirection and reorganization of our existence as a community and as individuals. Primarily we must live the life of social beings, with the responsibility and dedication of our best efforts for the *klal*, the community. Only then can we afford to invest in our own individual aims and goals.[69]

In brief: America must be turned into a center for decentralized Jewish flourishing on a global scale, and this can only be accomplished through a similar shift on the local scale; each individual must turn themself into a center for decentralized social and communal work. Schneerson certainly appreciated the American spirit of individual initiative and entrepreneurship. But he wanted to turn it inside out, directing it away from the narrow concerns of the private domain and harnessing it in the cause of the collective future of Jewish education and life.

In an interview with the Yiddish literary writer and journalist Ascher Penn, Schneerson outlined a three-point strategy, with a particular focus on young American Jews.

The three points are as follows:

1) Go to the young people.
2) Give young people the whole truth.
3) Give up the defensive position and move over to the offensive; give up the conviction that Judaism in America is in a difficult situation.[70]

According to Penn's analysis and testimony, Schneerson's own persona invoked a particular kind of resonance in young Jews from all kinds of backgrounds:

> The fact is that the young Jews of America almost instinctively felt that in Rabbi Menachem Mendel Schneerson they had a person who understands them. This perhaps explains why the young students of the New York universities and colleges often come to the Lubavitcher with various questions about Judaism…However busy he is, he always received them in the happiest, one might even say, the friendliest manner. Entire groups from Columbia, New York College, City College, as well as students from the various rabbinical seminaries have visited him.[71]

Penn attributed this mutual affinity to the Rebbe's own youth—he was still in his forties when he became rebbe, with a beard still "black as pitch"—and also to his wide-ranging knowledge of the secular sciences, his fluency in various European languages, his education at the

University of Berlin, and his subsequent graduation as an electrical engineer in Paris. Among other Hassidic rebbes in New York he was certainly something of an anomaly. As the columnist H. Fierst put it in the Yiddish daily *Forverts*, "unlike the Polish or Galician rebbes, who dress everyday in satin caftans and fur hats [*shtreimlen*], the new Lubavitcher Rebbe dresses in simple clothing, like one of the people...A genius in [Torah] learning, he is additionally a worldly man, and is very knowledgeable in general."[72] In Penn's judgment this combination of attributes and experiences was especially suited to America, and enabled Schneerson firstly to engage young American Jews in a language that they understood, and secondly to understand what these young people were looking for.

Schneerson told Penn that in his estimation the events of World War Two initiated a spiritual awakening for American Jews, "the end of materiality...an end to the rule of the dollar," and a new sense of "their holy mission to play the highest role as leaders of Torah Judaism...everywhere." Accordingly, a spiritual revitalization was already under way, and it was succeeding because "we came to young Jews with precisely what they were seeking." Schneerson's idea of what young Jews were seeking, as transcribed by Penn, is at once extremely traditional and extremely counterintuitive:

> When speaking to young people they are actually not looking
> for something lightweight. They are not frightened away by difficulty. And in this respect Judaism, authentic true Judaism, is
> the same as everything else in life. No one likes it when they are
> given something that is not whole, that is not authentic...American youth do not want a "fifty-fifty" Judaism...It may indeed
> be true that oftentimes the young person cannot take on the entire one hundred percent of Judaism. In the meantime he takes
> on say fifty percent, or even less. But he knows that he is walking on the right path and that he has the real goods...[73]

Rather than trying to adapt Judaism to the new American climate, Schneerson believed that the preservation of traditional Judaism in its fullest and most challenging form was in fact the more viable alternative. The aspirationalism of 1950s America needed to be infused with a meaning and purpose beyond the pursuit of individual material success, otherwise it would indeed come to embody an iron cage, a

constricting sameness enforcing the domestication of the spirit generally. For Jews in particular it would spell a bland assimilation into the
cookie-cutter perfection of middle-class American suburbia. A com-
promising, "fifty-fifty" Judaism would actually be unattractive to the
young and idealistic seekers of the American Jewish community. The
majority of young people want the challenge of authenticity even if
they know that they may not be able to live up to all of the obligations
imposed by the divine authority of the Torah. A little bit of truth, a little bit of an authentic whole, is more attractive than a less demanding
religious form that is fundamentally compromised and inauthentic.

The same principle underlies another element of his strategy, which
might be described as personalized non-denominationalism. As he put
in his interview with Kranzler:

> There is not a single Jew, as far as he may seem or thought him-
> self to have drifted from the center of Yiddishkeit, who does
> not have some good point, some particular mitzvah which by
> nature or by inclination he may promote. This spark of good
> in each soul can and must be utilized for the good of the Jew-
> ish community and, in turn, for the good of the person who
> does it. For this reason the Rebbe, my father-in-law, called not
> only on Orthodox Jews for cooperation in this work...but he
> drew on all types of Jews who had the power and will to con-
> tribute some aspect, some particular skill or capacity towards
> the offensive for Jewish education and the Torah life.[74]

On the one hand, Schneerson rejected the Reform and Conservative
movements as inauthentic expressions of Judaism, and would not recognize the religious authority of their rabbis. But what mattered more was
the individual efforts of individuals, and in his view these efforts should
always be embraced, encouraged, and never dismissed as inauthentic,
without any concern for that person's shortcomings in some other area
of Jewish practice. Witness for example his warm correspondence with
Louis Finkelstein, chancellor of the Jewish Theological Seminary and
titular head of the Conservative movement. In a letter addressed to him
in the autumn of 1960 he applauded Finkelstein's activist promotion of
Jewish learning and practice, and went on to argue that although some
of Finkelstein's older colleagues might look askance at such populism,

this should not concern him, because "your listeners and students will certainly side with you, and in the United States particularly, the fathers listen to the sons and the teachers to the students."[75]

Schneerson's blindness to denominational boundaries on the individual level echoes the declaration of Chabad's founder, often repeated by Schneerson, that each action in fulfillment of God's commandments constitutes an eternal union with the divine, irrespective of what was done a moment before or a moment after.[76] In a similar vein Schneerson would cite Maimonides' statement that with one mitzvah the individual has the capacity to "overbalance himself and the whole world to the side of virtue."[77] Taken together this means that one action carries eternal value in its own right, and that it can also be transformative for the entire world.

While these strategies were deeply rooted in Schneerson's Hasidic ethos, and in his understanding of the eternal nature of Torah Judaism, he was also a keen analyst of the particular conditions of American culture. His focus on young people is a case in point, and his remark to Finkelstein is an example of his repeated contention that in the United States young people are the trendsetters for all forms of cultural change. He noted the increasing dissatisfaction with the conformities imposed by the postwar culture of suburban consumerism, and argued that young Jews were not interested in "fitting in" to the mundane social aspirations that their parents had embraced. Rather than seeing this as a threat to the perpetuation of traditional Judaism, he saw it as an opportunity for superlative success:

> When you go to young people and say to them: Listen!... Your job is to *change* the world, to make it better than it has been till now—it is the nature of the young person to *desire* this... We must only ensure that the new paradigm is one that was created by an "elder who has acquired wisdom," [that is, Torah] "which is your wisdom and understanding in the eyes of the nations," the truest wisdom in the world. The "elder who has acquired wisdom" must come to the young men and women and explain: Please listen, for all kinds of reasons we have not successfully transformed the Jewish world, and by extension nor the rest of the world, "to repair the world with the sovereignty of God." This is the mission that is placed upon your shoulders: If you throw yourselves into the effort with full

fire then you will achieve a revolution, a transformation from
one extreme to another!...They should not merely go a few
steps, to the degree that the "elder" directed them, for he too
might become afraid of what he has done...The Torah need
not be afraid of the world; rather its role is to run the world—
even such a world as this, where the elders have already made
peace with their assumption that the situation will remain as
is and that it is impossible to change anything...[78]

The last two sentences in this excerpt show just how much faith
Schneerson had in the youthful perpetrators of the coming revolution;
while the "new" paradigm must be hewn from the "old" Torah, the
youth must take the new paradigm to the ultimate extreme without
paying heed to the inherently conservative fears that even a visionary
"elder" might harbor.

It is striking that Schneerson delivered this talk in 1958, just as the
beatnik phenomenon was becoming an issue of controversy in American
public discourse.[79] While some dismissed the beatnik heralds of America's countercultural revolution as morbid, mad, and ultimately nihilistic,
they actually saw themselves as spiritual protesters, seeking to break out
of the mechanistic formulas that had come to define American society
and religion. As the scholar Stephen Prothero has argued, "the beats'
flight from the churches and the synagogues...never ceased to be a *search
for* something to believe in, something to go by."[80] It was this search that
Schneerson was referring to when he told Ascher Penn that the secret to
Chabad's success was that "we came to young Jews with precisely what
they were seeking." He believed that an unapologetic Judaism, imbued
with Chabad's mix of activism and inner-worldly spirit, was precisely
what young American Jews were unconsciously yearning to discover.[81]

Allen Ginsberg, the iconic beat poet, once wrote that "Judaism is a
technique for altering human consciousness so that Holy Light can enter
the body."[82] Prothero further notes that "the two major affirmations" of
Ginsberg's spirituality were "the sacralization of everyday life and the
sacramentalization of human relationships."[83] The degree to which these
conceptions of Judaism and spirituality mirror those of Schneerson himself is uncanny. But mirror images, we should note, are always inversions.
Hasidism upheld the ethos of "in all your ways know Him"[84] since its
inception, and Schneerson paid particular attention to the body as the

ultimate medium of divine union, and to the sacralization of interpersonal relationships as the bedrock of all spiritual achievements.[85] Accordingly, Ginsberg's affinity with Hasidism—and Chabad in particular—was certainly a distorted one, but it ran far deeper than the superficial resemblance that he himself acknowledged and that has long been noted by journalists and scholars.[86] He and other young seekers might have been agnostic as to whether or not their quest even had a destination, but Schneerson was quite sure that what they were really missing was Hasidism.[87]

It seems an audacious claim to make, that Hasidism, with its all-embracing regime of laws and customs, could compellingly compete with the free-wheeling spirit of the 1950s and 1960s counterculture. But Schneerson wasn't joking. For all that the hippie lifestyle was antithetical to Torah law and life he nevertheless recognized it is an authentic expression of the universal spiritual search, an attempt to shatter the iron cage imposed by America's materialistic culture of conformist aspirationalism. Moreover, he really did see the ritual strictures of the Torah lifestyle as channels for a sustainable transformation of human consciousness—a transformation that was not artificially stimulated and passively experienced, but rather actively attained, internalized, and owned by the individual.[88]

In a public talk at a 1967 gathering celebrating Chabad's "day of redemption" (*Yud tet kislev chag hage'ulah*) Schneerson argued that "the current troubles and disturbances of all kinds, the uproar that has been raised in recent years over all kinds of injustices, which has even brought to what is called in this country juvenile delinquency" are all rooted in a "lack of conciliation between mind and heart."[89] This is a reference to a central psychological insight in Schneur Zalman of Liadi's *Tanya*, "the mind rules the heart…by the nature of its constitution…such that via will-of-mind each person is able to hold back, and reign over, the spirit of desire."[90] For Schneur Zalman, who laid out the axioms of the Chabad system, this means that so long as one has the right set of cognitive tools—including a thorough knowledge of, and faith in, the singular and unified being of God, as well as the discipline to cultivate a constant regime of divine cognizance and critical self-awareness—one can always act as God wills rather than as the heart desires or as social expectations demand. Through Chabad's cognitive-behavioral system, all one's thoughts, words, and actions can be harmoniously calibrated and divinely inspired.[91]

Crucially, however, this is not merely a system of contemplative therapy. Instead it is unapologetically and unrelentingly action-orientated. It is a system driven by obligation, by the mission to realize the divine will, which is synonymous with the 613 commandments of the Torah. It is by living in accord with these commandments that one's life, including all bodily activities, becomes manifestly absorbed in the singular unity of God. Ritual observance is therefore the fundamental mechanism for the regulated conciliation of the mind and the heart, aligning all aspects of life with the universal telos of mystical union.[92] In this 1967 talk Schneerson explained that of all the Jewish rituals this is best symbolized by the commandment to bind tefillin on the head, corresponding to the mind, and on the upper arm, alongside the heart. Herein, he argued, lay the practical path for the repair of the current social ills that were causing so much turmoil. "Thereby one's capacities for action and emotion—the desires of the heart—are bound up with straps of holiness" such that there is no longer a need "to run away to Greenwich Village, Hippy-Land, or even San Francisco."[93]

In the early 1970s Elliot Lasky toured as a music promoter with the Rolling Stones, and was staying in the home of Chip Monck when a friend introduced him to Zen Buddhism. Paradoxically, this brought Lasky to confront his own identity as a Jew. A few days later he walked up to Schneerson as he entered the central Chabad synagogue at 770 Eastern Parkway in Brooklyn, NY, saying that he had a question. "Ask," Schneerson invited. Here's how Lansky recalls their brief exchange:

> Our eyes were locked, it's just the two of us…and I asked him, "where is God?" and the Rebbe answered me "every place," and I said "I know, but where?" and the Rebbe answered again "every place, in everything; in a tree, in a stone," and I say to the Rebbe "I know, but where?" and he said something that really blew me away…"In your heart, if this is how you are asking."

Lasky then asked Schneerson if it was not true that "whether you are a Jew, or a Black man, or an Indian there is only one God for all of us?" Schneerson did not reject this universalistic vision, but responded by emphasizing the unique mission of each people: "The essence of the black man is to be what he is as a black man, and the essence of the Indian is to be what he is as an Indian, and the essence of the Jew is tied to

God Almighty through Torah and its commandments." The profound simplicity and seriousness of Schneerson's response was such that Lansky had to fight back tears as he recalled this life-changing encounter. After a few weeks of further soul searching he began putting on tefillin on a daily basis and studying *The Code of Jewish Law* (*Kitsur shulchan arukh*), as Schneerson had advised him, and ultimately he adopted a complete Jewish lifestyle.[94] Lasky's account could certainly be taken as evidence of Schneerson's personal charisma. But it is also testimony to his far-sighted social vision. For two decades he had consistently argued that the rebellious spirit of American youth would be the grounds for a grassroots Jewish renaissance and a radical recommitment to the rigors of Jewish practice. Now, in 1972, "the baal teshuvah movement" had become an empirically recognizable phenomenon.[95]

2.5—Women as Agents of Change in America and Beyond

IN THE ABOVE-CITED 1967 talk Schneerson also connected his more local analysis of the American counterculture with a broader analysis of cultural change in America, and of America as an international exporter of culture. What emerges here is a theory of social transformation that begins with the individual and progressively extends outward, transforming family life, communal life, local politics, national policy, and ultimately the entire culture of global society. We might think of the single action of a single individual as a stone dropped into the smooth waters of a lake, sending concentric ripples of water that extend outward across the entirety of its surface. Indeed, this is a theorization that echoes in countless talks delivered by Schneerson throughout the decades of his leadership.

In this particular talk he focuses on the cultural trope of the American Jewish mother as the driver of educational aspiration for her children. An article in the *American Sociological Review*, published in 1969, claimed that this "phenomenon is as conspicuous in social science as in urban folklore," and argued that it was true not only for Jews but for the American middle class more generally.[96] This has usually been understood as an expression of social anxiety, and has also been seen as a misogynistic caricature of Jewish women as overbearing social climbers.[97] Schneerson, however, interpreted it as emblematic of a deep strain of feminine

power and of maternal authority that he perceived to be embedded in
American culture. Combined with America's global role as an exporter
of capital and culture, moreover, the maternal authority of Jewish wom-
en could provide a catalytic mechanism for universal transformation:

> In America it is customary that the attitude regarding education
> is mainly determined by "the mainstay of the home" (Psalms,
> 113:9), that is, the wife and the mother. Now, America is the na-
> tion to which the eyes of all are raised, since it is from here that
> both financial and spiritual resources are disseminated. Accord-
> ingly, the way that educational policy is to be established here,
> especially among Jews, will constitute a model for the educa-
> tion of young people wherever they live, including in the Land
> of Israel... The nature of the world today is such that the nation
> that is the source of financial resources has the ability to be the
> opinion leader of greatest authority... Since in America it is "the
> mainstay of the home" who makes the decisions regarding ed-
> ucation it follows that she has an additional responsibility: The
> form of education that she established in her home will influ-
> ence her neighbors, first her immediate neighbors and thereby
> her neighbors in a far off community, even extending to Jews
> across the sea. May it be willed that in this manner too the rul-
> ing of Maimonides will be fulfilled, that the individual and the
> entire world will be overbalanced to the side of virtue.[98]

In the wider context of Schneerson's theorization of Torah life and
learning as the alternative counterculture that American Jewish youth
are really seeking, this is a call for Jewish mothers to correspondingly
embrace an alternative educational aspirationalism. Rather than priori-
tizing secular education above all else, and providing a Jewish education
circumscribed by the minimalistic requirements of social expectation,
it is within the power of Jewish women to take the initiative and disrupt
the educational status quo. By pre-empting the spiritual restlessness
of their children, Schneerson argued, they would save themselves the
trouble, confusion, and heartache associated with youthful rebellion.
They would also transform the prioritization of Jewish education into
the normative social aspiration, first in their own communities, and
then throughout the world.

This discussion of women as agents of cultural change is by no means an isolated one. As the historian Ada Rapoport-Albert has discussed at some length, one of Schneerson's first acts upon taking the mantle of leadership was to establish the international Lubavitch Women's Organization, explicitly calling on women and girls to see themselves not merely as wives and daughters of Hasidim but as members and representatives of Chabad in their own right. Rapoport-Albert dwells extensively on Schneerson's mystical theorization of women's special affinity with the divine and with the messianic redemption, as well as on the application of this theorization in the empowerment of women as actors in the community as a whole, rather than in their own personal lives and homes alone.[99] The following remarks, excerpted from a 1958 talk, demonstrate that this was not unrelated to his keen appreciation of the new dimensions of social transformation unfolding in American public life:

> With regard to matters of leadership in this country, especially on the political left, women have weighty opinion…Many communal initiatives are openly led by women, and even those things that are openly led by men are really driven by the women behind the scenes…Whenever men don't have the discipline to do the right thing, the women need to mix in and tell their menfolk how to conduct themselves. This is especially so with regard to mitzvot, as the Talmud says, women have a more beautiful approach to the mitzvot than men…They know that they live in God's world, and that every inch of the world is a letter of God's name…which entirely transcends nature.
>
> Since we are in a generation where women have much to say and much to do, when they will use their power and influence they will uproot the *pe'or* idol worship described in this week's Torah reading… The wisdom of the women builds the house of Israel…Just as the exodus from Egypt was in the merit of the righteous women of that generation, so it will be in the messianic era. By using their influence in the generation prior to the messianic advent they will erect the supernal temple and draw it down below…[100]

Schneerson's reference to the role of women on the political left is especially striking. This was an era when women were coming to national prominence on both sides of the political aisle. But this seems to express a more specific acknowledgment, and even admiration, of the progressive achievement of organizations like the League of Women Voters that were then achieving real political results. It is noteworthy that it was precisely during this period that the League adopted a grassroots strategy of education and empowerment, which replaced a hierarchical model that relied on the weight of expert opinion leaders.[101] Similarly, Schneerson was a consistent advocate for the advance of Jewish education for women, recognizing that education is the key to personal empowerment and agency.[102]

It is also notable that the timing of the above-cited talk, and of Schneerson's mobilization of Hasidic women, preceded the rise of second-wave feminism in the 1960s. What Rapoport-Albert aptly describes as Schneerson's "counter-feminism" was not a defensive reaction, nor mere mimicry. Characteristically, he was one step ahead of the zeitgeist; rather than waiting to react against it he took the initiative and carried his vision forward with the additional momentum of the rising cultural wave.

2.6—From Self-Transformation to Global Transformation

FROM THE MID-1970S and on, a change can be detected in Schneerson's discussions of America. In the first decades of his leadership he spoke mainly about the unique challenge and opportunity for Jews in America. But as he began to address larger and larger audiences, and as Jews became more confident in the role they could play in American society, Schneerson began to speak in more universal terms. Increasingly he appealed to the American nation, and to its elected representatives, to recognize and embrace its geopolitical role as an exporter of charity and justice on a global scale.

A series of talks delivered on the twenty-fifth anniversary of his predecessor's passing throws this shift into sharp relief. Schneerson began by elaborating on the process by which a single individual, beginning with the individual work of self-transformation, can progressively become a transformative influencer and a leader for larger and larger groups of people. Here Schneerson's concentric model of social influence, as outlined above, is mapped onto the political life of American society; he provides a step-by-step guide leading from the personal obligations of a private citizen to the collective obligations of the presidency. Strikingly, this political frame is shot through with biblical and rabbinic phrases, signaling that the obligations of the private citizen, and likewise of the president, are not to any earthly authority, but rather to God:

> No one is born a president, nor a sovereign, nor a leader. Initially you are only sovereign over your own self and your personal space. This sovereignty begins as soon as you are obligated by the mitzvot [at the age of twelve for girls and thirteen for boys], already then you have a mission to become sovereign over the "small city which is the body"[103]...
>
> Later, once you grow up, you become sovereign over your entire family...But here an additional difficulty arises, you must train yourself to put the protection of the family before the needs of the self. You have already become accustomed to sovereignty over your own body, and now you must recognize that you have an even more important mission; that the collective—in this case, the family—comes before the individual. As the Talmud establishes, when there is a conflict between an individual and a collective the law is decided in accord with opinion of the collective[104]...In the end this will turn out for the good of the individual, as an individual, as well.[105]
>
> Likewise when a person becomes influential and a leader for a larger constituency: You have become accustomed to being a leader over your own personal group...working faithfully for their benefit. But as soon as you are elected and appointed as leader or president over a larger entity, which incorporates within itself many subgroups, you must confront an even greater challenge. Then you are given the capability to overcome that challenge, not to fight for any one group against the interests of the majority of the other groups. On the contrary, you will explain to yourself and those around you that when the individual is at odds with the collective the law is in favor of the collective.[106]

The key to being a leader, according to Schneerson, is twofold. First, gain sovereignty over your own self. This itself requires discipline, the toil and challenge of overcoming the crass and worldly instincts of the body, of transforming bitterness into sweetness and darkness into light within the personal realm.[107] Second, put the interests of the collective, of the majority, before those of the individual, or of the minority sub-group that you previously represented.

Though this might seem a simple formula, it doesn't take much to discern that it projects a noble ideal of service that is rarely realized in modern political life. As Schneerson argued on other occasions, campaigns should be the time for debate between political parties, but once the votes are in, the elected nominee must undergo a transition, setting local interests, and even party interests, aside. Once the nominee occupies presidential office, the nominee must strive to act in good faith as the representative of the entire nation, and the nation must strive to support the collective agenda advanced by the nominee.[108] This is only possible if the elected leader has first achieved sovereignty over the self, for without the hard work of self-transformation it is impossible to put public interest ahead of personal interest. On this reading, personal character and public leadership are inseparably intertwined in a way that acts as a counterbalance to the partisan instinct that is all too often the governing factor in American politics. Schneerson's theorization of political praxis and its moral underpinnings is a sober counterpoint to the increasing reduction of personal identity to partisan affiliation, which leads to what some scholars have described as an "emotional" or "affective" form of political polarization.[109] For Schneerson, personal identity and affect must be brought under the reign of disciplined intellection in order for a person to become a faithful leader of a plurality of individuals. This echoes the classical Chabad precept that "the mind rules the heart,"[110] and provides a religious template for political tolerance.[111]

As already noted, Schneerson's discussion in his 1975 talks, and elsewhere, are not purely political. In describing the highest form of sovereignty he uses the Talmudic phrase "a leader above whom there is no one but God,"[112] and accordingly conceives of a nation's leader as one who is empowered from on high "to carry out the mission as is required."[113] For him, the mission of such a leader is not merely to act on behalf of the people, but also to act on behalf of God. Moreover, Schneerson immediately applies his model of political leadership to Jewish leadership as well. As a case in point he cites the example of his predecessor, arguing that at each stage of his career Rayats took on the responsibility of championing the religious needs of ever wider constituencies: As a young man he set his personal spiritual priorities aside in order to become an educator, later he set his educational priorities aside to become the leader of Chabad, and finally he even set the priorities of that particular group aside to ensure that the basic spiritual needs of the American Jewish community were being met.[114] Schneerson further emphasized that the ultimate purpose of this process, which needs to be emulated and continued by the disciples of Rayats, is to create "a dwelling for God in the lower realms" (*dirah lo yitbarakh betachtonim*), which is here equated with the realization and recognition of divine sovereignty:

> The sovereign of all sovereigns, the Holy One blessed be He, should be recognized [in the world]...such that wherever one turns one sees divinity, because everything is being conducted with charity and justice, and with Judaism—Torah study and mitzvah performance. Then it will certainly be achieved that "I shall give peace into the land" (Numbers, 26:6), in the simple sense—in the Holy Land—and in the broader sense, in the entire world around us. This will allow us to disseminate Judaism, and to disseminate charity and justice with greater magnificence and might, and with exceedingly great success.[115]

For Schneerson there is but one continuum of sovereignty, namely divine sovereignty, and it governs the mission of the individual and the nation alike. This too can be read as a counterbalance to the general trend in American politics. In an era when religion and politics were increasingly seen to be in tension with one another, and in which religion was increasingly reduced to a political tool, Schneerson argued that politics should be seen as a tool for the collective mission imposed upon society by God.[116] Of course, such a theorization raises the specter of theocratic coercion and the usurpation of personal autonomy. But with his insistence on the centrality of personal autonomy and moral agency, that is clearly not what Schneerson had in mind. In his theological discourse autonomous choice (*bechirah*) is theorized as the highest measure of religious value and commitment.[117] From a political standpoint too he did not seek to impose a particular religious creed, but rather to encourage a personal sense of responsibility to God that could freely give rise to a collective sense of beholdenness.

Schneerson's politics, in this regard, were in equal measures non-coercive and religiously aspirational. This rests on a subtle distinction of the kind that zealots, whether religious or antireligious, are usually quick to miss. But the following comment, regarding the constitutional separation of religion and state, is very telling:

> The intention in that which is inscribed in the Constitution...is that no one shall be forced to adopt the beliefs of another, and that no priority shall be given to one over another. But God forbid that it shall be said to mean that the nation can provide funding for anything, and the singular exception for which state funds cannot be used is to bring the call to young people...that the world is not a jungle...that there is a God.[118]

Here we see that it was this basic sense of divine sovereignty, rather than a specific religious denominationalism, that Schneerson felt to be fundamental to the ethos of the United States, and fundamental to the success of any civilized society. The separation of religion and state provided the latitude for a non-coercive religiosity to flourish freely.

We should also note that his reading of the Constitution, especially as reflected in this talk, seems to be rooted in a strong personal identification with America's origin story, and in particular with the pilgrims who made the treacherous journey across the Atlantic in search of a refuge from religious persecution. Schneerson argued that this history predisposed the American nation to the proliferation of a collective and non-coercive religious aspiration, which should rightly be facilitated by the nation's domestic and international policies:

> They fled here in order to worship God according to their understanding and without impediment and interference. They fled here with the confidence and trust that God would lead them...Certainly this indicates the path by which the nation should conduct itself, in accordance with this foundation...Upon that foundation and in accord with that spirit the entire edifice must be built...In each event they saw specific providence (hashgachah pratit), culminating with the miracle [marked to this day by Thanksgiving], as is well known in the historical narrative of this country...[119]

The Hasidic nature of Schneerson's theorization of this American origin story is emphasized here by the reference to the principle of specific providence (*hashgachah pratit*), according to which even the most apparently insignificant occurrence is orchestrated by God. In the Chabad tradition this is understood to be one of the cardinal theological innovations of the Baal Shem Tov, the founder of Hasidism, and it is linked to Chabad's particular notion of divine union within the world.[120] In arguing this point Schneerson drew a line of comparison between Abraham, the founding father of Judaism, and the pilgrim fathers who paved the way for the founding of the United States. According to the Hasidic interpretation, Abraham taught that God's singular being is actually united within the world, and that God should not be perceived merely as a transcendent deity. In Schneerson's view the story of the pilgrim fathers indicates that the United States was founded on the same principle:

> Abraham taught that…it is not that there are two separate entities, the world being independent and God being independent, only that they come together from time to time. Rather "there is no place empty of God" (*Tikunei zohar*, 92b)…The nation was founded on faith in God, and not faith in a transcendent God, merely found somewhere in the seventh heaven…rather the manner of their faith was such that it permeated their day to day lives, and their day to day conduct.[121]

Schneerson merged Chabad's own history of religious persecution, followed by refuge and flourishing in America—along with Chabad's theosophical ideology—with the national-origin story of the United States. On this basis, he charted a vision for the collective mission of the nation in direct parallel with Chabad's own mission, and with explicit ramifications for a range of policy issues. His approach to America's domestic policy issues will be discussed in Chapters 5 and 6, but what is most relevant here is his notion of America as the new center of global geopolitics and economics, and his notion of the divine mission that this special status signals:

> When we speak of a great nation that in recent years has gained the ability to have an impact throughout the world…it is also

certain that this imposes a special responsibility and merit, both with regard to its own affairs and also with regard to its global influence. This is a counter to the erroneous opinion in previous generations that we can isolate and limit ourselves, sufficing with domestic concerns...Since we see that in every corner of the globe they listen to and reckon with that nation [the United States]—so long as they speak with full vigor, certainly via pleasant means, but with true confidence—God forbid that they should isolate themselves, and say "what relationship is there between me and this trouble?"...Since we see that we have the capability to be influential it is certainly by providence...[122]

Here we have a vision of America not only as a destination for refugees, but also as an exporter of refuge, a nation that is duty-bound by God to wield its power "via pleasant means," thereby bringing charity and justice to those who need it, wherever they might be. On other occasions Schneerson made it clear that by "pleasant means" he meant "quiet diplomacy," warning that "noise and propaganda" lead to "opposition and stubbornness."[123]

"Each nation," Schneerson wrote in edited remarks published in 1978, "is a member of the Family of nations, and all must live together in the world, which is like one organism. When any part of an organism ails, it affects the whole body; strengthening any part of the body strengthens the whole." In this vein Schneerson went on to explicitly praise President Jimmy Carter for holding recipients of foreign aid to a higher standard of human rights, and for dismissing the notion that the United States should not treat such concerns as merely an "internal matter" outside of America's own interests. He additionally advocated that such aid should be invested specifically in economic, educational, and cultural concerns rather than in military aid to nations that would use it to make war rather than to make peace.[124]

Today, scholars and policy makers have much to say about the dangers of American isolationism and of American interventionism alike.[125] Many might take issue with Schneerson's own political stance on a whole range of concerns. Yet his notion of intervention "via pleasant means," and out of a sense of national duty before God, provides an alternative paradigm that is as intriguing as it is idealistic. What indeed would geopolitics look like if international diplomacy was dominated by leaders with a personal and collective sense of universal duty, of beholdenness not merely to their own national interest, but to a God who is at once transcendent and immanent throughout the world? In the ideal America of Schneerson's vision, partisan politicians would first transform themselves into visionary mystics, and would then work with tactful diligence to bring refuge, charity, and justice to every corner of the globe.

Schneerson's explicit engagement with the political realm, and his use of satellite television to broadcast his public talks to audiences across the nation, invites comparison to the televangelists who came to prominence during the Reagan era.[126] Indeed, when it came to domestic policy their views sometimes bore a superficial resemblance to his. Yet as we have noted, he insisted that religion should never become a politically partisan tool. He spoke about policy, not about party, and saw these policies as a way to construct an ideal society rather than as a way to avoid divine punishment. While it is often claimed that Hasidim vote as a bloc in accord with the dictate of their leaders, Schneerson never named a partisan choice in an American election, though he vocally encouraged people to vote.[127] He spoke not of the particular president of the day, but of the chosen incumbent of the office of the presidency, whether that person was Ford, or Carter, or Reagan, or Bush. Moreover, in his talks he did not simply invoke the brute authority of scripture. Instead, he weaved complex sociological arguments that drew on his keen powers of observation and social analysis, on the broad Jewish tradition of legal and philosophical argumentation, and on the more specific Chabad tradition of kabbalistic and Hasidic theorization.

Perhaps most significantly, Schneerson's vision of America's divine mission was fundamentally universalistic, embracing all individuals as central actors within the concentric constellations of collective society. As we have already seen, his notion of America as the new center was one that leveled the normative hierarchies of religious virtue and sought to facilitate a decentralized flourishing of Jewish life, and of universal charity and justice. Though on the geographic plane his starting point was the United States, his real goal was to reenchant the world.

Notes

1. For a short documentary, including original documentation and eyewitness testimony regarding Schneerson's arrival in New York, see "The Rebbe and Rebbetzin Arrive in America (28 Sivan, 5701—June 23, 1941)," *Chabad.org*, <chabad.org/1558408>.

2. Menachem Mendel Schneerson, *Kuntras binyan mikdash me'at* (Brooklyn, NY: Kehot Publication Society, 1992), 9. Also see Yosef Yitzchak Schneerson, *Sefer hasichot 5703* (Brooklyn, NY: Kehot Publication Society, 2010), 41; Menachem Mendel Schneerson, *Sefer hasichot 5749*, Vol. 2 (Brooklyn, NY: Kehot Publication Society, 2003), 549.

3. For an exhaustive record of Schneerson's early life, up to the period of his initial move to Berlin, see Boruch Oberlander and Elkanah Shmotkin, *Early Years: The Formative Years of the Rebbe, Rabbi Menachem M. Schneerson, as Told by Documents and Archival Data 1902-1921* (Brooklyn, NY: Kehot Publication Society, 2016). For details of his enrollment at Berlin's Humboldt University see *ibid.*, 283 and 345.

4. See *Kovetz khaf-ches sivan* (Brooklyn, NY: Kehot Publication Society, 1991), pages 11-19.

5. For a representative example, see Menachem Mendel Schneerson, *Igrot kodesh*, Vo. 3 (Brooklyn, NY: Kehot Publication Society, 1997), 457-458.

6. See Samuel C. Heilman and Menachem M. Friedman, *The Rebbe: The Life and Afterlife of Menachem Mendel Schneerson* (Princeton, NJ: Princeton University Press, 2010); Chaim Rapoport, *The Afterlife of Scholarship* (Oporto Press, 2011).

7. Schneerson's personal journals, written before he became leader of Chabad, were found in a drawer of his desk following his passing in 1994 and were subsequently published by Agudat Chassidei Chabad and Kehot Publication Society, first as a series of pamphlets and later as a multivolume set in several editions. See Elliot R. Wolfson, *Open Secret: Postmessianic Messianism and the Mystical Revision of Menachem Mendel Schneerson* (New York: Columbia University Press, 2009), 15; "The Rebbe's Notebook: The Reshimot," *Chabad.org*, <chabad.org/1210901>. Select entries from these journals will be discussed below. For Schneerson's correspondence with his father see Menachem Mendel Schneerson (ed.), *Likutei levi yitschak—igrot kodesh* (Brooklyn, NY: Kehot Publication Society, 1985); for his correspondence with his father-in-law, see esp. Yosef Yitzchak Schneerson, *Igrot kodesh*, Vol. 15 (Brooklyn, NY: Kehot Publication Society, 2011). For examples of his correspondence with Yosef Rosen see his own *Igrot kodesh*, Vol. 1 (Brooklyn, NY: Kehot Publication Society, 1997), 1-2; Vol. 21 (Brooklyn, NY: Kehot Publication Society, 1998), 1-6; Menachem Mendel Schneerson, "Choveret 33," in *Reshimot*, vol. 1 (Brooklyn, NY: Kehot Publication Society, 2012), 510-522.

8. For the specifics of Benjamin's movements and activities during these years see Howard Eiland, *Walter Benjamin: A Critical Life* (Cambridge, MA: Harvard University Press, 2014); for those of Schneerson see Eli Rubin, "The Rebbe: An In-Depth Biography of a Scholar, Visionary and Leader," *Chabad.org*, <chabad.org/2619397>. Also see Shaul Magid, "When Will the Wedding Take Place? A Little Known Discourse of the Seventh Lubavitcher Rebbe," in *One God, Many Worlds: A Festschrift in Honor of Rabbi Zalman Schachter-Shalomi, z"l*, ed. Netanel Miles-Yepez (Boulder, CO: Albion Andalus, 2015), 95-106.

9. Published in Walter Benjamin, *Illuminations: Essays and Reflections*, ed. Hannah Arendt, trans. Harry Zohn (New York: Schocken Books, 2007), 253-264. For a broad discussion of the reception of this work and its meaning see Ronald Beiner, "Walter Benjamin's Philosophy of History," *Political Theory* 12, no. 3 (Aug., 1984): 423-434. See also Jacob Taubes, "Seminar Notes on Walter Benjamin's 'Theses on the Philosophy of History,'" in *Walter Benjamin and Theology*, eds. Colby Dickinson and Stéphane Symons (New York: Fordham University Press, 2016), 179-214; Stéphane Symons, *Walter Benjamin: Presence of Mind, Failure to Comprehend* (Leiden and Boston: Brill, 2013), 13-50; Michael Lowy, *Fire Alarm: Reading Walter Benjamin's On the Concept of History*, trans. Chris Turner (London and New York: Verso, 2016).

10. On the centrality of the messiah and its meaning in Schneerson's thought see Wolfson, *Open Secret*. For a brief comparison to Benjamin's conception see *ibid.*, 286, and 398 n. 99.

11. See Howard Eiland, "Walter Benjamin's Jewishness," in *Walter Benjamin and Theology*, ed. Colby Dickinson and Stéphane Symons (New York: Fordham University Press, 2016), 113-143.

12. Scholem's journal entry for November 3, 1917, as cited in Eric Jacobson, *Metaphysics of the Profane: The Political Theology of Walter Benjamin and Gershom Scholem* (New York: Columbia University Press, 2003), 25. Cf. Eiland, "Walter Benjamin's Jewishness," 129.

13. *Talmud bavli*, Sanhedrin, 98a.

14. Cf. the comment regarding "Son of Zakai," *Talmud bavli*, Sanhedrin, 48b.

15. Cf. *Talmud bavli*, Yoma, 86a: "Great is repentance for its brings *healing* to the world."

16. This is the secondary title of the founding work of Chabad Hasidism, more commonly known as *Tanya*, by Schneur Zalman of Liadi. Cf. Chapters 20-24, where it is explained that "the creation of all the worlds, upper and lower,...and their sustenance...is nothing more than the word of God and the spirit of His mouth that is vested in them" and that it is only due to "the spirit of folly and forgetfulness" that a human being can be brought to sin.

17. Cf. *Talmud bavli*, Brakhot, 61b: "Fish of the sea die as soon as they are raised onto dry land..."

18. Menachem Mendel Schneerson, journal entry marked "Lisbon, Sivan 16, 5701" (June 11, 1941), published in "Choveret 11," in *Reshimot*, vol. 1 (New York: Kehot Publication Society, 2012), 128.

19. *Talmud bavli*, Sanhedrin, *ibid.*

20. Schneerson, journal entry marked "Lisbon, Sivan 16, 5701," 128-129.

21. *Ibid.*

22. Benjamin, *Illuminations*, 264.

23. *Ibid.*, 257-258. Cf. the closing remarks in Beiner, "Walter Benjamin's Philosophy of History"; Susan Handelman, "Walter Benjamin and the Angel of History," *Cross-Currents* 41, no. 3 (Fall 1991): 344-352.

24. See Eiland, "Walter Benjamin's Jewishness," 133, for the comment that Benjamin's "religiosity was virtually indistinguishable from his nihilism."

25. Benjamin, *Illuminations*, 258. Cf. Jacobson, *Metaphysics of the Profane*, 50: "The rhythm of messianic nature leads to...a praxis of nihilism, meaning a retreat from worldly participation in favor of an abstract and categorical realm of messianic reflection, embodied in a 'mystical' understanding of history."

26. Eiland, *Walter Benjamin*, 673-675.

27. Benjamin, *Illuminations*, 255.

28. Leviticus, 21:1.

29. *Bamidbar rabbah*, 19:4.

30. Menachem Mendel Schneerson, Journal entry marked "Chukat. Vichy 5700" (July 1940), published in "Choveret 49," in *Reshimot*, vol. 2 (New York: Kehot Publication Society, 2012), 111.

31. Maimonides, *Mishneh torah*, Yesodei hatorah 1:1.

32. Schneerson, Journal entry marked "Chukat. Vichy 5700," 111-112.

33. See Numbers, 19, and Mishnah, Parah.

34. Schneerson, Journal entry marked "Chukat. Vichy 5700," 113.

35. *Ibid.* The wordplay between *mitsvah* (commandment) and *tsavta* (bond) can be found in the early Hasidic work *Magid devarav leyakov* (Korets, 1781), #133, as well as in many later Chabad texts. Cf. Chayim Vital, *Pri ets chayim*, 29:3.

36. Proverbs, 3:6.

37. *Mishnah*, Avot, 2:12.

38. Menachem Mendel Schneerson, Undated journal entry, published in "Choveret 44," in *Reshimot*, vol. 2, 63.

39. Benjamin, *Illuminations*, 263.

40. *Ibid.*, 261.

41. *Ibid.*, 262.

42. Cf. especially the closing comment in Elliot R. Wolfson, "Open Secret in the Rearview Mirror," *AJS Review* 35, no. 2 (November 2011): 417-418, that for Schneerson "the futurity of waiting for the messiah to appear is not a matter of chronoscopic time at all, but a mental state whereby and wherein one realizes that what is to come intermittently is already present perpetually. All one needs to do is to open the door..." See also the overlapping oral presentation, Elliot R. Wolfson, "Habad Messianism and the Present Future," *YouTube.org*, <https://www.youtube.com/watch?v=dM-yQeuLS3w>, and the relevant discussion of the relation of the messianic to the present in *idem.*, *Open Secret*, 276-289.

43. First published in pamphlet form in 1948, this letter subsequently appeared in Yosef Yitzchak Schneersohn, *Sefer Hamamarim 5708-5709* (Brooklyn, NY: Kehot Publication Society, 1986), 232-236; *idem.*, *Igrot kodesh*, Vol. 2 (Brooklyn, NY: Kehot Publication Society, 2016), 492-498; *ibid.*, Vol. 15 (Brooklyn, NY: Kehot Publication Society, 2011), 137-143.

44. Yosef Yitzchak Schneersohn, *Igrot kodesh*, Vol. 15, 112.

45. Cf. Shalom DovBer Schneersohn, *Igrot kodesh*, Vol. 1 (Brooklyn, NY: Kehot Publication Society, 1982), 161.

46. See *Genesis rabbah*, 12:3; *Tanchuma*, Va'eira 15. The significance and implications of these rabbinic sources are discussed innumerable times in Chabad texts. For a representative example see the discussion and citations in Menachem Mendel Schneerson, *Likutei sichot*, Vol. 15 (Brooklyn, NY: Kehot Publication Society, 2006), 77.

47. See Albert Einstein, *Relativity: The Special and The General Theory—A Popular Exposition*, trans. Robert W. Lawson (London: Methuen & Co., 1920).

48. Various manuscript versions of this discourse have been collected in the two volumes of Schneur Zalman of Liadi, *Mamarei admor hazaken 5562* (Brooklyn, NY: Kehot Publication Society, 2012). Here we follow the text as it is cited in Rayats' letter: Yosef Yitzchak Schneersohn, *Igrot kodesh, Vol. 15*, 141.

49. Cf. Chayim Vital, *Ets chayim*, Gate 1 (Igulim veyosher), and Gate 43 (Tsiyor olamot), Ch. 2. A full justification of the claim that Schneur Zalman might be prefiguring Einstein must be left aside for the meantime. For the moment we must suffice with the clarification that we understand him to be invoking an alternative to the classical notion of the celestial spheres, and rejecting theories of gravitational attraction.

50. Schneur Zalman of Liadi, *Mamarei admor hazaken 5562*, Vol. 1, 293 and 310.

51. *Ibid.*, 310; Yosef Yitzchak Schneersohn, *Igrot kodesh*, Vol. 15, 142.

52. Yosef Yitzchak Schneersohn, *Igrot kodesh*, Vol. 15, 142.

53. Schneur Zalman of Liadi, *Tanya*, Ch. 36. See Faitel Levin, *Heaven on Earth: Reflections on the Theology of Rabbi Menachem M. Schneerson, the Lubavitcher Rebbe* (Brooklyn, NY: Kehot Publication Society, 2002).

54. See Shalom DovBer Levine, *Toldot chabad be'artsot habrit* (Brooklyn, NY: Kehot Publication Society, 1988), 86.

55. *Ibid.*, 37-86.

56. *Ibid.*, 88-94. Shalom DovBer Levine, *Toldot chabad bepolin, lita, velatviya* (Brooklyn, NY: Kehot Publication Society, 2011), 77-82.

57. Yosef Yitzchak Schneersohn, *Igrot kodesh*, Vol. 2, 331.

58. Menachem Mendel Schneerson, "Choveret 11," in *Reshimot*, Vol. 1, 128.

59. Menachem Mendel Schneerson, *Likutei sichot*, Vol. 33 (Brooklyn, NY: Kehot Publication Society, 1999), 275-278.

60. Menachem Mendel Schneerson, *Torat menachem sefer hamamarim melukat*, Vol. 2 (Brooklyn, NY: Kehot Publication Society, 2004), 338.

61. See for example, Menachem Mendel Schneerson, *Torat menachem hitvaduyot*, Vol. 13 [5715, I] (Brooklyn, NY: Kehot Publication Society, 1999), 323. Cf. Schneur Zalman of Liadi, *Torah or* (Brooklyn, NY: Kehot Publication Society, 2001), 4a.

62. Kranzler was educated in philosophy at the University of Würzburg, and in sociology at Columbia University, and later taught sociology and sociology of education at Johns Hopkins University. He authored children's books and sociological studies of Jewish communities in America. See Tzvi Hersh Weinreb, "Dr. Gershon Kranzler: Tiferet Personified," *Jewish Action* (Winter 5761/2000). His interview with Schneerson first appeared in the Sept-Oct., 1951 issue of *Orthodox Jewish Life*. An edited and somewhat abridged version appears at *Chabad.org* <chabad.org/66877>, and it was published in Hebrew translation in *Kfar Chabad Magazine* 1406: 28-31.

63. *Kfar Chabad Magazine* 1406: 28-29.

64. Mordecai M. Kaplan, *A New Zionism* (New York: Herzl Press and the Jewish Re-construction Press, 1959), 178. On the centrality of Zionism in the formation of American Jewish identity in the post-Holocaust era, see "Zionism and American Jews," *MERIP Reports* 29 (Jun., 1974): 9.

65. See Arthur Hertzberg, "American Zionism at an Impasse: A Movement in Search of a Program," *Commentary Magazine* (Oct. 1, 1949) <https://www.commentary magazine.com/articles/american-zionism-at-an-impassea-movement-in-search-of-a-program/>.

66. See, for example, Menachem Mendel , *Igrot kodesh*, Vol. 3 (Brooklyn, NY: Kehot Publication Society, 1997), 403 and 561, for examples of instructions to emigrate either to the United States, Canada or Australia, and likewise *ibid.*, Vol. 4 (Brooklyn, NY: Kehot Publication Society, 1997), 1023, 213, and *ibid.*, 349, where he advises that economic opportunities in Australia and South Africa are likely to be more favorable than in the United States and Canada.

67. *Ibid.*, Vol. 4, 410-411.

68. For another iteration of Schneerson's views, countering the narrative of secular nationalism as the key to Jewish continuity, and in favor of a multiplicity of Jewish centers, see Shalom Lavin, "Yokhiach veyehav: sicha im harabi milubavits bebruklin," *Dvar*, Oct. 11, 1959.

69. *Kfar Chabad Magazine* 1406: 29.

70. Ascher Penn, *Iydishkeit in amerike*, Vol. 1 (New York: Shulsinger Bros., 1958), 71.

71. Ibid., 69-70. For a transcript of one of these discussions with college students, held in 1952, see "What Is the Purpose of Life? Notes from Conversations with the Rebbe, 1952," *Chabad.org*, <chabad.org/664336>. Also see, "The Rebbe Speaks to Young Israel Intercollegiate Students 1961," *Chabad.org*, <chabad.org/392193>.

72. H. Fierst, "Der nei'er lubavitsher rebi," *Forverts* (Jan. 26, 1951). <http://jpress.org.il/Olive/APA/NLI_heb/SharedView.Article.aspx?href=FRW%2F1951%2F01%2F26&id=Ar00203&sk=771F345E>.

73. Penn, *Iydishkeit in amerike*, Vol. 1, 70-71.

74. *Kfar Chabad Magazine* 1406: 30.

75. Menachem Mendel Schneerson, *Igrot kodesh*, Vol. 19 (Brooklyn, NY: Kehot Publication Society, 2003), 442-443.

76. *Tanya*, Ch. 25.

77. Maimonides, *Mishneh torah*, Laws of Teshuvah, 3:4.

78. *Torat menachem hitvaduyot*, Vol. 25 [5719, 2] (Brooklyn, NY: Kehot Publication Society, 2003), 39-41.

79. It was in 1958 that Norman Podhoretz published his critique of the Beats, "The Know Nothing Bohemians," in *Partisan Review*, with Allen Ginsberg responding in *The Village Voice*. This was also the year in which Herb Caen of the *San Francisco Chronicle* coined the term Beatnik in an article titled "Pocketful of Notes."

80. Stephen Prothero, "On the Holy Road: The Beat Movement as Spiritual Protest," *The Harvard Theological Review* 84, no. 2 (Apr., 1991): 210.

81. See for example, Menachem Mendel Schneerson, *Torat menachem hitvaduyot*, Vol. 51 [5728, I] (Brooklyn, NY: Kehot Publication Society, 2013), 341: "The younger generation are *waiting* for someone to come and set before them a challenge... accept upon yourself the yoke of heavenly sovereignty, of Torah and mitzvot, and not in order to imitate someone or do someone a favor, but because in this *you will find yourself*."

82. Letter to Max Gartenberg, cited in Harold Cantor, "Allen Ginsberg's 'Kaddish': A Poem of Exorcism," *Studies in American Jewish Literature* 2, no. 2 (Winter 1976), 11.

83. Prothero, "On the Holy Road," 214.

84. Proverbs, 3:6. Cf. Tsippi Kauffman, *In all Your Ways Know Him: The Concept of God and Avodah be-Gashmiyut in the Early Stages of Hasidism* (Ramat-Gan: Bar Ilan University Press, 2009).

85. The body as the ultimate locus of divine union is a recurring theme in Schneerson's teachings. For a representative example, see Menachem Mendel Schneerson, *Torat menachem sefer hamamarim melukat*, Vol. 4 (Brooklyn, NY: Kehot Publication Society, 2012), 200-201. On the centrality of the interpersonal see below, Chapter 4.

86. For Ginsberg's own references to Hasidism and Chabad see "Allen Ginsberg, Montreal, 1969 Q & A–8) (Judaism and Krishna)," *AllenGinsberg.org*, <https://allenginsberg.org/2016/03/allen-ginsberg-montreal-1969-q-a-8-judaism-and-krishna/>. Also see Richard Kostelanetz, "Ginsberg Makes the World Scene," *The New York Times*, July 11, 1965 <https://archive.nytimes.com/www.nytimes.com/books/01/04/08/specials/ginsberg-scene.html>: "Ginsberg... looks and sounds, one immediately thinks, like a Hasidic rabbi... his outlook remains more similar to that of Martin Buber and Hasidism than to the Jewish rationalistic tradition exemplified by Freud..."; Stephen Fredman, "Allen Ginsberg and Lionel Trilling: The Hasid and the Mitnaged," *Religion & Literature* 30, no. 3 (Autumn, 1998): 67-76.

87. In an interview conducted by Jewish Educational Media, Yosef Krupnik recalled that in a personal audience he had with Schneerson in the mid-1960s the latter spoke of the affinity between the hippies and the Hasidim, in the course of which he mentioned Ginsberg by name. See, "Jewish Counterculture, 1967," *Chabad.org*, <https://www.chabad.org/462845>, timecode 2:22.

88. See, for example, Schneerson, *Torat menachem hitvaduyot*, Vol. 51, 341-342: "This too is symbolized in the straps of the tefillin... one might ask, when you want to impact someone's heart and intellect what do you need straps for?!... One should explain with intellect, speak to the feelings in his heart, and there is no need to bind him [with tefillin]? But the reason is that first and foremost a person must *bind* themselves, must *resolve* to actualize the will of God, and then he is assured that afterwards he will also achieve deep understanding... They will indeed bind themselves with straps of holiness, and not because that is what the neighbor does... [but because] they are seeking a path in life, trusting that the truth of this will become clear."

89. *Ibid.*, 328.

90. *Tanya*, Ch. 12.

91. *Ibid.*, Ch. 25.

92. *Ibid.*, Ch. 36.

93. Schneerson, *Torat menachem hitvaduyot*, Vol. 51, 331.

94. Elliot Lansky, "'But Where Is God?'" *Chabad.org*, <Chabad.org/2289725>. For additional details about Lansky's journey and its implications for himself and his family see *idem.*, "My Journey from the Fast Life Back to My Jewish Roots," *Chabad.org*, <chabad.org/2627353>.

95. See M. Herbert Danzger, *Returning to Tradition: The Contemporary Revival of Orthodox Judaism* (New Haven and London: Yale University Press, 1989), 71, where it is stated that "the term ba'alei t'shuva was not used until in 1972" [*sic*]. In truth Schneerson had been consistently using the term from the very beginning of his leadership. Although the term is found in earlier Hasidic texts and is indeed rooted in rabbinic texts, he was explicitly laying down the theological ground for the embrace of the new influx of returnees to Jewish practice that the coming years and decades would yield.

96. Mariam K. Slater, "My Son the Doctor: Aspects of Mobility among American Jews," *American Sociological Review* 34, no. 3 (Jun., 1969): 359.

97. See Aviva Cantor, *Jewish Women / Jewish Men: The Legacy of Patriarchy in Jewish Life* (New York: HarperCollins, 1995), 207-231; Brygida Gasztold, "Self-Sacrificing and/or Overbearing: The Jewish Mother in the Cultural Imagination," *Scripta Judaica Cracoviensia* 11 (2013): 161-174, and esp. 167: "In the American milieu, where she [the mother] was confined to the realm of domesticity, her self-esteem was connected with her children's career, especially as she bore the responsibility for socializing them."

98. Menachem Mendel Schneerson, *Torat menachem hitvaduyot*, Vol. 51, 399-401. See Maimonides, *Mishneh Torah*, Laws of Teshuvah, 3:4.

99. Ada Rapoport-Albert, *Hasidic Studies: Essays in History and Gender* (Liverpool: Littman Library of Jewish Civilization, 2018), 448-456.

100. Menachem Mendel Schneerson, *Torat menachem hitvaduyot*, Vol. 23 [5718 III] (Brooklyn, NY: Kehot Publication Society, 2007), 170-172.

101. See Abby Scher, *Cold War on the Home Front: Middle Class Women's Politics in the 1950s* (PhD thesis, The New School for Social Research, 1995), esp. 278-297. For more on the changing role of women in America during the early decades of Schneerson's tenure, see William H. Chafe, *The American Woman: Her Changing Social, Economic and Political Roles, 1920-1970* (London: Oxford University Press, 1972), 199-244.

102. On this topic see Ilan Fuchs, "'Women Shall Encircle Man': Women's Torah Study in the Teachings of R. Menachem Mendel Schneerson" in idem., *Jewish Women's Torah Study: Orthodox Religious Education and Modernity* (New York: Routledge, 2014), 128-158.

103. This phrase follows Kohelet, 9:14, and Nedarim, 32b Cf. *Tanya*, Chapter 9.

104. Brachot, 9a.

105. On the notion that putting the collective before the individual is ultimately beneficial for the individual as well, see below, Chapter 4.

106. Menachem Mendel Schneerson, *Sichot Kodesh 5735*, Vol. 1 (Brooklyn, NY: Vaad Hanachot Hatemimim, 1986), 325-326

107. *Ibid.*, 325. The language used here is drawn from the Zohar via *Tanya*, Ch. 10.

108. For a particularly developed discussion in this vein, see Menachem Mendel Schneerson, *Sichot Kodesh 5741*, Vol. 2 (Brooklyn, NY: Vaad Hanachot Hatemimim, 1986), 168 and on. This talk was delivered just a few days before the inauguration of Ronald Reagan, and Schneerson spoke at length about the importance of expressing gratitude to the outgoing incumbent, Jimmy Carter, for his service, irrespective of harsh disagreements with his policy. See esp. 176-177: "Even though prior to the the election there was a situation of plurality (pluribus), not only quantitatively but qualitatively, such that each held positions in opposition to those of the other party, including about who should be elected...[nevertheless] after the elections have already taken place, the intentions is that this plurality should be formed into a united entity (e pluribus unum)...Although he was elected by the majority and there was a minority against him...once he is elected he becomes a representative of the minority as well...with complete equity..."

109. On the long history of "polarization" in American politics, and the newer phenomenon of polarized political identity, see Emily J. Charnock, "Party Polarisation in the United States" *Political Insight* (Sept. 2018): 4-7. For a more substantive assessment of the latter issue see Lilliana Mason, "Losing Common Ground: Social Sorting and Polarization," *The Forum* 16, no. 1 (June, 2018): 47–66.

110. *Tanya*, Ch. 12.

111. On the question of the relationship between political tolerance or intolerance and religion, as reflected in various scholarly fields of political science, religious studies and sociology, see Marie A. Eisenstein, "Religion and Political Tolerance in the United States: A Review and Evaluation," in *The Oxford Handbook of Religion and American Politics*, edited by James L. Guth, Lyman A. Kellstedt, and Corwin E. Smidt (Oxford, UK: Oxford University Press, 2009), retrieved Sep. 13, 2018, from <http://www.oxfordhandbooks.com.libproxy.ucl.ac.uk/view/10.1093/oxfordhb/9780195326529.001.0001/oxfordhb-9780195326529-e-15>.

112. Horayot, 11b.

113. Menachem Mendel Schneerson, *Sichot Kodesh 5735*, Vol. 1, 326.

114. *Ibid.*

115. *Ibid.*, 327.

116. For a general overview of the use and abuse of religion in American politics see Harold Perkin, "The Tyranny of the Moral Majority: American Religion and Politics since the Pilgrim Fathers," *Cultural Values* 3, no. 2 (1999): 182-195.

117. See, for example, Menachem Mendel Schneerson, *Torat menachem sefer hamamarim melukot*, Vol. 3 (Brooklyn, NY: Kehot Publication Society, 2002), 71.

118. Menachem Mendel Schneerson, *Sichot Kodesh 5735*, Vol. 1, 330.

119. *Ibid.*, 329.

120. See J, Immanuel Schochet (ed.), *Keter shem tov hashalom* (Brooklyn, NY: Kehot Publication Society, 2016), 266, 464-468. Also see Schneur Zalman of Liadi, *Tanya*, Part 2, Chapters 1 and 2.

121. Menachem Mendel Schneerson, *Sichot Kodesh 5735*, Vol. 1, 328-330.

122. *Ibid.*, 329.

123. Menachem Mendel Schneerson, *Torat menachem hitvaduyot 5743*, Vol. 4 (Brooklyn, NY: Kehot Publication Society, 1990), 1735. For further examples and a discussion of Schneerson's application of these principles in the case of Soviet Russia, see Eli Rubin, "Soviet Jewry: Quiet Diplomacy, Covert Activity," *Chabad.org*, <chabad.org/2619818>.

124. Menachem Mendel Schneerson, "Education Is the Cornerstone of Humanity," published as a full page ad on Monday, September 11, 1978, in *the Washington Post*. For the text of the ad see "Education Is the Cornerstone of Humanity: On the Inauguration of 'Education Day USA'—April 18, 1978," *Chabad.org*, <chabad.org/816460>. On September the 18th Carter wrote to Schneerson saying that he had read the ad and "am grateful for your support and blessing." A facsimile of the letter is viewable here: https://w3.chabad.org/media/images/398/eSgm3986555.jpg

125. On the many meanings of these terms and on their use in political and historical discourse see J. Simon Rofe, ed., "Isolationism and Internationalism in Transatlantic Affairs," *Journal of Transatlantic Studies* 9, no. 1 (Mar., 2011).

126. On Schneerson and Chabad's use of media in the wider context of American religious media see Jeffrey Shandler, *Jews, God, and Videotape: Religion and Media in America* (New York: New York University Press, 2009), 230-252.

127. Ahead of the 1980 presidential election, for example, he encouraged everyone who had the right to vote to use it but added that he would not interfere regarding the question of who to vote for. See *Sefer hasichot 5741*, Vol. 1 (Brooklyn, NY: Vaad Hanachot Hatemimim, 1986), 827. The single exception to this rule concerns the 1988 election in Israel, which involved the split of the main Orthodox party due to a small faction who wished to cut Chabad off from the rest of the Orthodox community. In the words of the Chabad spokesman, Yehudah Krinsky: "the decision to endorse Agudah was an unprecedented step forced upon him [Rabbi Schneerson] by the Khomeini-like effort [of Rabbi Schach] to excommunicate a whole body of the Jewish people." See relevant discussions and citations in Robert O. Freedman, "Religion, Politics, and the Israeli Elections of 1988," *Middle East Journal* 43, no. 3 (Summer, 1989): 406-422. For portrayals of the Hasidic voting block in popular media, see John Kifner, "Birth of a Voting Bloc: the Hasidim and Orthodox Organize," <https://www.nytimes.com/1989/05/02/nyregion/birth-of-a-voting-bloc-the-hasidim-and-orthodox-organize.html>, and Urie Heilman, "The Hasidic Bloc Vote: Bernie and Hillary's Empire State of Mind and Other NY Campaign Notes," https://www.jta.org/2016/04/12/news-opinion/politics/the-hasidic-bloc-vote-bernie-and-hillarys-new-york-state-of-mind-and-other-notes-from-the-ny-primary-campaign.

CHAPTER 3

THE SOCIAL CONSTITUTION
OF HASIDISM AND THE
DIVINIZATION OF THE COSMOS

3.1—The Tsadik, the Community, and
Hasidism as an Antidote to Alienation

TODAY THE LIBRARY of Menachem Mendel Schneerson's published writings and oral teachings fills well over a hundred volumes. But his very first publication, *Hayom yom*, appeared in 1943 and continues to be singled out for special attention by those who hold him in esteem.[1] It consists mainly of short aphorisms and anecdotes set out in a yearlong calendar of daily readings. In the not impartial judgment of his father-in-law, this slim volume is "packed with pearls and diamonds of the greatest and best quality" and is "a true work of Hasidic culture."[2] If nothing else, these entries provide us with direct insight into the principles of Hasidic lore that Schneerson himself judged to be of most fundamental relevance to Hasidic life. It is also undoubtable that these anecdotes and aphorisms have continued to play a central role in the shaping of the collective ethos of Chabad right up to the present day.[3]

We have already observed that Schneerson was a keen-eyed social analyst and strategist. What concerns us in the present chapter is his vision of the social constitution of Hasidism itself. In Schneerson's view he was not merely intervening in the broader currents of social change, but was applying, developing, and disseminating a Hasidic teaching that was not only revolutionary in a spiritual or religious sense, but which was even more essentially transformative in a social sense. The following anecdote, cited in *Hayom yom*, encapsulates this conception with characteristic verve:

> The original hasidim of Schneur Zalman of Liadi once gathered together, circa 1784 to 1787, and the topic of their discussion was that the Rebbe's innovation is that we are not alone. In the past the rebbe—the head of the academy or the scholar of genius—was alone, and the students were alone too. The path of Hasidism established by the Rebbe is the great and holy innovation that the rebbe is not alone and the hasidim are not alone.[4]

Loneliness, or alienation, has long been identified by theorists and sociologists as one of the maladies of the human condition, especially in the modern period.[5] Here it is claimed that the primary innovation of the Hasidic path pioneered by Schneur Zalman of Liadi is that it constitutes an antidote to loneliness. While the veracity of the anecdote itself cannot be independently ascertained, its substance does stand up to scrutiny when read through a broad methodological prism. In recent years a growing body of scholarship has begun to amass that revives and credibly revises what was previously dismissed as an overly romantic view of Hasidism as foregrounding social concerns as well as ideological and religious ones.[6] Indeed, scholars have always understood that social questions were key to a proper understanding of the phenomenon we call Hasidism. But time and again they found themselves unable to disentangle themselves from the perceived tension between Hasidism's mystical and social dimensions. This is a false dichotomy, however, and it largely depends on the unwillingness of academic scholars to take the indigenous ideas of Hasidism on their own terms, insisting on fitting them into the neat boxes imposed by modern disciplinary categories.[7]

Hasidism deserves to be understood not only as a social movement, but also as an intellectual tradition that analyzes social ideas. Hasidism provides theoretical models that are *alternative* to those provided by the modern traditions of sociology and critical theory.[8] As an example we have before us the figure of the rebbe or the tsadik, the spiritual and social leader who is one of the most recognizable features of every Hasidic group. Gershom Scholem identified the tsadik with the more general figure of the prophet, "the man whose heart has been touched and changed by God."[9] In this he was correct. But he was wrong to juxtapose the tsadik with the traditional rabbinic leader, "the scholar, the student of the Torah" who needed nothing more than deeper knowledge of the law.[10] As Maoz Kahanah and Ariel Mayse have recently shown, the most prominent leaders of the emergent Hasidic movement in the last decades of the 18th century—Schneur Zalman of Liadi among them—were at once prophetic charismatics and also scholarly interpreters of rabbinic law and lore.[11]

Similarly, Scholem is quite right to argue (following Martin Buber) that "the originality of Hasidism lies in the fact that mystics…turned to the people with their mystical knowledge."[12] But he is wrong to claim that these mystics "had attained their spiritual aim" prior to turning to the people.[13] The contrary is true; the spiritual or mystical aims of the Hasidic masters could not be attained in solitude, but *only* through being in the midst of the people. This is precisely what set the emergent Hasidic movement apart from earlier Jewish mystical circles and traditions. What Scholem regarded as a wondrous paradox actually has a quite simple explanation: The mystical aims of Hasidism do not stand in tension with communal life. Hasidic mysticism is fundamentally social; it is experienced collectively, and is indeed *an experience of collectivity.*

Through a close reading of Schneur Zalman's teachings, Leah Orent has now shown that, for him, the love between the individual soul and God is a communal Jewish experience. The sense of being an individual standing apart from the community, which generally governs the human experience, is actually a result of the exile and imprisonment of the transcendent soul within the earthly body. To achieve a personal mystical experience, in other words, is to overcome bodily individuation, to overcome loneliness and alienation, and to participate in the "Song of Songs," the collective song that contains all the individual songs of the Jewish people.[14]

The specific intimations of the anecdote published by Schneerson in *Hayom yom* can be illuminated through a reading of a text that appears on the very first page of the authoritative compendium of Schneur

Zalman's oral discourses, *Torah or*. Here the nature of leadership, that
is, the role of the tsadik, is scrutinized through an interpretive analysis
of the biblical Moses, the archetypal Jewish leader, and his relationship
with the Jewish people:

> We find in the case of Moses that following the sin of the
> golden calf a thousand lights were taken from him, and this
> is hinted to by the sages in what they wrote on the verse, "Go,
> descend." (Exodus, 32:7.)—"Descend from your greatness. I
> did not give you [Moses] greatness except on account of the
> people of Israel." (*Talmud bavli*, Brakhot, 32a.) This is because
> the people of Israel are as a foot to Moses, as it is written,
> "Six hundred thousand are the nation's feet, in whose midst
> I [Moses] am." (Numbers, 11:21.) Meaning that they encom-
> passed him and were as a head to him even though they were
> certainly as his foot.[15]

Moses, in other words, is only a leader "in the midst" of the community. The leader is only given greatness on account of the community,
and therefore the community plays a role relative to the leader that is
analogous to that of the head which tops the human body. The head
imbibes sustenance for the human body, provides knowledge, vision,
and direction to the human body. The leader, likewise, is sustained and
provided with spiritual illumination on account of the people. If the
people sin, falling from their spiritual station, then "a thousand lights"
are taken from Moses too, though he could in no way be faulted for
their transgression. The people and the leader are inextricably bound
together. In the formulation found in *Hayom yom*, "the rebbe is not alone
and the hasidim are not alone."

Some scholars have argued that Schneur Zalman's *Tanya* presents a
rigid social hierarchy, according to which the righteous leader is on a
spiritual and moral plane that entirely transcends that of ordinary people.[16] But this text, along with many others, shows us that his conception
of leadership was far more complicated and sophisticated. Certainly, the
very notion of leadership is hierarchical. But in the Chabad conception
the function of a leader is—in Naftali Loewenthal's phrase—to "communicate the infinite," so that all people can practice techniques that
enable them to become absorbed within God's all-encompassing being.

The crucial role of the tsadik, within the cosmic hierarchy, is to be the conduit through which the hierarchical distinction between heaven and earth is erased.[17] In this text we see, moreover, that the spiritual stature of the tsadik is itself constituted by his role within the community. Likewise, we can add, the communal structure of Hasidism is itself constituted by the role of the tsadik therein. Simply being in the tsadik's presence inspires a sense of self-effacement on the part of individual members of the community, and of self-sublimation within the collective. Thereby a sense of non-hierarchical fellowship is constructed, forming the basis for the central ideal of Hasidic communal life.[18]

Less than two weeks before suffering a stroke in 1992, Schneerson published and distributed an edited discourse that would come to be regarded by his disciples as akin to his spiritual last testament. The question of the relationship between the leader and the community is one of its central themes, and a close reading yields many rich points that are worthy of consideration. What is most relevant here, however, are two passages that emphasize the degree to which the leader's ultimate goal must be (a) to erase all hierarchical distinctions, and (b) to empower the community with the tools to accomplish what the leader can never achieve alone.

> Even if one is on an extremely lofty spiritual level…by dint of the fact that such revelation does not illuminate the world generally, it is clear that even one's personal revelation is bounded. For when the unbounded revelation of the infinite is disclosed its revelation extends to every place, and so long as there is one place (even a marginalized corner) where the revelation of divinity does not shine it is a bounded revelation. This explains the Zoharic aphorism cited by R. Schneur Zalman of Liadi that "even if one tsadik would completely reconcile with God the messiah would come in that generation." For through reconciliation (*teshuvah*) the unbounded revelation of the infinite is drawn forth, and such a revelation would extend everywhere.[19]

The truly successful tsadik, accordingly, is not a solitary figure at all, nor a figure whose spiritual experiences utterly transcend the grasp of ordinary people. On the contrary, the experiences of a truly successful tsadik will be utterly universal, illuminating even the most marginalized corner of the earth. Indeed, this discourse espouses a socio-mystical vision that is staggering in the scope of its ambition. The proximity of its publication and distribution to the end of Schneerson's term as a fully functioning, living tsadik makes this passage all the more poignant. In a passage close to the end of the discourse he seems to gesture at the possibility of his own absence with even more specificity. Earlier he had cited his father-in-law's teaching that "the feet (analogous to the people) bring the head (analogous to the teacher) to a station that the head cannot arrive at independently."[20] Speaking of his father-in-law he concludes the discourse with the further argument that:

> His work to arouse and reveal the faith that is within every Jew, by dint of the essence of the soul, is in such a manner that afterwards they will be able to accomplish their mission independently, to the extent that they shall be an eternal luminary invulnerable to any alteration…and thereby we merit, very imminently, the true and complete redemption.[21]

The leader, like the head, cannot arrive at the ultimate goal independently. But a truly successful leader can empower the people to such a degree that even *afterward*—when the leader has already departed—they can continue to work independently and eternally, thereby arriving at the ultimate success, the universal phenomenon of the true and complete redemption.

This last testament is nothing short of remarkable, and it also goes a long way to explaining the continued success of Chabad in the quarter century since Schneerson's death. On the one hand it places the tsadik at the center of the cosmic drama. On the other hand it argues that the ultimate test of the tsadik's success depends upon the tsadik's absence.[22] It is small wonder that the tsadik is compared to Moses; to Moses who was at once the greatest of all the prophets (Deuteronomy, 34:10) and the most humble of all men (Numbers, 12:3); to Moses who once demanded that God preserve the Jewish people, despite the gravity of their sin, "or else erase me from your book" (Exodus, 32:32). According to Schneerson, it emerges, without the people there can be no Moses. Moreover, the ultimate goal of Moses is to sublimate his own identity by disseminating it and implanting it within each member of the Jewish nation. Just as personal experience must ultimately be synonymous with universal experience, so leadership must ultimately empower each member of the community with the independent wherewithal to achieve success.

3.2—The Rebbe's Mission Statement: The Three Loves That Are All One

Upon accepting the leadership of Chabad in 1951, Schneerson offered a self-described "statement." The centrality of Hasidism's social dimension—and particularly of interpersonal love—could not be clearer:

> The first thing people want to hear is a statement, and the procedure is that it must contain something innovative, something provocative. I don't know if this is provocative, but if you want to hear a statement, the Rebbe said that there are three things: There is love of God, and there is love of Torah, and there is love of the Jewish people, and these three things are all one. This means that it is impossible to distinguish between one and the other, for they are all one, as a single essence… [and] when one grasps hold of something that is a part of the essence one grasps the essence in its entirety… Accordingly, everyone must know that when you grasp hold of love of God, one cannot make do with that, and one cannot grasp hold of that if you don't also grasp hold of love of the Torah and love of the Jewish people. But, on the other hand… if we begin with love of the Jewish people, which seems to be a logical commandment, one will eventually achieve love of Torah and love of God… One must also see to it that one's love of the Jewish people should not only be constituted in giving food to the hungry and water to the thirsty, but also… in bringing Jews to love of Torah and love of God.[23]

This is a tremendously rich passage, and its status as part of Schneerson's definitive mission statement renders it worthy of special consideration. Rather than privileging love of God over love of one's fellow, as one might expect from a religious leader, Schneerson makes love of God entirely dependent on love of the Torah and love of one's fellow Jew. It is likewise striking that love of the Torah and love of the Jewish people are mentioned in the same breath, and are later linked together. To love one's fellow is not merely to look after their physical needs, but also to look after their spiritual and religious needs. As has already been discussed in the previous chapter, Schneerson saw the Torah—its study, and the practice of its commandments—as the only viable means by which Jewish survival would be ensured. Love of God alone, without any anchor in the physical world, is additionally judged to be empty of any substance. The substance of such love can only be constructed in the realm of living social reality, via love of Torah and love of the Jewish people.

There is a stark realism at play here; feelings and ideals are only endowed with meaning if they are attached to the terrestrial realm of activity and interpersonal relationships. This realism is grounded in the metaphysical belief that (1) the eternity of both the Torah and the Jewish people results from their shared oneness with the eternal God, and (2) that it is within the reality of this physical world that the eternal truth of God can best be affirmed. This underscores the way in which Schneerson sharpened the central Chabad doctrine that the ultimate telos of existence is specifically the creation of "a dwelling in the lower realms" (*dirah betachtonim*), and particularly this physical world which is the lowest of all realms. By token of this theological realism, earthly love of one's fellow human being constitutes a firm enough foundation to assure that open love of God will shortly follow. Likewise, that love can legitimately be expressed simply in the provision of "food to the hungry and water to the thirsty," though it should ideally extend into spiritual concerns as well, thereby overcoming the cosmic gap between heaven and earth.

This discussion of interpersonal love brings us to the question of Jewish particularism. Or, to put the shoe on the other foot, just how inclusive was Schneerson's social vision? When he talks about "love of the Jewish people," is it to be taken in a narrow, exclusionary sense, or can it be understood to apply to humanity at large?

This is a question that has already been discussed with great seriousness, depth, and erudition by Elliot Wolfson, who shows that Schneerson's paradoxical conception of Jewish chosenness and universal responsibility cannot easily be parsed. Wolfson nevertheless concludes that from a "relatively early date, the Seventh Rebbe was pondering the manner in which non-Jews can participate in the holiness attributed to Jews" and that "this vision only intensified in the years of his leadership."[24]

A clear statement of the universal principle of human kinship is found in a letter addressed by Schneerson to a representative of the Republic of Poland's Council for Polish Jewish Relations:

> The first man, Adam...was created as a single individual...One of the reasons—our sages declare—is that it was God's design that the human race, humans everywhere and in all times, should know that each and all descend from the one and the same single progenitor, a fully developed human being created in the image of God, so that no human being could claim superior ancestral origin; [and] hence also find it easier to cultivate a real feeling of kinship in all interhuman relationships.[25]

In this, Schneerson was following the example of Schneur Zalman of Liadi, who had already taken significant steps to "deconstruct the boundaries of love."[26] In Chapter 32 of the latter's foundational work, *Tanya*, the biblical imperative to "love your fellow as yourself" is read far more inclusively than it had been by previous rabbinic authorities and is rooted in the notion that "we all share a single father." The traditional halakhic position is that this commandment only applies to "your fellow in Torah and the commandments," thereby narrowing the imperative of love to pious Jews, and excluding Jewish sinners as well as non-Jews.[27] But Schneur Zalman forcefully argues that the imperative of love must be extended even to sinners:

> It was concerning this that Hillel said, "be a disciple of Aharon, love peace etc., love creatures and bring them close to Torah," (Avot, 1:12) meaning that even those who are far from God and His service, and are therefore called by the designation 'creatures' alone, we must draw them with strong cords of love, and thereby one might be able to bring them close to Torah and service of God, and if not, you have not thrown away the reward for the commandment to love your fellow.[28]

In a talk delivered and published in 1991 Schneerson cited this passage and explicated its universal significance:

> The commandment "raise up the lights" (Numbers, 8:2) was
> transmitted specifically to Aharon the High-Priest (who also
> fulfilled it in actuality) because Aharon's quality was...[to]
> "love creatures and bring them close to Torah": He has love
> even for "those who are far from God and His service, and
> are therefore called by the designation 'creatures' alone"
> (their only merit lies in the fact that they were created by
> God), and he brings them close to Torah...—even those who
> are found on the lowest possible station—...to the point that
> they become "a flame rising independently," (Rashi, ad loc.),
> and through achieving this among the Jewish people (that
> even the "creatures" shall "rise independently") this capac-
> ity is drawn into the world as well, such that even the lowest
> part of the world shall be illuminated, and in the manner of
> "a flame rising independently."[29]

Here the distinction between Jew and non-Jew is significantly reduced. The injunction to "love creatures and bring them close to Torah"
is extended to Jews and *thereby* to all people, so that the entire world is
ultimately illuminated by the Hasidic doctrine of interpersonal love.
This coheres with Schneerson's argument, expressed elsewhere, that
all Torah precepts that are self-evidently conducive to the construction and maintenance of a civilized society apply to all of humanity,
even if traditional Jewish sources do not often make the universal relevance of these precepts explicit.[30] In the above-cited mission statement,
he expressly noted that "love of the Jewish people...seems to be a log-
ical commandment," thereby opening the way for this precept to be
understood as applying to all people, and not just to Jews.[31]

Schneerson's 1991 talk is additionally significant because it provides
a powerful statement on the transformative power of love. He envis-
ages a world in which even the "lowest" elements of society no longer
need to be coerced into good, civilized behavior, but are instead motivated to take the initiative themselves, becoming a force for good as
"a flame rising independently." This can be achieved when we follow
the example of Aharon the High-Priest, whose service as the lighter

of the temple menorah was not unconnected to his identity as the personification of love. When the world is transformed by interpersonal love—rather than via normative forms of authority, social engineering, or control alone—goodness and light do not need to be imposed, policed, or enforced. When the world is transformed by love, each of its inhabitants is empowered to excel in independent unison.

The symbolism of the independently rising flame vividly portrays the multi-dimensional character of Schneerson's conception of love. True love between one person and another runs straight through to the divine soul, to the divine spark, that is within each individual.[32] Accordingly, interpersonal love does not merely extend horizontally, between individual members of society, but instead rises upward as well, extending vertically into what Schneur Zalman of Liadi described as "their root and source in the living God." In introducing a vertical dimension to social relations, Hasidism anchors the process of social transformation beyond normative social categories and within a larger, macro process, which sociologists do not usually want to talk about. The radical power of this larger conception is easily grasped when we take Schneerson's mission statement on the three loves that are "all one" to its ultimate conclusion; to enter into a loving relationship with your fellow human being is to enter into a loving relationship with God.[33]

This brings us to the third pillar upon which this cosmic vision stands. Love of your fellow and love of God are also understood to be synonymous with love of Torah. For many, this is the most difficult part of Schneerson's vision to swallow. Why is the Torah, along with its myriad commandments and the associated laws that govern every aspect of orthodox Jewish life, so essential? Isn't the socio-mystical axis enough? Indeed, doesn't this relegate Schneerson to the ranks of all the other conservative religious leaders who simply can't let go of the ancient laws mandated by the Bible, and which seem to be obsolete in contemporary society?

Naturally Schneerson was often asked questions of this kind, and he did not fail to respond. Of particular relevance in the present context is a talk in which he discussed the centrality of the Torah and its commandments, not only to a relationship with God but to interpersonal relationships as well. His argument is rooted in an extensive critique of the superficiality of interpersonal relationships that are not predicated on a shared commitment to do the will of God. Here he drew on the request made in the High Holiday liturgy that all of creation "shall form one fellowship (*agudah achat*) to actualize Your will with a complete heart." On his reading:

> This doesn't mean that a united fellowship might exist anyway, while lacking the purpose "to actualize your will." Rather, such a fellowship can only exist if its purpose is "to actualize your will."…Whereas with regard to other causes…though people may be bound together regarding a specific enterprise, they nevertheless remain separate entities for the following reasons:
>
> 1. In all their other affairs they have no relationship, for their opinions are not the same, and they are indeed utterly different in essence. This one is distinct and that one is distinct. It is only with regard to one particular thing that they have united, and only with regard to that particular thing and with the particular faculties that relate to it.
>
> 2. Even regarding that specific endeavor itself they are also not truly united, meaning that even in this specific endeavor they are two separate entities. Since in the totality of their identities they are two separate people (as explained above), even when it comes to this specific endeavor, each of them acts in a way that is circumscribed by their own existence and their own feelings. It is only on the superficial level that they act in concert.
>
> 3. Even insofar as they are superficially united regarding this specific endeavor, this too is not something that will last. Since in their fundamental being they are separate from one another, and for each of them their own fundamental being and their other concerns are a greater priority and more important than this specific endeavor, as soon as this specific endeavor will come into conflict with their own being they will separate from one another and even the superficial fellowship will dissolve.
>
> Indeed, we have tangibly seen in the case of many such fellowships, which apparently seemed to be strong fellowships,

and in the end, when some conflict transpired with the individual existence of the members, these fellowships fell apart
and nothing remains of them.[34]

This superficiality can only be overcome, according to Schneerson,
when interpersonal love is constituted vertically as well as horizontally,
and this can only be achieved through the revelatory power of the Torah and its commandments:

> When the fellowship is formed in order "to actualize your
> will with a complete heart," meaning for the sake of Torah
> and the commandments, then the Torah reveals the essence
> of the soul, and on the part of the essence of the soul all Jews
> are literally one entity.[35]

This brings us to one of the cornerstones upon which the entire
edifice of Schneerson's thought is built, and which was already very
fully developed in the writings of Chabad's fifth rebbe, Shalom DovBer
Schneersohn of Lubavitch (1860-1920, known by the acronym "Rashab"). Rashab's most systematic work constitutes a phenomenological
interpretation of all the various modes of religious practice and experience that are encompassed by Torah study and mitzvah observance.
His central argument is that the particular properties of each of these
modes, as well as the entire lifestyle that they construct together, constitutes a phenomenological experience of the essence of divine being.
In other words, the revelatory power of Torah study and mitzvah observance is such that it makes the presence of God tangibly accessible
within the normative world of human life and experience.[36]
    It is impossible to understand Schneerson's worldview with-
out this fundamental axiom; the Torah-prescribed practices of
traditional Jewish life provide the essential medium for the phenomenological manifestation of the divine. This axiom is all-pervasive, and
we shouldn't be surprised that it is central to his conception of Hasidism's socio-mystical constitution as well: The phenomenological
manifestation of Hasidism's socio-mystical core can only be discovered
through the embodied study of Torah and the embodied practice of its
precepts in personal and social life.[37] This explains the third dimension of Schneerson's mission statement; neither love of God nor love of

your fellow can be properly grasped without love of the Torah. Torah is the revelatory channel that draws the divine essence of interpersonal love into the open, and disclosing what otherwise remains a merely metaphysical truth, namely that no two individuals are really separate from one another; in their essence they are each fundamentally one with God and one with one another.

Schneerson goes so far as to argue that if an individual feels himself to be a separate entity, entirely independent of his fellow, he must realize that: "he is still standing at the very beginning of spiritual work and development, for if his spiritual work would be true then the Torah and the commandments would have revealed the essence of his soul in which all are one entity."[38] By the same token, Torah can reshape the fundamental dynamic of all our social endeavors:

> It is consequently a good idea that any fellowship, for whatever purpose it is convened, should incorporate at least some element that is related to Torah and the commandments. This element should be the foundation of the fellowship, through which it will be held together as a lasting fellowship dedicated to whatever voluntary purpose it was convened.[39]

This suggestion illustrates the way in which Schneerson's conception of the relationship between the religious realm and the secular realm stands in direct contrast to the normative conception that seeks to keep these realms apart from one another. As the Russian Jewish poet Yehudah Leib Gordon put it in one of his most famous lines, "Be a man on the street and a Jew at home."[40] Gordon wanted Jews to engage with the civic realm merely as people, preserving their religious and cultural heritage only in the private domain, thus bifurcating modern public life from the preservation of ancient lore and custom. But Schneerson wanted Jews to be Jews in the street as well, to permeate and strengthen their civic endeavors with the eternal power of the Torah and the shared mission that all of creation "shall form one fellowship (*agudah achat*) to actualize Your will with a complete heart."

In Schneerson's view, it is clear, Hasidism's social constitution should extend its transformative phenomenological power to all areas of human endeavor. Indeed, his messianic mission was nothing less than the resacralization of human life and society, and ultimately the entirety of existence, in all its aspects. It is due to this activist conception of Hasidism, as much as to any other factor, that Chabad presents a contemporaneous alternative to secularization that is no less modern and, for many, no less compelling.

Scholars of Hasidism would do well to pay more attention to the centrality of the social in Hasidism's sacred project. Given the right conditions its socio-mystical constitution can be a source for the re-animation and resacralization of society from within. Put differently, Hasidism is at once a social form and a religious form, providing an all-encompassing blueprint according to which individuals and families build communities and orientate themselves within the cosmos. It can be ghettoized from wider society, as in the case of Satmar, and thereby reductively define itself by the ways it cuts itself off from wider culture. Alternatively, it can embed itself as an engaging and alternative cultural force within the wider society. It was the latter path that Schneerson chose, and he recognized that the new political and cultural context of postwar America provided the right conditions for a Hasidic resacralization of society and culture to succeed.

3.3—The Farbrengen: A Practice of Communicative Openness and Interchange

HAVING DISCUSSED THE theoretical basis of Schneerson's socio-mystical vision of Hasidism, and of his own role as a Hasidic leader, we now turn to the primary practice by which he realized that vision in the social life of his community, namely the "farbrengen."

Farbrengen is a Yiddish word that means "gathering," but which has the more specific connotation of spending quality time in good company and lively conversation.[41] In Chabad Hasidism this meaning is given even greater specificity. The farbrengen is not merely a social occasion in a secular and recreational sense, but rather a sacred institution that plays a central role in the cultivation and absorption of the socio-mystical ethos of Hasidism.[42]

The farbrengen has been succinctly described by the ethnographer Damián Setton, based on research he did in the Chabad community of Buenos Aires, and much the same can be observed in Chabad communities the world over:

The ritual consists of a gathering where people sit around a table and put forth three central components: *nigunim* (melodies),
mashke (alcohol), and the words of the Torah. The nigunim are
religious melodies...The singing of nigun involves a performance where specific parts of the body are utilized. The actors
balance back and forth, elevating their voices and beating the
table with their fists or open hands, manifesting the passionate
dimension of religiosity. The nigunim that are sung in the farbrengens are purely melodic without any lyrics.[43]

Naftali Loewenthal has framed the farbrengen within his larger
theorization of Chabad's tradition of communication, and of Chabad's
mission to communicate the infinite. Significantly, he also relates it to
the analysis of communication typologies set forth by Jürgen Habermas. Loewenthal notes that "there are a number of different kinds of
farbrengen, some of which can still be seen today," and argues that the
discourse of a farbrengen is one in which hierarchical norms are in some
way transcended, creating "a sense of openness and freedom."[44] From
this perspective the melodies and the alcohol can be seen as accessories
to the third and most central component, namely the communication
of Torah. The first two components cultivate a heightened sense of
openness and freedom—and, we might add, of shared socio-mystical
experience—which allows for the communication of Torah in a form
that is quite different from normative teaching in a classroom setting.

Loewenthal, following Habermas, outlines three forms of communication: (1) "A rigid command structure, as of a king to his subject or master
to servant."; (2) Rational argument in terms of accepted norms...the
more enlightened teacher...engages in rational discussion with the class
in order to convince them of the rightness of the instructions."; (3) "The
norms themselves are transcended, and have to be justified from a universalistic point of view. Teacher and class together redefine the school
rules, starting with the question of whether or not rules are necessary."[45]
Chabad texts, according to Loewenthal, take the radical step of questioning all the axioms of religion, albeit in order to uphold them, and
accordingly enter into "the third category of communication, the point
at which one might ask: why should there be Divine commands at all?
Why should God care what people do? Why did God create the world?
And what do you mean by 'God'?" Loewenthal further argues that this

communicative "openness" is seen "more clearly, if elusively and enigmatically" in the farbrengen, whose discourse is marked by the dynamic of empathy, "the capacity to see oneself in the other fellow's situation."[46]

Indeed, farbrengens are sometimes held on a completely equitable basis, among friends or colleagues. In these instances no one assumes the position of a teacher or mentor in relation to an audience. Instead all participants freely share their minds, responding, interjecting, and above all empathizing. In a treatise on interpersonal discourse penned by the aforementioned Fifth Rebbe of Chabad, Rashab, the centrality of this kind of exchange is underscored:

> It is a foundation and great fundamental…that they should connect and speak to one another…for you cannot insist that the truth is in accord with your own intellection when you hear the insight of your friend and you truthfully debate one another. Thereby they come to the truth of the matter.[47]

At first blush, the farbrengen might seem to be a Hasidic version of the philosophical banquet described in Plato's *Symposium*. But at a farbrengen philosophy is no mere abstraction; the participants are not simply engaged in an intellectual game whose object is an entertaining display of cleverness, logic, or clarity. As Rashab goes on to intimate, the chief object of the farbrengen is that each of the participants attain a clearer reckoning of where they stand in matters of personal worship (*avodah*). Through open and empathetic discussion with their fellows, in other words, they can better see themselves as they stand in relation to God. This distinction is expressed in the farbrengen's confessional dynamic. As Rashab says, "It is a foundation and great fundamental…in matters of personal worship that they reveal the flaws of their hearts to one another, and discuss this."[48] He continues to explain that this kind of confessionalism enables participants not merely to identify their flaws, but also to experience meaningful and therapeutic regret, and moreover to curate solutions and cooperatively resolve to implement them. He further underscores that this process can only be successful if it stands on a foundational spirit of self-effacement:

> All this occurs when the individual has humility (*bitul*) and is able to unite with—and bring himself close to—his fellow. But

> when asserting one's existence egotistically, one is by default
> utterly unable to reveal the flaws of one's heart to the other. Or
> if thinking the other to be very inferior, how then can one re-
> veal to him all one's issues, and what will it help?...The main
> factor is that he is fundamentally unable to unite with the oth-
> er...and is not at all receptive to the argument of the other, to
> honestly listen and to assess it without extraneous bias.

Here we see that the communicative openness that Loewenthal
identifies also encompasses an openness to criticism, to spiritual vulnerability, and to spiritual progress.

Loewenthal describes another form of the farbrengen in which "one
person may have the role of 'guide,' but what this person says can progress to a further stage at which both guide and the other participants
are together discovering something new." There is an equalizing factor at play here according to which what the guide says is shaped and
drawn forth by the listeners. They might also respond or interject, thus
assuming the role of a "guide" or "mentor" in relation to the "guide"
and "mentor." Given this empathetic interchangeability, along with the
open-endedness it introduces, it is hardly surprising that Loewenthal
describes the farbrengen as having achieved "the status of a kind of art-
form" within the Chabad community.[49]

What we are especially concerned with here, however, is a farbrengen of a different sort entirely, a farbrengen in which it would seem that
the normative command structure of master and pupil can never be
overcome. This is the form of farbrengen at which the tsadik—in this
case Menachem Mendel Schneerson, Chabad's Seventh Rebbe—presides. Lowenthal argues that in this model too the definitive sense of
openness is preserved because the tsadik's purpose is to communicate
something universal, namely the all-encompassing infinitude of God,
and make it resonate within the hearts and minds of his listeners. Paying particular attention to a farbrengen led by Rashab at his court in
the Russian town of Lubavitch, circa 1913, Loewenthal describes it as
a "numinous shared event...creating a bridge between mystical belief,
resolute observance of the Law and the openness and quest for freedom
associated with modernity."[50]

Building on these remarks, we might intervene with our argument that Hasidism should rightfully be understood as fundamentally

socio-mystical in its phenomenological constitution. In light of this conception, it can be further suggested that it is specifically in the farbrengen, among the gathered Hasidim, that the rebbe is transformed into a font of divine illumination and communication. The farbrengen is itself instrumental in the construction of a socio-mystical dynamic in which the shared quest for the divine can be realized. The sense of openness and freedom, of universality and even democracy, is accordingly not at odds with the awesome station, the pedestal, upon which the tsadik is placed. On the contrary, as we have already seen in Schneur Zalman of Liadi's teachings, the luminous station of the tsadik can only be achieved in the midst of the people. This means that even the tsadik is subject to the communicative interchangeability of the farbrengen, in which all participants must be open to impart, to receive, and—most importantly—to share. The rebbe does not merely speak, communicating to his Hasidim, but is also a recipient of the numinous sense constructed by the very collectivity of the occasion.

In previous eras, the form of farbrengen where the rebbe presides was a relative rarity. Rashab, for example, would generally lead a farbrengen on three fixed occasions throughout the year.[51] His main means of communication was not the farbrengen but the oral delivery of a formal Hasidic discourse (a "mamer") each Friday evening, at the onset of Shabbat.[52] The Seventh Rebbe, by contrast, turned the farbrengen into the primary medium of interaction with his Hasidim. This practice began in the 1940s, when his father-in-law and predecessor, Rayats, instructed him to lead a farbrengen once a month on Shabbat after the morning prayers.[53] He continued this for the next fifty years, and would also lead farbrengens on special occasions that fell during the week, such as on the Chabad festival of *Yud tes kislev*, or on his own birthday.

The fact that Schneerson so often held weekday farbrengens is of particular value to researchers. Hundreds of audio recordings have been preserved, including of the 1951 farbrengen at which he accepted the leadership of Chabad. Video recordings of complete farbrengens date from the early 1970s, and many of them are freely available on the internet.[54] This allows scholars, as well as contemporary Hasidim, to access these events not only via the written transcripts of what was said but from the vantage point of a cameraman in the room. In comparison to a video, the textual imprint of a Hasidic teaching is a pallid reduction of a communicative interchange whose dimensions extended far beyond mere words. Schneerson's Hasidic "teachings" must properly be understood to include performance, and the distinct social dynamic embodied in the tightly packed audience, together with the expectant atmosphere that prevails, the enthused singing, and the heartfelt Hasidic toast of "*lechayim!*" ("to life!"), together with the Rebbe's individualized response, "*lechayim livrakhah!*" ("to life and to blessing!").

Schneerson's farbrengens quickly developed a distinctive format of their own. Most weekday farbrengens were several hours long, beginning at eight or nine in the evening, and continuing past midnight. On some occasions the farbrengens went on till four or five the following morning. As an example, we will take a closer look at the farbrengen held on April 15, 1981—in honor of his seventy-ninth birthday—as preserved in video form:[55]

As Schneerson enters the hall the crowd rises and the singing intensifies. The camera follows him as he strides swiftly to a red upholstered chair behind a long, white-covered table on a raised dais facing the crowd. Senior Hasidim are also seated on the dais, as are honored guests, including rabbis and elected officials. A senior rabbi (Efraim Eliezer Yolles of Philadelphia) approaches Schneerson as he reaches his seat, and his whispered words are acknowledged with a warm nod and a smile. Schneerson takes his seat, and the singing subsides. A moment later he begins speaking, a microphone on the table before him amplifying the vigor in his voice. This is the first of eight talks that he will deliver that evening, interspersed with interludes of song, and ranging between 15 minutes and 45 minutes each. Between talks Schneerson also scans the crowd, rapidly locking eyes with individuals and vigorously nodding in personal greeting as they raise small cups and wish him "*lechayim!*"[56]

In a sense it is these mini interactions, these rapid moments of one-on-one greeting and wordless exchange, that convey the essence of the farbrengen. This is at once a mass event and a deeply personal one. The farbrengen is the collectivization of embodied individuals in shared reception of the divine, and the medium for that reception is not simply the Rebbe himself, but rather the interface between the Rebbe and each individual hasid. The Rebbe is not merely charismatic, but is rather a communicator of charisma, and the transfer of charisma is achieved through all and any of the farbrengen's elements: through the wave of the Rebbe's arm to the beat of a lively tune, or the sing-song cadence of his speaking voice—which has a rhythm reminiscent of poetry, prayer, and trance music—as much as through the content of his delivery.[57]

3.4—Communicative Interchange and the Divinization of the Cosmos

THE CONTENT OF Schneerson's delivery is always Torah, but his conception of Torah is one that encompasses the entire world. This echoes Abraham J. Heschel's formulation in his classical volume on the biblical prophets: "The main task of prophetic thinking," and, we may add, of prophetic speech, "is to bring the world into divine focus."[58] At any given farbrengen Schneerson might offer a scholarly exposition on Maimonides' code of Jewish law, a deconstruction and reinterpretation of Rashi's seminal medieval commentary to the Bible, or an incisive theological discourse drawing on classical works of Jewish philosophy, Kabbalah, and Hasidism. On the very same occasion he might also offer critical commentary on the latest international crisis—touching on security, economics, and diplomacy—and also deliver a sharp analysis of American domestic policy questions, with particular reference to education, criminal justice, or new technological developments. All of these discussions will be laced with references and citations from the length and breadth of biblical, rabbinic, and Hasidic literature. None of these discussions will be entirely theoretical or abstract. The focus is constantly on the individual and collective work of divinizing the self and the world. The explicit discussions of current events and world affairs broaden the scope of Schneerson's Torah teachings, and broaden the scope of the farbrengen's socio-mystical interaction so that the entire cosmos is therein embraced.[59]

This conception of Torah as the portal for cosmic embrace and reciprocal interchange is articulated in the opening talk of the 1981 farbrengen described above, which acts as a preface and prism through which all the subsequent talks of the evening are refracted:

> The Torah begins with the letter *bet*, which the Midrash tells us is the first letter of the word *brachah*, meaning blessing...Everything in Torah does not merely extend from above to below,

or from below to above—being either in the aspect of recipient or of giver—but is rather a complete existence that encompasses both dynamics. Likewise, when a Jew, and indeed any being, receives blessing from God—drawn below from the Source of Blessing—it is followed by a response, an "opening with blessing" on the part of the recipient, which is an ascent from below to above...This means that God desired that all things...should be complete, such that when one receives something...God gives the capacity to the recipient—whether we are speaking of any entity in general, or of a Jew especially—that, as our sages say, all things offer song to God, as the *Midrash shirah* specifies all the verses sung by the various different creations in the world. And this offering of song is a form of blessing, recognition and thanks due to God who creates them and sustains them. In initiating praise of God it is as if one becomes a giver and a provider in relation to God.[60]

In Hasidism, blessings are usually regarded as being within the purview of God and of the Rebbe. Blessings are bestowed from on high.[61] But here Schneerson argues that such one-sidedness is insufficient and incomplete. A complete blessing, a Torah blessing, is a reciprocal and interactive one, in which all of creation is raised up to stand in communicative interchange with God. This principle of reciprocity is one that Schneerson articulated and expanded upon on many other occasions, and it is central to his theorization of the role of the individual and of the community within society, a topic to which we will return in the next chapter.

What is most significant in the present context, however, is how this theorization is manifest in the praxis of the farbrengen: Schneerson's opening talk, as cited here, is not merely a discussion *about* the meaning of blessing, but is itself a *performance* of its content. Schneerson is responding to the blessings he has received from God over the course of his life, and responding to the blessings he has received from Hasidim and well-wishers as he enters his eightieth year. He is also bestowing blessings upon God and upon all who extend blessing to him and who look to him for blessing in return. His words, his Torah discourse, become the medium via which this cosmic exchange of blessings is enacted, and via his words the scope of this exchange—the scope of the farbrengen itself—is explicitly expanded to include all of God's creations.

Schneerson's embrace of new media technologies—and particularly video, which has already been noted—served to expand the collectivizing communication of the farbrengen even further, temporally and geographically. Now, nearly a quarter century after Schneerson's death, viewers across the world can still feel part of this occasion, can be drawn into the rhythm of the event, and become enthused by its communicative charisma.

Technology's capacity to extend the farbrengen beyond the constraints of time and space was well understood by Schneerson and by the global network of Chabad Hasidim. From 1970 and on, a group of yeshiva students based in Brooklyn, London, and Israel set up an international phone "hook-up" system to broadcast Schneerson's farbrengens to Chabad communities around the world.[62] Later they would be broadcast on the WEVD radio network and on satellite TV. In the 1990s satellite technology would be utilized to create an interactive farbrengen and celebration via live video link, connecting simultaneous gatherings across the globe with the gathering led by Schneerson in New York.[63] As Jeffery Shandler notes, "Menachem Mendel Schneerson is distinguished among hasidic leaders for the way in which he situated technology within his view of humankind's relationship to God and to the universe."[64]

Speaking of the use of the telephone, radio, and other media used to transmit Torah, Schneerson paid particular attention to the physical mechanism through which sound waves are transformed into electrical current and then converted again into sound, citing this as a tangible example of the divinization of the world:

> There is an advantage in the fact that the voice comes via a metal coil (and is not actually the voice of a *person*), for this provides the capacity and opportunity to reveal the singular essence [*yechidah*] (the Singularity of the world [i.e. God in whose singular being the world is encompassed]) within the world, even within metal which is *inanimate*—such that even inanimate matter that remains in its inanimate station and status, changes (and vibrates internally) and transfers "the word of God."[65]

It is not merely people—sentient human beings—who are enfolded within the cosmic farbrengen via technology, but even the inanimate stuff of the cosmos itself is thereby made transparent to its singular essence, which is nothing less than the singular being of God's own self.

In a talk delivered during the Chanukah Live celebration held on December 1, 1991, Schneerson spelled out his expansive conception of the event's socio-mystical significance in the clearest possible terms:

> There is a lesson to be learned from the fact that we make a satellite [event] at the onset of Chanukah—and in such a way that whoever wishes, whether Jew or non-Jew, can set the [television] machine to witness how one single Jew has the ability to shed light upon the entire world, such that it need not take any time for that light to arrive everywhere in the world...We saw just now that a child...lit a single candle in a single location in the world, and in the same instant it was seen across the entire world...taking an unlit candle and making it luminous with the light of Torah and God's commandments. Moreover, during the days of Chanukah one becomes increasingly more radiant...thereby illuminating one's entire environment...As we see tangibly via the satellite that is being used now—it allows us to speak together with Jews in Moscow, with Jews in New York, Jews in India, Jews in Japan, Jews in the Land of Israel, or in Australia, and so forth—and thereby when we speak here in New York about Jewish life, Torah study, and practicing the commandments—one of which is "love your fellow as yourself," and another being "charity," to help out another who is needy—one can immediately transmit and transfer money via satellite to the bank...so that the bank can immediately release a large amount of money in accord with their needs...And the same applies to [the transmission] of good spiritual counsel...or an explanation of the meaning and intention of a Torah topic more generally...[66]

Here again we encounter the symbolism of the lit flame, but now it is combined with the new symbol of the satellite, which at once orbits in the heavens and is the medium for global interconnectivity on earth. Through this symbol Schneerson developed the theme of cosmic communicative interchange considerably in three talks delivered that evening, arguing that the instant interconnectivity achieved by the combination of satellite technology and Torah is in fact replicable in every positive action that we do. Just as a word of Torah can now inspire a person on the other side of the globe without a moment's pause, so charitable aid can be instantly transferred anywhere as soon as it is needed. Schneerson further emphasized that even where no technology is involved a seemingly insignificant act can likewise be recast as an act of cosmic union: "When a small child drinks a small glass of water, and first blesses the One 'whom all is created by His word,' that bit of water is thereby connected with all the manifold things that are created by God's word, for they all depend on being used for blessing."[67] This is a conception that enlarges the farbrengen's scope not only to include the entire world on the macro level, but to include everything in the world on a micro level as well.

One thing that is not always obvious from watching the videos of these farbrengens is that women too were participants. As described by the ethnomusicologist Ellen Koskoff, who first attended one of Schneerson's farbrengens in 1973, the women's gallery almost completely encircled the synagogue hall, and was filled with tiered wooden benches. Tinted screen windows prevented the women from being seen by the men below (and by the cameras), but on some occasions the men's bleachers were so high that the last tier of men was "mere inches from the women on the first tier of the gallery."[68] Koskoff writes that the women's participation in the farbrengen is "more modest in its expression" yet "no less exciting," and "their intensity...matches that of the men below them."[69] Koskoff also takes note of farbrengens held between female peers, and offers a strong ethnographic investigation of gender performance in music in the Chabad community.[70] In the present context, however, we should further note that Schneerson would deliver special addresses to women several times a year. These addresses were not full farbrengens, but they had special features of their own. After the address the women were often given the opportunity to go up to the dais, exchanging a quick word with the Rebbe and receiving a dollar directly from his hand, which for most men was impossible at a regular farbrengen. On these occasions the women would sit in the main synagogue hall, while the men listened and watched from behind the tinted windows of the women's gallery. These addresses have likewise been preserved in audio and video recordings.[71]

Another variation of the farbrengen was introduced in 1981. By this point the great number of people seeking to meet with Schneerson was too great, and with very few exceptions, his practice of receiving people for "private audiences" (*yechidut*) was brought to an end. It was replaced with the "collective private audience" (*yechidut klalit*), in which Schneerson would speak to specific groups who would gather in the main hall of the synagogue. These groups might consist of bar mitzvah boys, girls who were graduating high school, soon to be married couples, and guests from Israel, France, or England (on these occasions the Rebbe would speak in Hebrew, French, or English rather than in Yiddish). In the latter cases men and women would both gather in the main synagogue, separated only by a double row of tables, which were arranged to create a walkway and space for a low dais with a table and chair for the Rebbe to sit to address the audience of collective individuals.[72] When some protested at this collectivization of the *yechidut*, Schneerson responded in a written note that in fact "now every farbrengen is like a *yechidut for one who so desires.*"[73]

On December 20, 1990, the main synagogue was packed with thousands of children for that year's Chanukah Live celebration. On this occasion most of the men were relegated to the street outside, where they watched the proceedings on a giant screen. The tinted windows of the women's gallery were opened to allow a better view, and a female Japanese photographer by the name of Chie Nishio was able to position herself directly above the Rebbe's dais. She was perfectly poised to capture the lit candles of the synagogue's oversized menorah in the foreground, with Schneerson leaning on his lectern and watching one of the screens set up to face him. He is surrounded by male cameramen, a few senior Hasidim, and throngs of children.[74]

At the evening's conclusion the Rebbe handed out rolls of coins to be distributed among the crowd, and then waved over the cameramen and photographers to personally hand each of them a coin as well. Then he turned to his left and glanced upward to where Chie Nishio was standing. Taking a roll of coins in his right hand he walked to the edge of the dais and stretched his arm upward toward the open window of the gallery above. Nishio snapped one final photo before transferring her camera to her left hand and reaching down with her right to receive the Rebbe's gift.[75] The farbrengen had expanded to a global scale, but Schneerson had not lost sight of the individual.

Notes

1. Menachem Mendel Schneerson, *Hayom yom* (Brooklyn, NY: Kehot Publication Society, 1943). On the circumstances and significance of its original publication see Avraham Rosen, "'Today Is the Day': Reading Between the Lines of the Lubavitcher Rebbe's Holocaust Era Calendar," *Chabad.org*, <chabad.org/1902777>.

2. Yosef Yitschak Schneersohn, *Igrot kodesh*, Vol. 7 (Brooklyn, NY: Kehot Publication Society, 1983), 231.

3. See Avraham Rosen, "'A Calendar for all Occasions': How Hayom Yom Became a Jewish Classic," *Chabad.org*, <chabad.org/3772406>.

4. Schneerson, *Hayom yom*, entry for the 22nd of Iyaar.

5. For a recent contribution to the discourse on alienation and its significance for modern thinkers see Rahel Jaeggi, *Alienation*, with a foreward by Axel Honneth (New York: Columbia University Press, 2014). See also Philip Slater, *The Pursuit of Loneliness: American Culture at the Breaking Point* (Boston: Beacon Press, 1990); Bertell Ollman, *Alienation: Marx's Conception of Man in a Capitalist Society* (Cambridge, UK: Cambridge University Press, 1976), and Robert J. Coplan and Julie C. Bowker (eds.), *The Handbook of Solitude: Psychological Perspectives on Social Isolation, Social Withdrawal, and Being Alone* (Malden, MA: John Wiley and Sons, 2014).

6. For a critique of the arguments of Israel Halpern and Yeshayahu Schachar that contemporaneous non-Hasidic sources are more oriented toward social justice than Hasidic ones see Marcin Wodziński, "The Socio-Economic Profile of a Religious Movement: The Case of Hasidism," *European History Quarterly* 46, no. 4 (September, 2016): 668-701, esp. 672. Also see Haviva Pedaya, "Lehitpathuto shel ha-degem ha-hevrati-dati-kalkali behasidut: hapidion, hahavurah veha-aliyah leregel," in *Dat ve-kalkalah: yahasei gomelin, shay le-Ya'akov Kats bi-melot lo tish'im shanah: kovets ma'amarim* (Jerusalem: Zalman Shazar Center, 1995), 311–373; Naftali Loewenthal, "The Hasidic Ethos and the Schisms of Jewish Society," *Jewish History* 27, no. 2 (December, 2013): 377-398; Leah Orent, "Religious Experience and the National Community—The Version of R. Shneur Zalman of Liadi," *Studies in Spirituality* 13 (2003): 99-117.

7. For an extensive discussion of the theoretical background, and of the disciplinary shift we propose, see Philip Wexler, *Mystical Sociology: Toward Cosmic Social Theory* (New York: Peter Lang, 2013). The essence of our thesis is encapsulated in the following paragraph: "It is difficult for those of us trained in classical, modernist sociology to imagine that religion could be the subject, and not simply the object of social understanding…to see mystical discourse, as a contemporary intellectual foundation for social analysis…Now, as the "newer" religious and critical side of classical sociology becomes more professionally acceptable—even as more traditional interpretations are utilized by fields such as Jewish mystical studies—we can now more fully recognize the religious foundations of sociology…[and] to show, with examples, how mystical Jewish texts offer social analytic resources…" (*Ibid.*, 115-116). Below we will develop this argument with particular application to Chabad Hasidism, and to the leadership of Menachem Mendel Schneerson, through a reading of primary and secondary sources, as well as through an analysis of the social form of Schneerson's own leadership practices.

8. *Ibid.*, esp. 52-53.

9. Gershom Scholem, *Major Trends in Jewish Mysticism* (New York: Schocken Books, 1941), 334.

10. *Ibid.*, 333.

11. Maoz Kahanah and Ariel Even Mayse, "Hasidic Halakhah: Reappraising the Interface of Spirit and Law," *AJS Review* 41, no. 2 (November, 2017): 375-408. This bears out a broader argument made by Elliot Wolfson to the effect that this combination is actually characteristic of Jewish mysticism more broadly. See Elliot R. Wolfson, *Venturing Beyond: Law and Morality in Kabbalistic Mysticism* (Oxford and New York: Oxford University Press, 2006), 262-263: "The particular path of the Jewish mystical experience leads out of the specificity of this one tradition, but it does so in a manner that compels walking the path repeatedly to find the way out. If one contemplates the possibility of following the path to get beyond the path definitively, then one is off the path and thus will never get beyond the path. To traverse the path of law one must travel the path of law."

12. Scholem, *Major Trends*, 342.

13. *Ibid.* In this Scholem follows the classical Weberian model of prophetic charisma, according to which the prophet first attains spiritual stature in solitude and only secondarily sets out to inspire a religious movement. For a more thorough discussion and critique of Scholem's attempt to develop a sociology of Jewish mysticism, largely following the work of Ernst Troeltsch on Christianity, see Philip Wexler, *Mystical Sociology*, 87-108.

14. Leah Orent, "Religious Experience and the National Community." For the discussion of "the song of songs" see Schneur Zalman of Liadi, *Likutei torah, Shir hashirim*, 2b. Cf. the relevant treatment of the same text, Eli Rubin, "Creating Space for the Song of Songs: How to Overcome Self-Doubt and Discover a Different Way to Pray," *Chabad.org* <chabad.org/2961615>. The locus classicus of Schneur Zalman's understanding of embodiment as the cause of individuation and mystical experience as the key to interpersonal love is his *Likutei amarim — tanya*, Chapter 32, and Eli Rubin, "Habad Hasidism and the Mystical Reconstruction of Society," in *Jewish Spirituality and Social Transformation*, edited by Philip Wexler (New York: Herder and Herder, 2018), 63-68. See also *idem., Mystical Sociology*, 138-140.

15. *Torah or*, 1b.

16. Nehemia Polen, "Charismatic Leader, Charismatic Book: Rabbi Schneur Zalman's Tanya and His Leadership," in Suzanne Last Stone, ed., *Rabbinic and Lay Communal Authority* (New York: Yeshiva University Press, 2006), 53-64. For a more sophisticated reading of the relationship between the theorization of the tsadik in *Tanya* and the socio-historical realities of Hasidism during the period in which it was written, see Ada Rapoport-Albert, *The Problem of Succession in the Hasidic Leadership with Special Reference to the Circle of R. Nachman of Braslav* (PhD thesis, University of London, 1974), 15-16. In her estimation Schneur Zalman considered the socio-historical figures called "tsadikim" in his time (including himself) to belong to the intermediate category of beinonim, which itself is subdivided into many gradations, rather than to the highly idealized category of the tsadik as described in *Tanya*. At the same time, she is quite clear that in Chabad, like in other

Hasidic groups, the tsadik, was nevertheless seen as an utterly unique personality, and that this phenomenon remained no less central to the social reality of the Chabad movement. For more general discussions of the role of the tsadik in Hasidism, see S. Ettinger, "The Hasidic Movement: Reality and Ideals," *Journal of World History* II, nos. 1– 2 (1968): 251-266; Samuel H. Dresner, *The Tzaddik* (New York: Schocken Books, 1974); Arthur Green, "Typologies of Leadership and the Hasidic Zaddiq," in *idem.*, *The Heart of the Matter* (Philadelphia: The Jewish Publishing Society, 2015), 167-203.

17. See Naftali Loewenthal, *Communicating the Infinite: The Emergence of the Habad School* (Chicago: University of Chicago Press, 1990), esp. 3-4.

18. This point was articulated by Schneerson himself. See Menachem Mendel Schneerson, *Torat menachem hitvaduyot 5743*, Vol. 1 (Brooklyn, NY: Kehot Publication Society, 1990), 543: "Among Hasidim the image and picture of the Rebbe is always imprinted before their eyes...Since [it is as if] the rebbe himself stands before him, how can he call anyone by any title...therefore they would call [the famed Hasid and scholar, Rabbi Dovid Tzvi Chein of Chernigov,] by the [diminutive] name Dovid Hirshel [sans any honorific]." Also see the relevant discussions in Loewenthal, *Communicating the Infinite*, 64, and Wexler, *Mystical Sociology*, 68. More on the significance of the Hasidic gathering (the "*farbrengen*"), with the rebbe or tsadik as its focal point, will be said below.

19. Menachem Mendel Schneerson, "Mamar ve'atah tetsaveh 5741—kuntras purim katan 5752," in *Sefer hamamarim melukatim*, Vol. 3 (Brooklyn, NY: Kehot Publication Society, 2012), 39-40. See relevant citations there.

20. *Ibid.*, 34.

21. *Ibid.*, 43.

22. The only precedent for the survival and success of a Hasidic group without the appointment of a new tsadik is the case of Braslav. See Ada Rapoport-Albert, *The Problem of Succession in the Hasidic Leadership*, for an extensive treatment of this example. In her estimation, "while the theoretical basis for the continuation of a distinct Braslav group after his death can be found in the teachings of R. Nachman, the actual survival of the circle was primarily due to the organisational genius of R. Nathan Sternharz." (Ibid. 243.) Following the theorization developed here, we might suggest that in the case of Braslav the absent leader has been rendered present through the utter dedication of his student and scribe, Nathan, to the faithful preservation and dissemination of his master's visionary teachings. This a form of mutual effacement of self, a mutual presence via absence, which allows for the eternal preservation of the rebbe / hasid relationship in idealized form. Cf. *ibid.*, 302: "R. Nathan did not preach his own teachings, but rather he repeated a long and complicated Torah of his dead master...Had he entertained any ambition to become a full successor to R. Nachman and a Zaddik in his own right he would have immediately asserted his independence by preaching his own 'Torah'. But R. Nathan saw it as his duty merely to spread R. Nachman's teachings in the world."

23. See *Sichot kodesh 5711* (New York: Vaad Hanachot Hatemimim, 1985), p. 123.

24. See Elliot R. Wolfson, *Open Secret*, pp. 224-264.

25. For the text of this letter see, "No Human Being Can Claim Superior Ancestral Origin," *Chabad.org*, <chabad.org/1075121>. For the Talmudic source see *Talmud bavli*, Sanhedrin, 37a.

26. For this phrase and for some elements of the discussion that follows see Eli Rubin, "Habad Hasidism and the Mystical Reconstruction of Society," in *Jewish Spirituality and Social Transformation*, edited by Philip Wexler (New York: Herder and Herder, 2019), 68-72. Also see Wexler, *Mystical Sociology*, pp. 67-69.

27. See Maimonides, *Mishneh torah*, Hilchot aval, 14:1; Hilchot de'ot, 6:34; Hilchot rotse'ach, 13:14.

28. Schneur Zalman of Liadi, *Likutei amarim tanya*, Chapter 32.

29. Menachem Mendel Schneerson, *Torat menachem hitvaduyot 5751*, Vol. 3 (Brooklyn, NY: Kehot Publication Society, 1993) 342.

30. Menachem M. Schneerson, *Torat menachem hitvaduyot 5746*, Vol. 4 (Brooklyn, NY: Kehot Publication Society, 1990), p. 254. See also *idem.*, *Likutei sichot*, Vol. 38 (Brooklyn, NY: Kehot Publication Society, 1999), p. 28.

31. Cf. *Sefer hachinukh*, Commandment #243: "The root of this commandment is known, for as one does to his fellow so his fellow will do to him, and thereby there shall be peace among creatures."

32. Schneerson often affirmed that all human beings, not only Jews, possess a divine spark, a point that is already explicated by Schneur Zalman of Liadi. See Menachem Mendel Schneerson, *Torat menachem hitvaduyot 5720* (Brooklyn, NY: Kehot Publication Society, 2004), p. 401; *idem.*, *Torat menachem hitvaduyot 5744*, Vol. 4 (Brooklyn, NY: Kehot Publication Society, 1990), 2308; *idem.*, *Likutei sichot*, Vol. 21 (Brooklyn, NY: Kehot Publication Society, 1983), p. 107; Schneur Zalman of Liadi, *Tanya—igeret hakodesh*, Epistle 25, 138a-142a.

33. On the "the vertical dimension" and its introduction to social theory see Anthony J. Steinbock, *Phenomenology and Mysticism: The Verticality of Religious Experience* (Bloomington: Indiana University Press, 2009); Philip Wexler, *Mystical Sociology*, 54, and 128-129.

34. Menachem Mendel Schneerson, *Torat menachem hitvaduyot*, Vol. 21 [5718, I] (Brooklyn, NY: Kehot Publication Society), 99-100. The translation here follows the Yiddish transcript of this talk as published in *idem.*, *Sichot Kodesh 5718-5719* (Brooklyn, NY: Vaad Hanachot Hatemimim, 1985), 36-38.

35. *Ibid.*

36. See Shalom DovBer Schneersohn, *Yom tov shel rosh hashanah 5666* (Brooklyn, NY: Kehot Publication Society, 1991). For some aspects of Menachem Mendel Schneerson's development of this conception see Eli Rubin, "Intimacy in the Place of Otherness: How Rationalism and Mysticism Collaboratively Communicate the Midrashic Core of Cosmic Purpose," *Chabad.org*, <chabad.org/2893106>. See also Naftali Loewenthal, "'The Thickening of the Light': The Kabbalistic-Hasidic Teachings of Rabbi Shalom Dovber Schneersohn in Their Social Context," in Jonatan Meir and Gadi Sagiv (eds.), *Habad Hasidism: History, Thought, Image* (Jerusalem: Zalman Shazar Center, 2016), 7*-43*.

37. For Schneerson's own elaboration of this point, and of a specific teaching of Rashab, in the continuation of his discussion of fellowship see Menachem Mendel Schneerson, *Torat menachem hitvaduyot*, Vol. 21 [5718, I], 103-106; *Sichot Kodesh 5718-5719*, 41-43.

38. Menachem Mendel Schneerson, *Torat menachem hitvaduyot*, Vol. 21 [5718, I], 98; *Sichot Kodesh 5718-5719*, 37.

39. Menachem Mendel Schneerson, *Torat menachem hitvaduyot*, Vol. 21 [5718, I], 100; *Sichot Kodesh 5718-5719*, 37-8.

40. See Michael Stanislawski, "Gordon, Yehudah Leib," in *YIVO Encyclopedia of Jews in Eastern Europe* (9 August 2010), accessed 19 October 2018, <http://www.yivoencyclopedia.org/article.aspx/Gordon_Yehudah_Leib>.

41. See the relevant entries in Solon Beinfeld and Harry Bochner (eds.), *Comprehensive Yiddish-English Dictionary* (Bloomington: Indiana University Press, 2013), 518.

42. For some preliminary remarks on this score see Wexler, *Mystical Sociology*, 68.

43. Damián Setton, "The Consumption of Alcohol in the Lubavitch Movement in Buenos Aires: Diversity of Meanings." *Revista de Antropología Iberoamericana* 8, no. 3 (Sept.-Dec., 2013): 354-355.

44. Naftali Loewenthal, "Hasidism and Modernity: The Case of Habad," *Proceedings of the World Congress of Jewish Studies* 11C(2) (1993), 111-113. For a descriptive overview of the various forms of the Farbrengen, focusing on the end of the 19th century and the beginning of the 20th century, see Naftali Brawer, *Resistance and Response to Change: The Leadership of Rabbi Shalom DovBer Schneersohn (1860-1920)* (PhD Thesis, University College London, 2004), 230-238.

45. Loewenthal, "Hasidism and Modernity," 111-113. Cf. Jürgen Habermas, trans. Thomais McCarthy, *Communication and the Evolution of Society* (London: Heinemann Educational Books, 1979), 1-5, 154-158, 208-210, n. 2.

46. In his discussion of empathy Loewenthal cites and quotes Daniel Lerner, *The Passing of Traditional Society* (New York: Free Press of Glencoe, 1964), 49-50. On Chabad's own theorization of empathy see Eli Rubin, "'The Pen Shall Be Your Friend': Intertextuality, Intersociality, and the Cosmos—Examples of the Tzemach Tzedek's Way in the Development of Chabad Chassidic Thought," *Chabad.org*, <chabad.org/3286179>.

47. Shalom DovBer Schneersohn, *Kuntras hicholtsu* (New York: Kehot Publication Society, 1948), section 10. See the relevant discussion in Eli Rubin, "Purging Divisiveness, Embracing Difference: Rabbi Shalom DovBer Schneersohn's Manifesto against Self-Righteousness in Interpersonal Discourse," *Chabad.org*, <chabad.org/3800391>.

48. Schneersohn, *Kuntras hicholtsu*. The confessionalism of the farbrengen, which takes place between peers, should not be confused with the phenomenon of confession before the tsadik that has been described in the scholarly literature, especially in the case of Bratslav. See David Biale et al., *Hasidism: A New History* (Princeton, NJ: Princeton University Press, 2018), 191.

49. Loewenthal, "Hasidism and Modernity," 112.

50. *Ibid.*, 112-113.

51. See the relevant discussion and citations in Brawer, *Resistance*, 233.

52. *Ibid.*, 224.

53. See the testimony of Leibel Posner, "In All Your Ways, Know Him," *Chabad. org*, <chabad.org/1393813>; *idem.*, "The King and the Pawn," *Chabad.org*, <chabad. org/462840>.

54. "The Farbrengen Series: Chassidic Gatherings with the Rebbe," *Chabad.org*, <chabad.org/2143216>.

55. About half of the farbrengen were released, with subtitles, in DVD format as *Farbrengen: Yud Aleph Nissan, 5741—1981* (New York: Jewish Educational Media, 2012). A selection that runs for one hour and seventeen minutes can be viewed on the Internet, "Pre-Passover Farbrengen: A 1981 Satellite Feed of a Gathering with the Rebbe," *Chabad.org*, <chabad.org/1809252>. The complete audio record- ing of the farbrengen is available from *Chabad.org*'s "Public Address Archive," at <https://www.chabad.org/therebbe/sichoskodesh_cdo/year/5741/month/1/day/ 11/cat//x/42/y/15>.

56. For an ethnographic descriptions of farbrengens led by Schneerson, see Ellen Koskoff, *Music in Lubavitcher Life* (Urbana and Chicago: University of Illinois Press, 2001), 3-14.

57. See Wolfson, Open Secret, 29. On trance in Hasidism see Jonathan Garb, *Shaman- ic Trance in Modern Kabbalah* (Chicago: University of Chicago Press, 2011), 99-118. With particular reference to Schneerson's farbrengen see Susan Handelman, "A Man Apart," *Cross Currents* 45, no. 2 (Summer 1995): 239: "When he [Schneerson] spoke Torah, it was not just another lecture, a flow of words; there was something magnetic about the Rebbe's presence. Each talk was complex but beautifully structured and full of startling insights…" The magnetism described by Handel- man suggests that the cadence of his speech, together with his personal charisma, produced a semi-hypnotonic state in his audience.

58. Abraham J. Heschel, *The Prophets* (New York: Jewish Publication Society of America, 1962), 24.

59. For similar remarks regarding the content of Schneerson's talks see the relevant description of Schneerson's farbrengen in Handelman, "A Man Apart."

60. This translation was based on the video recording cited above. For a published transcript see Menachem Mendel Schneerson, *Sichot Kodesh 5741*, Vol. 3 (Brooklyn, NY: Vaad Hanachot Hatemimim, 1986), 101.

61. See Wodziński, "The Socio-Economic Profile," 689.

62. See Mordechai Lightstone, "How 1970s Chassidic Hackers Created a Worldwide Broadcast Network: The Backroom of a Brooklyn Landmark Building Served as the Global Hub for Jewish Connectivity," *Chabad.org*, <chabad.org/3422879>.

63. The first Chanukah Live intercontinental broadcast took place in 1989. For foot- age from these events see ""Chanukah Live" Celebrations: Live Broadcasts of Chanukah Celebrations and Menorah Lightings Across the Globe," *Chabad.org*, <chabad.org/3153123>. Also see Maya Balakirsky Katz, *The Visual Culture of Chabad* (New York: Cambridge University Press, 2010), 221-223.

64. See Jeffrey Shandler, *Jews, God, and Videotape: Religion and Media in America* (New York: New York University Press, 2009), 250-252.

65. Menachem Mendel Schneerson, *Torat menachem hitvaduyot 5747*, Vol. 1 (Brooklyn, NY: Kehot Publication Society, 1990), 126. Round brackets and emphasis appear in original text.

66. For a video recording of this talk see "Lights, Camera, Action!: 1st Night of Chanukah, 5752 · December 1, 1991," *Chabad.org*, <chabad.org/604927>.

67. The audio recording of this talk is available at the following URL: <chabad.org/555115>.

68. Koskoff, *Music*, 6-8.

69. *Ibid.*, 13.

70. *Ibid.*, 13, 120-140, 152.

71. Audio recordings of these talks can be found via the following URL: <https://www.chabad.org/search/results.asp?searchword=n%27shei&t=120>.

72. See *Kovetz hayechidut* (Brooklyn, NY: Vaad Talmidei Hatemimim, 2010), 30-31. Audio recordings are available at the following URL: https://www.chabad.org/therebbe/sichoskodesh_cdo/year//month//day//cat/Yechidus/x/47/y/18.

73. *Ibid.*, 38. Emphasis in the original.

74. This photo was published on *Slate.com*, <https://compote.slate.com/images/b2ca32ff-c7d5-471c-b8f3-72aceo0703ec.jpg>, accessed Oct. 24, 2018. See Jordan G. Teicher, "A Glimpse Inside Crown Heights' Hasidic Community in the '90s," *Slate.com*, Nov. 18, 2014.

75. For a video of this moment see "Distributing Chanukah Money: December 20, 1990 · 8th Night of Chanukah, 5751," *Chabad.org*. For the photo taken by Nishio as the Rebbe reached up toward her, see Samuel G. Freedman, "Brooklyn's Lubavitch Community: A Culture Captured by the Ultimate Outsider," *The New York Times*, Nov 28, 2014 <https://www.nytimes.com/2014/11/29/nyregion/brooklyns-lubavitch-community-a-culture-captured-by-the-ultimate-outsider.html#>. *The New York Times* incorrectly dates the photo to 1988.

CHAPTER 4

⟨≈≋≋≋⟩

THE PRINCIPLE OF RECIPROCITY
BETWEEN SELF, COMMUNITY,
AND COSMOS

4.1—The Reciprocal Dynamic of Giving and Receiving

A KEEN SOCIAL analyst and a master of social practice, Menachem
Mendel Schneerson was also an original social theorist. That is, he
articulated a fully formed theory of the ideal principle by which society should function, namely the principle of reciprocity. This is a
theory that defies reduction to either of the two poles of modern social discourse, and is not merely a compromise between them; it is at
once individualistic in orientation (as is capitalism) and collectivistic
in orientation (as is socialism). Its fundamental tenet is that individuals
can only achieve personal success and happiness through engaging in
a reciprocal dynamic of giving and receiving. It is through meaningful
reciprocity that constellations of relationships are built, which coalesce
into vibrant communities greater than the sum of their parts. What is
crucial here, for Schneerson, is that it is just as important to receive as
it is to give. Moreover, the dynamic between giving and receiving is
such that each comprises the other. Social interchange, in other words,
should ideally carry an inherent mutuality according to which all participants are empowered and endowed with dignity. The novelty of

Schneerson's concept is sharpened when we note his insistence that the fundamental motive of reciprocity lies in the happiness and joy experienced by an individual who successfully satisfies the needs of another. This goes beyond the conventional notions of reciprocity, whether they be altruistic or utilitarian, in that the benefit received is not simply a byproduct of the contribution made but is actually built into the very act of giving itself.[1]

Here is how Schneerson articulated his concept of reciprocity in a talk delivered in the summer of 1971:

> As soon as one becomes aware of the existence of another Jew, the first thing is to realize that this is not merely circumstantial. Rather, this is by divine providence, and it is certain that these two elements are at play: 1) that he can thereby gain something from the existence of the other Jew who he has become aware of, and 2) that there is probably some way in which he can also help the other Jew. This is because the entire order of creation is set up such that there shall be no recipient who is merely a recipient, and no giver who is merely a giver...no wealthy person who is merely wealthy, and no poor person who is merely poor. As the sages tell us, just as the wealthy person bestows something upon the poor person, so the poor person bestows upon the wealthy person. On the contrary, "more than the householder provides to the pauper is provided by the pauper to the householder." (*Vayikrah rabbah*, 34:8.) And just as this is so with charity in its normative sense, so is it also in the case of spiritual charity...One person's role is to help another spiritually, another's role is to help people physically, as *The Code of Jewish Law* tells us, "Everyone is obligated by the commandment to give charity, even a pauper." (*Yoreh de'ah*, 248:1.)[2]

We have already encountered the underlying principle of reciprocity in Schneerson's own practice as a Hasidic leader, as discussed in the preceding chapter. Here, however, we must take particular note of his emphasis that every person has both a need and an ability to give, and likewise both a need and an ability to receive. This takes us beyond the particular case of Hasidism and its practices, into the wider application of Schneerson's conception of reciprocity to the dynamics of social life, particularly in the areas of economics, interpersonal encounters, and the relationships between self, community, and cosmos.

The ability to give is an asset, but according to Schneerson it is also a vulnerability, a neediness. The capacity to give is native to the human soul, and it aches to be exercised. This philanthropic neediness complicates the normative conception of the relationship between the giver and the recipient; the needy recipient should actually be understood to be in a position of power and dignity, bestowing upon their would-be benefactors an opportunity to exercise their capacity to give. The need and ability to give also imposes an obligation; the wealthy individual is indebted to the pauper who provides the opportunity for self-transcendence, for human interaction, recognition, and reciprocity.[3]

Of course, this recalls Marcin Wodziński's analysis of the Hasidic conception of wealth, as described in Chapter 1, namely that it is regarded "as belonging to the people of Israel as a whole rather than to individuals, and as a gift from God conditional upon the practice of charity."[4] But Schneerson's concept of reciprocity goes far beyond this, because it reverses the normative concept of who plays the role of giver and of receiver in a charitable exchange. Furthermore, the concept of reciprocity does not merely concern monetary or economic interchange, but also spiritual, intellectual, and emotional interchange as well. This is a point to which we will return below. For the moment it is important to first clarify the full implications of Schneerson's theorization of the reciprocal dynamic of giving and receiving.

We have already noted that in Schneerson's view everyone needs the opportunity to give to others, to act charitably. Likewise, every person also needs the opportunity to receive. To be a recipient of spiritual or material charity is to be needy in one respect or another. But rather than seeing such neediness as a deficiency, as something to be ashamed of, Schneerson reframes it as a form of giving, of taking care of the needs of the other, of completing the other. It is an opportunity for both participants in the exchange to become whole, to be reciprocally completed, indeed to become more complete than the narrow constraints allowed by the circumscriptions of individuality. To deny your neediness as an individual is to deny a facet of your humanity that should rightly be regarded as an asset rather than as a flaw. As humans we have the capacity to be receptive, to open ourselves to the gifts of others, to become bigger than ourselves. And this capacity is itself a gift, not a failing.[5]

Per the passage cited above, no one has the right to reduce their perception of someone else, or of their own self, to the unequivocal category of "rich person," or of "poor person." Everyone is rich in some way that is enormously valuable, and likewise everyone has the dignity of being deficient, and therefore receptive, in some way that is equally integral to who they are as a human being. Notions of wealth and of neediness need to be critically deconstructed and reconstructed in more sophisticated terms; thereby a new framework can emerge in which imbalances can be rebalanced, and in which relationships of joyous and graceful reciprocation can be cultivated and cherished.

Schneerson's theory of social reciprocity leads to a conclusion that is as contrary to the socialist paradigm as it is to the capitalist one. The unyielding accumulation of personal wealth is certainly seen as a miserable preoccupation for the rich as well as for the poor. But the completely equal distribution of wealth is similarly regarded as a starkly dystopian option. This conclusion is made explicit in a letter addressed by Schneerson to a certain Dr. D. Elkanah, dating from 1956:

> I received your letter of May 15th with pleasure, and enjoyed reading about your interest in the teachings of Hasidism, [and] certain details of your thoughts about it, especially regarding joy... With regard to the conclusion of your letter—in which you write that the redemption cannot be complete until "the needy disappear from the earth" (Cf. Deuteronomy, 15:11) and all people work collectively, with mutual responsibility [and] without poor and wealthy—I do not concur with your opinion, because the nature of a person is that a feeling of true happiness comes to a person when he is able to do something for the good of another, and this is only possible when one is rich and the second is poor. However, this does not contradict your valid complaint regarding the injustice of the massive divide. And as it is explained in the teachings of Hasidism, every creation, if only it acts in concert with its telos, is not merely a recipient but also a giver. Meaning that if one is poor in a given respect, one

is rich in another respect…Even regarding the Creator and
manager of the world our Torah tells us that it is as if He is
sometimes a recipient and not only a provider…as the sages
said, "toil for the needs of the Supernal One."[6]

Schneerson unequivocally recognizes the injustice of the massive
gap between rich and poor. At the same time, he argues that to utterly
eradicate any and all imbalances would be to eradicate the possibility
of true happiness. Accordingly, he rejects the notion that in the utopian
era of "complete redemption" the fundamental notions of rich and poor
will be entirely replaced with a collective system of mutual ownership and complete equality. Instead he envisions a reciprocal society in
which each individual is empowered to achieve true happiness through
making a meaningful contribution to the welfare of others. Reciprocally, happiness can be provided to others through being a gracious and
appreciative recipient of their gifts in turn. This ideal is not a static
state of personal completeness (as in the capitalist model), nor a static state of collective sameness (as in the socialist model). It is rather a
dynamic state of constant imbalance and rebalance, of interpersonal
interaction and expansion, of give-and-take, with each individual attaining a sense of personal fulfillment via the unique contribution they
are empowered to make to the lives of the people around them. Life
does not come to a standstill in the messianic age. Instead it is elevated
beyond the vices of egotism and injustice so that individuals can flourish in meaningful reciprocity and joyous communion.

4.2—Encountering the Other, Encountering the Divine

IN A TALK delivered in 1980 Schneerson articulated a more spiritual
dimension of this reciprocal model, one that goes beyond economic
considerations in the simple sense and extends into the realm of education and the exchange of knowledge. Just as he sought to complicate
the normative juxtaposition of the wealthy person with the pauper, so
he sought to complicate the normative juxtaposition of those who are
deemed to be authoritative teachers ("wealthy in knowledge") and those
who are deemed to be in need of being taught ("poor in knowledge").[7]
Thereby he provided a transformative paradigm through which every

interpersonal encounter can be endowed with edifying meaning and ultimate significance.

As is so often the case, Schneerson's discourse on this topic is refracted through the prism of traditional Torah sources, centering here on a Talmudic tale about an encounter between the sage Rabbi Elazar and "an ugly person." Elazar was the son of Rabbi Shimon bar Yochai, the hero of the collection of classical Jewish mystical texts known as the Zohar, and consequently a revered figure in Hasidism as well. Elazar is the quintessential exemplar of learned and mystical authority, of elitism. Having been raised in the image of his father, having studied with him in a secluded cave for twelve years in order to avoid the malevolent reach of the Romans, he was considered one of the select "masters of ascent," a spiritual giant. And it is from this elitist perch that he looks upon "the ugly man" whom he encounters, initially responding to his greeting in the third person, and going on to insult him:

> Rabbi Elazar, son of Rabbi Shimon, came from Migdal Gedor, from his rabbi's house, and he was riding on a donkey and strolling on the bank of the river. And he was very happy, and his head was swollen with pride because he had studied much Torah. He happened upon an exceedingly ugly person, who said to him: "Greetings to you, rabbi." But Rabbi Elazar did not reciprocate. Instead he said to him: "Worthless person, how ugly is that man. Are all the people of your city as ugly as you?" The man said to him: "I do not know. Go and say to the Craftsman Who made me: How ugly is the vessel you made." When Rabbi Elazar realized that he had sinned, he descended from his donkey and prostrated himself before him, and he said to him: "I have sinned against you; forgive me." (*Talmud bavli*, Taanit, 20a-b.)

In its original context the point of this story does not lie in the insight conveyed by the so-called ugly man, but rather in the teaching conveyed by Rabbi Elazar in the aftermath of the encounter: "A person should always be soft like a reed and he should not be stiff like a cedar." But Schneerson argues that a far more radical lesson can be drawn from the words of Rabbi Elazar's interlocutor, especially when they are read against the authoritative statement in the Mishnah:

> Ben Zoma said: Who is wise? One who learns from every person, for it is written, "From all my teachers I became wise, because your testimony speaks to me." (Avot 4:1, Psalms 119:99.)

Schneerson takes it for granted that Rabbi Elazar was surely familiar with Ben Zoma's teaching. Yet his spiritual achievements made him blind to the divine testimony embodied by the person whom he encountered upon the riverbank. Rather than seeing the divine he only saw ugliness and otherliness. Paradoxically, Schneerson emphatically argues, this failure did not occur despite Rabbi Elazar's stature, but rather precisely because he was a "master of ascent," "meaning that he not only witnessed mystical ascent but that he himself experienced it." It was precisely as a result of his profound mystical experiences, as a result of his familiarity with transcendent divinity, that he was incapable of recognizing the testimony to God that is immanent within the world and within every single one of its inhabitants:

> The whole concept of testimony only applies to something that is concealed. In the case of something that will be revealed, and certainly of something that is already revealed, the concept of testimony does not apply. And in the case of Rabbi Elazar divinity was all the more like "something revealed"…So it is not possible to say that Rabbi Elazar required testimony to God. Therefore all he saw is that this is an "ugly person" and he said "Worthless person, how ugly is that man etc."[8]

The very appellation "rabbi" means "teacher," yet Rabbi Elazar is himself in need of being taught that to be a teacher is to engage reciprocally. As the sage Rabbi Hanina puts it elsewhere in the Talmud, "I learned much from my teachers, from my friends more than from my teachers, and from my students more than from all of them." (*Talmud bavli*, Taanit, 7a.) When Rabbi Elazar meets a stranger and fails to reciprocate when greeted he betrays the very title "rabbi" in which he takes such pride. Luckily he has the presence of mind to recognize his error, and to take the resounding rebuke of his interlocutor to heart: "Go and say to the Craftsman Who made me: How ugly is the vessel you made." In Schneerson's paraphrase:

"Why do you not see the 'Craftsman' who is here, in me? Why
do you not see how I am a testimony to God, in which case
you would have found something to learn from me?"[9]

What Elazar needed to learn was that there is no value in merely
ascending beyond normative human perception and thereby perceiv-
ing divinity. The purpose of ascent is only realized when the mystical
experience can be reproduced on earth in the perception of transcendent divinity as it is immanently embodied in ordinary life, including
in the face of any and every individual whom you encounter. Schneerson underscores this point by invoking the midrashic imperative whose
emphasis in Chabad literature he brought to a climax, namely that the
purpose of creation is for humankind to make a "dwelling" for God in
"the lower realms."

We must not reject the world, but must make there a dwelling
place for God…We must therefore see in each thing in the
world how it is a testimony to God, "Your testimony speaks
to me." The "Craftsman" who is in each thing in the world [is
seen], and accordingly the person learns something from everything that he sees, [becoming] "one who learns from every
person," and even from inanimate things…[10]

Even the most learned Torah scholar, even the mystic who has attained the highest form of spiritual ascent, must approach the world
receptively. Yes, the scholar and the mystic certainly have a contribution to make to the world, indeed it is the mission of the Torah
and its adherents to repair and refine the world. But it can never be
forgotten that to give is also to receive, to teach is also to learn, to repair is also to be repaired. The scholar or mystic is a channel through
which divinity can flow down into the world from above. But divinity
also wells up from below, from the deepest recesses of the terrestrial realm; for it is precisely therein that the innermost essence of
divine being is most concretely implanted. To eschew the qualities
of receptivity and reciprocity is to reduce divinity to the top-down
perspective. True wisdom, by contrast, depends upon an openness
of mind, an openness to encounter divinity in every encounter. In
Schneerson's own words:

In order that one can learn "from every person," from every person without exception, there must be [receptivity to]
"Your testimony speaks to me." If a person only learns one
topic fully and then goes out into the world and sees something ugly, it may not necessarily be the case that this "ugly"
thing speaks to the same topic that he studied. It may be that
this "ugly" thing is relevant to an entirely different topic, and
accordingly he does not see in it anything of "Your testimony." Accordingly, he learns nothing from this thing. Whereas
if he has [receptivity to] "Your testimony speaks to me," then
it becomes His speech [i.e., the word of God]...When this is
the case, then in whatever he encounters and in whatever he
sees he will see how this is "Your testimony," and accordingly he will learn something from the encounter. Then he is a
"wise person" who "learns from every person," and from everything in the world.[11]

In Chapter 1 we noted Schneur Zalman of Liadi's intimation that the
physical world itself—like the visions of the prophets recorded in the
Bible—is nothing less than the revelation of the word of God.[12] Here
this paradigm is certainly articulated with greater breadth and expli-
cation, if perhaps not with the same boldness. More importantly, it is
applied not only to the world in general, but to every particular thing
encountered in the world, and more specifically to every interpersonal
encounter. Underscoring the inclusivity of this application, Schneerson
emphasizes that if "the Torah of truth" labels the person encountered
by Rabbi Elazar with the appellation "ugly," then he must truly have
been ugly, "meaning that he was bereft of any good attributes"; yet even
such a person must be seen as a living testimony to the Craftsman, to
God who freely chooses to create and sustain this person.[13]

Schneerson does not only follow Schneur Zalman of Liadi conceptu-
ally, but also echoes him methodologically; he provides a contemplative
strategy that can be applied as a positive lens through which we can approach an interpersonal encounter even with an ostensibly "ugly" person.
Citing earlier works of Jewish philosophy and ethics, Schneerson notes
that every human being is composed of the "four elements," classically
identified as fire, water, air, and earth. Fire and water are opposites, as
are air and earth, and yet they are miraculously combined in the human

body. (In modern scientific terms a similar argument could be made about the sheer complexity of the body and its functions, which somehow succeed in the simultaneous execution of infinite tasks of vastly different scope and purpose.)[14] Secondly, he invokes the miraculous union of mind and matter, referencing *The Code of Jewish Law* which echoes the Cartesian position that these are two fundamentally different substances whose union can only be achieved by dint of divine omnipotence.[15] To contemplate these two facts, says Schneerson, is to recognize that to encounter any human being is to encounter a living testimony to God and the magnitude of His works. This simple recognition alone should transform the way in which we encounter other people, undermining whatever presumptive judgmentalism we might harbor and opening us to receive whatever insight we might be able to glean from them. Every interpersonal encounter should be a reciprocal encounter. Every encounter with the other should be an encounter with the divine.[16]

4.3—An Encounter between Individuals Exceeds the Sum of Its Parts

THE PRINCIPLE THAT every encounter with the other should be an encounter with the divine leads directly to a second principle, namely that every social interaction exceeds the sum of its parts. Schneerson applied this principle in two practical areas with special frequency: firstly, in the realm of Torah education and spiritual investment in the community; and secondly, in the realm of marriage, the relationship between husband and wife.

Writing to a rabbi from Israel who was concerned that his activities as an educator were detracting from his ability to excel in his own Torah studies, Schneerson invoked and elaborated another Talmudic teaching:

> When someone who is wealthy in Torah helps someone who is poor in Torah...the eyes of both are illuminated (*Talmud bavli*, Temurah, 16a)...This implies far more than the dictum of the sage, "I learned much from my teachers, from my friends more than from my teachers, and from my students more than from all of them." (*Ibid.*, Taanit, 7a.) The latter dictum refers to what the individual learns in accord

with their own ability, as implied by the language "I learned."
By contrast the guarantee of the sages in the former dictum,
that "the eyes of both are illuminated by God"…refers to
illumination in accord with the ability of God, which is obviously immeasurably greater. My intention here is [to make
clear]…that [in this case] the abrogation of Torah study itself perpetuates Torah study, for thereby one's heart and
mind are made a thousand times more refined, such that in a
short span of time you will be immeasurably more successful in your studies.[17]

In keeping with the socio-mystical model described in Chapter 3 it
is specifically through connecting with another individual that one encounters the divine. The addressee assumes, quite intuitively, that any
investment of time and effort in the education of others will reduce his
personal Torah achievements. But Schneerson forcefully argues that
the contrary is true; by virtue of one's investment in the other, one
transcends one's own personal capacities, attaining the greater gift of
success that is within the provision of the divine.

Concerning marriage Schneerson would often cite another Talmudic statement, "man and woman, if they are meritorious the divine
dwells between them." (*Talmud bavli*, Sotah, 17a.) Following the interpretation of the famous medieval commentator Rashi, Schneerson
pointed out that the Hebrew words for man (*ish*) and woman (*ishah*) are
both composed of the word for fire (*esh*), plus one additional letter; in
the case of man the letter *yod*, in the case of woman the letter *hei*. These
two letters together form one of the biblical names of God. In other
words, it is specifically in the holy partnership of man and woman that
the name of God is made whole.[18] Their fiery union is a vessel for the
indwelling of God on earth, and it is therefore a union that is greater
than the sum of its parts. It is not simply a transactional partnership
between two individuals, but is rather a union that is endowed with
mystical and cosmic qualities, and graced by the infinite and eternal
power of God.[19]

Marriage might intuitively be thought of as requiring sacrifices on
the part of both parties, and is often parodied in popular culture for
the squabbles it can introduce. But Schneerson consistently advised
those who sought his counsel to look at marriage as something that

introduces transcendent divinity into the most basic structure of life; marriage enhances the happiness of both parties precisely because it allows them to overcome the strictures of individuality and selfishness. His advice to those who felt themselves to have been wronged by their marriage partners also emphasized the inherent reciprocity that marriage entails, which can manifest itself negatively as well as positively. In one letter to an aggrieved husband he wrote:

> When one thinks of one's wife, one must always recall that the entire collective of the Jewish people (*kneset yisra'el*)…is referred to as the wife of the King of Kings, the Holy One blessed be He. When one beseeches God that He shall conduct himself with his…beloved in a manner that fulfills the desires of their hearts for good, it is well known that the arousal from above [i.e., from God] depends on the arousal from below, therefore one must conduct himself in the same way in relation to one's own wife, as the Talmud says: "Honor her more than your own self." (*Talmud bavli*, Yevamot, 62b.) This is especially the case as we stand at the end of the era of exile and the complete redemption is close…at which time "the female shall transcend the male." (Cf. Jeremiah, 31:21.) This itself brings about a sense of honor and care relative to one's wife…Even if she has a flaw it is often the case that it actually stems from a flaw in the husband's conduct, which turns her into "the wife of a bandit" (*Talmud yerushalmi*, Ketubot, 2:9), but she can also become "the wife of a scholar who is like a scholar" (*Talmud bavli*, Shevu'ot, 30b).[20]

Here the principle of reciprocity is at play in two distinct ways. First, the husband's relationship with God reciprocally mirrors his relationship with his wife; he can only hope for God to treat him with empathy to the degree that he empathetically honors the needs and desires of his wife. This underscores that the scope of their relationship is not confined only to the interactions between the two of them as individuals, but also includes their shared relationship with God. Second, the husband must recognize that any flaws he perceives in his wife may in fact attest to his own flaws; by transforming himself from a metaphorical "bandit" into a metaphorical "scholar" his wife's flaws too will be reciprocally erased.

An additional manifestation of the principle that every interaction should be seen as greater than the sum of its parts can be gleaned from the example set by Schneerson himself. In the later years of his leadership, from the spring of 1986 onward, Schneerson made it his custom to distribute dollars and blessings on a weekly basis to anyone who wished to see him. (By then he was no longer accepting people for private audiences.) Each Sunday morning he would stand near the door of his study for several hours, and thousands would stand in line awaiting the few precious seconds when they would receive the Rebbe's undivided attention. Many of these encounters were captured on video, and it is clear to any observer that there was nothing perfunctory about them. Schneerson is completely present, looking into the eyes of each individual, and transferring a dollar from his hand to the hand of every man, woman, and child who comes by. Even small babies received their dollar directly, personally, rather than through the intermediate hand of their accompanying adult. The dollar was meant to be given to a charity of the recipient's choice, though most would give a different dollar to charity and keep the one received from the Rebbe as a talismanic souvenir.[21]

The significance of the dollar was also intended to underscore the fundamental reciprocity of the encounter; the recipient of Schneerson's blessing came away with the ability and the responsibility to bestow blessing upon a third party. The recipient was transformed into a giver, and thereby the Rebbe himself received the gift of impacting a wider circle beyond the single individual with whom he interacted in that moment. On one occasion, in 1988, Schneerson took the opportunity to explain the principle to the philanthropist and activist Ronald Lauder:

> It is my idea that [in] the first encounter of two Jews they should do something for a third Jew. And the first thing that they can do for the third Jew is to give charity. And that is the idea of giving [a dollar]: It is not much money, but it is an indication of what is [worthy] for every one of us to do. When any one of us meets a Jew, start by looking to do something that will benefit a third Jew.[22]

As the Chabad writer Tzvi Freeman has put it, the Rebbe was not merely distributing blessings, but was rather *investing* in each individual he encountered: "The dollar was not yours. It was the Rebbe's dollar that he wished to give to charity. Which charity? The charity that you would choose... The Rebbe was investing in you, in your ability to make the right choice and do something good. You and the Rebbe were now bound together in a single act of goodness: The Rebbe's dollar, your choice."[23] The Rebbe did not want people merely to receive from him. He wanted to give people the opportunity to do something for others, and for him as well. Here we have the articulation and the realization of the fundamental notion that a reciprocal relationship transcends the sum of its parts; the encounter between two people must immediately expand to include a third individual who isn't actually present. Thereby it not only empowers its participants but also locates them in a wider constellation of intersecting relationships, coalescing into community.

4.4—Undoing the Dialectic between Self and Community

RELATED BUT DIFFERENT to the dialectic between self and other is the dialectic between self and community. An example of Schneerson's conception of individual flourishing within the context of reciprocal community can be found in a letter he addressed to the Israeli trade unionist and politician, Kadish Luz. The latter was born in an area of Russia that was part of Chabad's heartland, and he supported the development of Chabad's agricultural village, Kfar Chabad, near Lod in central Israel.[24] In 1964 he sent Schneerson a copy of his book, *Avny derekh*, a semi-autobiographical account of the rise of Israel's kibbutz (agricultural-collective) movement. Having read the book Schneerson took the opportunity to offer a respectful but substantive critique of the socialist paradigm adopted by kibbutz communities. This critique is especially noteworthy as it drives to the heart of the tension between the need for a person to flourish as a distinct individual, on the one hand, and the counter need of the community to put the wants of the collective, and of the majority, before those of any single person. This goes beyond the problem of the interpersonal encounter between one individual and another, as described above, and foregrounds the encounter between the individual and the community. Schneerson sets out the problem thus:

> In and of itself, the most apparent function of the commune
> is to equalize individuals of greater and lesser stature—

something that runs contrary to human nature. For with human beings, "just as their faces are different from one another, so too their minds and characters are different from one another." (Cf. *Tosefta*, Brakhot, 6:5.) A person thus finds satisfaction and fulfillment when he is given the opportunity to most fully actualize his potentials not so much in those areas which he shares in common with his fellows, but rather in those areas in which he individually excels relative to his contemporaries and his society, for this is his essence. At the same time, man is not by nature a recluse, and "it is not good for man to be alone." (Genesis, 2:18.) The human being seeks a social life as the context and means that will help him to attain personal completion.[25]

In the continuation of the letter Schneerson highlights the tension between the pros and cons of the suppression of competitiveness through the collectivist ethos of the socialist commune:

Another positive function of the commune is that it eliminates that jealousy and competitiveness that is so undesirable and often bring a deterioration of the relations between a person and his fellows, whereas collective activity usually draws the hearts closer together etc.

On the other hand, the purpose of the commune must not be to eliminate all competitiveness, since challenge and competition are among the chief stimulants toward greater effort and advancement on a person's part and an optimal utilization of one's abilities with alacrity etc. Rather, the commune should channel the competition to a higher plane. In other words, instead of the competition being for man's most basic, material needs—which is where the competition begins in an individualistic society—to the extent that, in the words of our sages, "Were it not for the fear of the government (i.e., the requirements of society) a man would swallow his fellow alive" (Avot, 3:2)—in a collective society the competition can be transferred to higher aims, whether to the procurement of supplements beyond one's basic needs or, on a higher level, to achievements in the life of the spirit.

What arises from all of the above is that the concept of the
collective and of collective life is not a goal and achievement
in its own right, but a step, facilitator and path to the development of the individuality and uniqueness of its members and
the realization of their individuality and uniqueness in the
best way and fullest measure.[26]

Remarkably, Schneerson does not seem to be opposed to the socialist ideals of the kibbutz movement. On the contrary, his critique is
framed entirely in constructive terms; he seems concerned to ensure
that the movement does not trip over its own feet, and to that end encourages an increased emphasis on the flourishing of the individual
as the ultimate telos of collective life. The socialist principles of the
kibbutz commune, he seems to argue, are not directly antithetical to
individual flourishing. On the contrary, if the provision of "basic needs"
is taken on by society as a collective responsibility, this will actually
empower people to excel as individuals in the higher orders of material and spiritual gain. Along these lines, socially responsible policies
are understood to suppress the undesirable and unjust corollaries of
competitiveness, and as a direct result allow competitiveness and individual excellence to come to the fore in more noble forms; that is,
in "the procurement of supplements beyond one's basic needs or, on
a higher level, to achievements in the life of the spirit." Collectivism
need not eliminate competition. On the contrary, collectivism can actually enhance the benefits of competition.

Herein, it might be suggested, lies the novelty of Schneerson's model: Capitalists and socialists alike tend to see the individual and the
collective as standing in inherent competition with one another. But
Schneerson argues that this is a fundamental mistake. On the contrary,
the individual and the collective are complementary to one another;
the collective can only be sustained when individuals thrive, individuals can best excel when the collective is well provided for. This
undoing of the common wisdom that individual flourishing and collectivism stand in competition to each other can be seen as an antecedent
to the argument set forth more recently by the philosopher Elizabeth
Anderson. She believes that the provision of communal equality does
not infringe upon the freedom of individuals, but rather secures it. As
she puts it: "the social condition of living a free life is that one stand in

relations of equality with others."[27] Replace the words "a free life" with the words "individual flourishing" and we arrive at the precise formula advocated by Schneerson.

In addition to the theoretical considerations outlined thus far, Schneerson goes on to highlight two additional considerations of utmost practicality for the success of the kibbutz movement. He argues that an emphasis on individuality will (1) better motivate individual members of the collective to put their own personal issues aside in order to advance their collaborative goals, thereby decreasing the likelihood of ill-will and a fall in morale; and (2) also help ensure that the second generation—the children of the pioneers, who grow up within a collective commune that is already well established—will not feel entirely stifled by the impositions of communal life. In other words, a focus on personal achievement and development can actually advance the initial attainment of the collective ideal and can go some way to answering the question of how the kibbutz movement might perpetuate its ideals beyond its pioneering stage.[28]

In the above letter to Luz, Schneerson's primary purpose is to uphold the principle of individual flourishing which he fears is in danger of being lost in the kibbutz collectives. In another letter, dating from 1961, we find Schneerson addressing a young man who is in danger of becoming so self-obsessed as to lose all sense of his responsibilities to society. Here he aims to uphold the principle of collectivism and reciprocity, and quite sharply seeks to shake the addressee from the narrow pitfalls of narcissism:

> Your whole letter—two and a half closely typewritten pages—is full of your own expectations and disappointments, as if everybody owes you everything, but no one has a claim on you.
>
> Yet even a brief reflection will clearly reveal that the universe we live in is ordered on a system of give and take, and the personal universe of the individual (the microcosm) must likewise conform to this system of reciprocal relationship. Consequently, when one disrupts or distorts this system, it must necessarily bring about a distortion in one's immediate surroundings, and especially in one's inner life.
>
> Now, judging by your own description... you have been gifted with more than the average measure of intelligence...

opportunities of education etc. In other words, you have been
on the receiving end, but—forgive me for being so blunt—it
did not occur to you, judging from your letter, that you might
owe something to the society; that you might have obligations
to participate in it actively and help to better it by putting to
good use some or all of the mental gifts and capacities with
which you have been endowed. Heaven knows that our society
is far from perfect and that there is much to be done in the way
of raising its standards of justice and morality. It is the basic
duty of everyone to contribute one's share towards this end.[29]

In this letter we see the further application of Schneerson's theory
of reciprocity, not only on the level of social community and organization, but also on the level of personal wellbeing. Though we don't know
precisely what was troubling his addressee, Schneerson makes it clear
that the "distortion" he is experiencing in his "inner life" results from a
social imbalance, indeed from a lack of engagement in social contributions for the good of others. The antidote to these inner, psychological
disturbances, accordingly, is not to engage in more navel gazing but
rather to replace self-concern with concern for others. In the continuation of the letter Schneerson provides two paths of action. The first is
prescribed universally:

> If the person turning to me with such a problem as you de-
> scribe were a gentile, I would say to him: You are too much
> wrapped up with yourself, with your own emotions and feel-
> ings and aspirations. Stop being concerned with your own
> problems. The way to cope with such an emotionally charged
> situation is to stop trying to cope with it. You must get away
> from yourself, and begin to think of others. It is time to begin
> an active participation in society; to give and to give gener-
> ously. The opportunities are many, and the need is great. You
> have your choice: social work, charitable, or even scientific.

The second path is a more particular one, but its orientation is the
same. The antidote lies in a purpose beyond the self, in a beholdenness
not only to society, but to God. In effect, Schneerson argues, the commitment to adhere to an all-encompassing regime of religious practice

can actually be therapeutic, especially in the modern world. The Jew has the same obligations to society as the gentile, but additionally has a further set of obligations to God:

> You are a Jew, and your obligations go beyond the above. You must <u>live</u> like a Jew in your daily life, the Jewish way of life, the way of the Torah and Mitzvoth, and you must use your influence with others in the same direction. Some people think the Torah and the Jewish way is "old fashioned," but they are both misguided and unscientific. Truth never gets "too old," can never get stale. Only falsehood, half truth and compromise can not last long; but truth is enduring and timeless.
>
> It may require courage and resolution to change one's way of life. But these are qualities with which youth is generously endowed, and you are a young man, nineteen, as you write. You are capable of facing this challenge boldly.

Here we have echoes of Schneerson's countercultural strategy for Jewish renaissance, which was discussed more fully in Chapter 2. But in the present context what is most relevant is that Schneerson's call for a bold and transformative commitment is also related to his principle of reciprocity. The all-embracing demands of the Torah and its commandments—especially as they are recast and illuminated by the ethos and teachings of Hasidism—provide a very specific path beyond the narrow constraints of individualism, and beyond the internal psychological imbalances that are the natural product of self-centered preoccupation. From this perspective, living a Torah-observant life not only makes one part of a community with a shared set of values, practices, and institutions, but also has the potential to endow all aspects of one's day-to-day affairs with a sense of cosmic engagement, explicitly placing the individual in a reciprocal relationship with God on an ongoing basis.

Before turning to the question of the relationship between self and cosmos it is worth pausing to reflect on one more example of the way Schneerson engaged with the question of the relationship between self, other, and community—this time from the perspective of Jewish law:

Based on the biblical verse "and you shall do what is just and good in the eyes of the Lord...that you may come and possess the good land" (Deuteronomy, 6:18) the Talmud rules that neighbors have the first right of purchase when a property is sold, to the point that another buyer must accept the neighbor's financial compensation and vacate the field even if a transaction has already been concluded.[30] On the face of it this simply means that the buyer should do the just thing and allow the neighbor to exercise his first right to purchase the field. But in a 1954 talk delivered on the tenth anniversary of his father's passing Schneerson suggested that the very fact of proximity creates a reciprocal transaction between neighbors, such that each actually has a measure of legal ownership in the other's property. The verse isn't merely advocating that potential buyers should allow the neighbor the first right of purchase. Instead the verse is establishing that "what is just and good" creates a de-facto contract that binds the entire community, and obligates the courts to uphold the neighbor's stake in the adjoining property. In an edited version of this talk, first published in 1976, Schneerson argued that this is in fact the opinion of the great medieval legal authority and philosopher, Maimonides.[31]

Without becoming distracted by the finer points of this issue and its implications, Schneerson's argument underscores the seriousness with which he regards the relationship between the individual and the other, the individual and the community. Neighborliness is not to be treated lightly, and proximity to another human being does not merely require us to be polite or nice. Neighborliness actually comes with legal obligations. Of course there are many other examples of this in Jewish law. But here it emerges that the reciprocal bonds of justice and community are so strong that our neighbors might be considered to have a real legal stake in our property, and we in theirs. To act for the good of others, even at the cost of personal inconvenience—as in the case of the buyer who must vacate his newly purchased property—is not merely applause-worthy or magnanimous, but a legal duty that cannot be evaded.

4.5—The Individual as the Fulcrum of Macrocosmic Purpose

To PLACE THE self in relation to the cosmos is to confront the ultimate existential question: Is my existence of any real consequence at all? It is arguably the greater awareness of the vastness of the world and the cosmos that has actually increased the sense of loneliness and futility

in our modern era of globalization, fueled by the rapid advance of communication technologies.[32] Contextualized by the big picture of the
entire cosmos, one might wonder whether anything thought, said, or
done can really matter one way or another?

This is a far greater predicament than that of the individual who
faces a tension between personal success and the success of the community. That is merely a local quibble, and it never throws the very
existence of the individual into question. To face the cosmos, however,
is to question your own existence and its significance. Much rides on
how the question is answered. Much rides on whether or not the question is even asked.

Not to ask the question, not to place oneself in relation to the cosmos, is to remain oblivious to anything beyond the narrow constraints
of your own bodily senses; to remain entirely preoccupied with the
narrowest possible conception of self. In *Hayom yom*, Schneerson's first
published work, he cites an aphorism attributed to his namesake, the
third rebbe of Chabad (Menachem Mendel of Lubavitch, 1789-1866):

> The kindness and special advantage that "God made man up-
> right" (Ecclesiastes, 7:29) to walk erectly, is that though he
> walks on the earth he sees the Heavens. Not so with beasts
> that go on all fours; they see only the earth.[33]

The ability to see beyond the constraints of personal and local perspective, in other words, is precisely what distinguishes the human from
the beast. And yet it is precisely what makes us human that can lead the
human to the greatest depths of despair and helplessness, or—worse—
to a state of uncaring inertia and laziness. The existential question thus
transmutes into a lame excuse. In a public letter penned ahead of the
Rosh Hashanah festival in 1964 (and appended to the above-discussed
letter to Kadish Luz) Schneerson speaks of those who evade their duty
with the erroneous argument "that it is impossible to transform the
world, or that their parents didn't give them the requisite education and
preparation, or that the world is immense and he is alone and how can
he possibly achieve anything?"[34]

The answer to this question or excuse, for Schneerson, lay in the
story of the creation of the first man (*adam harishon*) in the biblical book
of Genesis, a story that in classical rabbinic and kabbalistic teachings

is especially linked to Rosh Hashanah. Though popularly thought of
as the Jewish New Year and the anniversary of creation, according to
rabbinic sources it actually marks the sixth day of creation, the day
when man was created.[35] In Chabad literature much is made of this,
and indeed it endows the celebration of Rosh Hashanah with a significance that is far removed from the more prosaic celebration most
would associate with the New Year, and which provides an insightful
window into Schneerson's conception of the place of each individual
human being in the macrocosmos. The latter followed all his predecessors as Chabad rebbes in highlighting the intimations of a passage
that appears in the Rosh Hashanah liturgy: "This is the day of the beginning of Your work, a remembrance of the first day."[36] Here is how
Schneerson encapsulated the Chabad interpretation of the passage in
a discourse delivered in 1980:

> On the 25th of Elul the world was created, and Rosh Hasha-
> nah is the day of Adam's creation and the sixth day of creation;
> why then do we say of this day that it is the beginning of Your
> work? Also, why is Rosh Hashanah on the 1st of Tishrei and
> not on the 25th of Elul?...And the explanation of this is that
> the ultimate purpose of the creation of the world is that man
> shall draw forth revelation of the divine into the world by
> means of his effort...and this was begun and initiated on the
> day of Adam's creation...On the day of Adam's creation the
> revelation of divinity is begun and initiated.[37]

This is the opening passage of a long discourse on the sharp distinction between the world as it stood during the first five days of creation,
on the one hand, and the transformation of the world that only becomes possible with the creation of man on the sixth day. In a nutshell:
The creation of man introduces the possibility of cosmic reciprocity, of
cosmic joy, of ultimate revelation and fulfillment not only for creation,
but for God as well:

> Though "the world was created complete"...the complete-
> ness of the world as a creation from above [i.e., without the
> contribution of man from below] is with measure and lim-
> itation. But through the work of man a revelation is drawn

forth that transcends the measures and limitations of the world...the measures and limitations of the world are burst open, including the measures and limitation of the world as they were on the first day of creation, upon which God was alone in His world.[38]

Prior to the creation of man the world was complete. The only thing that was lacking was dynamism, the capacity for the world to exceed the sum of its parts, the capacity for the world to become receptive to a manifestation of divinity that entirely transcends the axiomatic conceptions of creation itself. This is a set of conceptions that binds God to the category of "Creator," a category that not only reduces God to the role the term describes but also relegates God to the peak of the cosmic hierarchy; only a provider and not in any way a recipient. God has created an entire world, but yet remains alone, transcendent, bereft of any relationship.

The crucial fulcrum of divine manifestation that is built anew each Rosh Hashanah, per earlier Hasidic and kabbalistic sources, is *malkhut*.[39] Literally, *malkhut* translates as "sovereignty," but it is also associated with the capacity to communicate intimately with another individual, and—most significantly—with the feminine aspect of the divine, and of the cosmos generally. This is not the place to attempt a full theorization of all these kabbalistic associations. Suffice it to say that here, and elsewhere, Schneerson highlights the paradoxical capacity of *malkhut* to both create the illusion of distance and overcome the illusion of distance. This is precisely what reciprocity is all about; to reciprocate is not to smother the other, but to acknowledge the other as other, to recognize their individuality, their distinct needs, and their distinct gifts.[40] It is precisely through carving out a cosmic sense of distance between man and God (signaled by the grandeur of divine sovereignty) that man and God can enter into a reciprocal relationship according to which the work of man raises up the entire world, making it transparent to the essence of divine being, which lies at its core. It is man who builds the fulcrum of divine sovereignty from within the world, ultimately revealing that the being of the world is nothing more and nothing less than the very being of the divine self.

In his public Rosh Hashanah letter of 1964 Schneerson spells out the practical implications of this kabbalistic conception:

> With the creation of man...the completion of creation is at-
> tained...because man is the creature who can, must and will,
> ultimately, bring all other elements of creation to their com-
> pletion. This will be achieved when man utilizes all of his
> own capacities, and all the capacities of nature—whether in
> the inanimate, vegetable or animal realms—to the fullest
> degree. Thereby every being in the entire creation will be
> brought into resonance with the will of the creator.[41]

Thus far it has been made clear that humankind, in general, has a
central purpose to play within the macrocosmos. It is only through
them that the ultimate purpose of creation can be achieved. But what
of each person as an individual?

It is precisely to underscore the cosmic significance of each individual that Schneerson so often invoked the Talmudic statement that
unlike all the other animals "man was initially created alone" as a
single individual, to teach us that "one person...is an entire world,"
and to teach us that like Adam "every individual is obligated to say
'the world was created for my sake.'" (*Talmud bavli*, Sanhedrin, 37a.) In
Schneerson's words:

> This shows us and emphasizes that one single person has the
> ability to bring the entirety of creation to its complete te-
> los...Even in our time, in whatever place and situation one
> might be found, one has the full capacity (and therefore also
> the duty) to strive and to attain the highest degree of comple-
> tion, and also to achieve the same for the entire world...Rosh
> Hashanah gives us the strength to fulfill our duty, for on this
> day the entirety of creation is renewed.[42]

From this perspective Rosh Hashanah emerges as a day upon which
man must look up from the narrow confines of the local, earthbound
perspective; a day upon which to "walk erectly" and "to see the heavens." Rosh Hashanah is a day to place oneself in the largest possible
context, at the center of the macrocosmos, rather than at its margins. It
is a day to take stock of the relationship between man and God, a day
for each human being to realize and recognize that they are indeed in a
personal relationship with God's own self. Rather than simply praying

for personal, individual needs and success, the individual instead prays that they be granted the spiritual and material wherewithal to execute their cosmic mission every day of the coming year, working diligently to imbue all aspects of the world with a sense of beholdenness to, and reciprocal union with, the divine sovereign.[43] Through this Hasidic prism a new light is shone on all the various liturgical and ritual elements of the special Rosh Hashanah prayers and practices, turning them into the medium via which renewed energy, resolution, and commitment are drawn by each individual into their life's work for every day of the coming year.

These are themes that Schneerson did not merely invoke on Rosh Hashanah, but on many occasions each year, throughout the decades of his leadership. The following excerpts from a talk delivered in the summer of 1984 are especially noteworthy for the complex negotiation that is presented between the cosmic power of each individual, and the increased advantage accrued when two or more individuals come together to constitute a collective, a community:

> When an individual comes and joins a crowd one might think: "Since there are so many Jews here, if so, what am I worth as an individual?" To this we respond, "Blessed is the one who comes." (Psalms, 118:26.) Though you are but one individual, even when you come to a place in which a crowd is found, your existence as an individual remains intact. Indeed a special blessing is extended to you: "Blessed is the *one* who comes."
>
> This is underscored by the saying of the sages, "for this reason man was created alone," in order that all future generations should know that anyone who descends from Adam—which refers not only to Jews...but to all the descendents of Adam, including non-Jews—is "a complete world"...
>
> When an individual comes and joins a crowd...then he accrues the additional station, merit, and blessing of the community. In addition to fulfilling his mission as an individual he also fulfills his mission as a part of the collective entity; thereby it not only becomes easier for him to fulfill his individual mission, but he also accrues an additional mission that can only be fulfilled by a collective entity, formed by several

individuals who join together "like one man with one heart"
(cf. Rashi to Exodus, 19:2) for a single purpose and telos, thereby creating an entirely new entity.[44]

It is perhaps natural to think that the participation of the individual
in a collective endeavor, in the creation of community, must come at
some personal cost. The individual must abdicate something of their
own status, curb their own talents and ambitions, in order to successfully integrate into the community. But Schneerson insists that this
is a misnomer. The crowd does not drown the individual, but buoys
and raises the individual to increased success. Community provides
context and resources through which the unique contributions of each
individual can resonate louder and be disseminated much further.
The stronger the community is as a whole, the better equipped will
its members be to thrive individually, each of them better supporting
and amplifying the particular mission of each of its other constituents.
Moreover, a community comprising a network of unique individuals
becomes an entirely new entity. A community, in contrast to a lone individual, is an entirely different kind of organism in which a diverse set
of individual limbs and tools can now be arrayed in collective harmony
and directed toward a goal that no single one of its individual members
could have hoped to attain alone.

Broadly, this conception echoes the position taken by Schneerson
in his letter to Luz. In the continuation of the talk, however, a third element is emphasized: an element that lies beyond the dialectic of the
individual and the community, but which is specifically articulated in
their encounter and union. It is precisely when two individuals join together that the traditional greeting is articulated, "blessed is the one
who comes in the name of God." It is in the coming together of individuals to form community that the name of God is invoked, and
specifically the name *havayah*, which has a double meaning: (1) The
One who "was, is, and will be" encompassing past, present, and future
"at once"; (2) The Creator. This, Schneerson explains, is an invocation
of the transcendent essence of God which is the ultimate ground of all
creation. In other words, the greeting and blessing uttered when two
individuals meet to form a community constitutes a revelation of "the
true being" of God's own self, thus bringing both the individual and
the community in line with their cosmic telos.[45]

4.6—The Transformation of Self and Cosmos in Theory and Practice

IN SCHNEERSON'S SYSTEM, it emerges, there are actually three concepts of the individual that function alongside one another, and in interaction with one another: (1) The individual as an individual, alone; (2) the individual as a part of the community, as a unique social actor; (3) the individual as a complete world, as a fulcrum via which the entire cosmic telos is realized.

In a sense, the individual as individual mirrors the completeness and the lonesomeness of God prior to the creation of man. The individual is complete, and yet is bereft of the dynamism of a relationship with an equal other. The principle of reciprocity could only come into play, on the purely human level, when the single man—according to rabbinic and kabbalistic sources, originally actually an androgyne—was "split" into a couple, man and woman.[46] Indeed, this "split" is directly associated with the construction of the fulcrum of *malkhut* on the sixth day of creation.[47]

The individual as a part of a community actually acquires the characteristic of community; the individual is transformed into the central cog in a network of central cogs, maximizing personal achievement through the power of the collective. This evokes an aphorism cited by Schneerson, as formulated by his predecessor: "An individual is a multitude."[48] An individual should never see themselves as *merely* an individual. Through the dynamic of reciprocity the individual can create a community of individuals. As a part of a collective community, a multitude, the individual accrues the full power of the collective. As such the individual can face the world, and the challenge of transforming its spirit and ethos, with the confidence that they can and will be successful. As the aphorism concludes: "An individual can create a multitude, and bring a multitude to life."[49]

Illustration of Schneerson's application of this principle in practice can be found in the counsel he gave to David Lapin, a South African rabbi who visited the Rebbe in 1976. At the time, Lapin had established both a business and a center for Torah study in Johannesburg. While successful in both areas he felt that he was becoming too overstretched and that perhaps it was time for him to quit the business altogether. Listening to Schneerson's "unlimited" vision of all that he could achieve if he maintained—and even increased—his activities in both realms, Lapin felt overwhelmed by the Rebbe's expectations. As he recalled in a 2015 interview, "It seemed almost unbelievable that anyone could expect that of one, certainly of me. I was a young person at the time." When he voiced his realistic conclusion that it was simply too much, Schneerson said,

> "I'll tell you your difficulty. You think that human interaction
> is like a chemical reaction, and it isn't. In a chemical reaction
> you have two elements, they react and you get some kind of
> third compound as a result. But…when people interact it's
> a nuclear reaction. In a nuclear reaction you've got to think
> in terms of a center spot and a sphere, and it reacts in all
> directions at the same time, and as the outer rings of that
> sphere become bigger and bigger the number of people you
> are touching gets bigger and bigger…So when you touch the
> heart of one person that's a nuclear explosion, because that
> person in turn touches so many other people."[50]

These words are Lapin's paraphrase, but in the Rosh Hashanah letter of 1964 that has already been cited (and elsewhere as well) Schneerson invokes the image of a nuclear explosion to make a very similar point.[51] Lapin followed the advice he received and came to see his own brief meeting with Schneerson as an example of the very phenomena described.

This brings us to the third conception of the individual, the individual as the fulcrum of the cosmic telos. To think of the individual in this way is to put each person into a reciprocal relationship not only with the individual members of their local community, nor merely with all members of the global society at any given time. It is rather to place the individual as the center of the entire cosmos and at the center of its entire history. "Every individual is obligated to say 'the world was created for my sake.'" (*Talmud bavli*, Sanhedrin, 37a.) Schneerson takes this statement with utter seriousness and clearly wanted to impress its powerful implications on everyone he could reach. In his many talks and letters this conception is refracted through the Hasidic lens that he inherited from his predecessors going all the way back to Schneur Zalman of Liadi.

Here we will take note of two of the many texts that are illustrative of the deep-rootedness of Schneerson's cosmic concept of the individual in classical Chabad teachings, and which will also help us to better understand the concept itself. First, a letter addressed by Schneur

Zalman to a hasid and physician named Yitshak of Dubrovna, offering guidance in the contemplative techniques that lead to the attainment of joy and awe before God:

> The main thing constantly is to make oneself be in awe before God, as it is says, "happy is the man who is constantly fearful." That is, one should believe that God fills the world, as it says "the heavens and the earth I fill," and as He created the worlds at the outset so he creates them every day, as is said [in the daily prayer liturgy], "He renews in his goodness, every day, constantly, the work of creation." For at the outset he did not create you by compulsion, but rather by His will. Without His will, existence would not continue even for a moment... Therefore one must immediately guard one's mind, like one's actions... that one shall be bound onto God constantly.[52]

It is noteworthy that much of this is specifically framed as a direct appeal to the reader personally, using the second-person "you." There are three points that Schneur Zalman wants us to consider: (1) God fills the world; (2) God is constantly recreating the world anew; and (3) the constant act of re-creation does not happen by default, but is driven by God's will.

Together, these three points drive home a clear conception of an immanent God who is neither static, disinterested, or generalized. On the contrary, God is dynamically engaged with the personal existence of each individual on a constant basis. "He did not create *you* by compulsion, but rather by His will." Contemplation and recognition of this belief, R. Schneur Zalman argues, will inspire a joyful sense of awe and purpose ("happy is the man who is constantly fearful") so that through all one's thoughts and actions "one shall be bound onto God constantly."

We now turn to a text by the fourth rebbe in the Chabad-Lubavitch line, Shmuel Schneersohn of Lubavitch, in which the cosmic power of "doing the will of God" is articulated through a dramatic upending of the normative hierarchies of kabbalistic cosmology, and indeed of the very concepts of time and creation. Crucially, he reads the last clause of the phrase "it is pleasurable before Me that My will is done"—which is placed in the mouth of God by the Talmudic rabbis—as "My will is *made*." To do the will of God is to *make* the will of God:

Man encompasses the upper and lower, meaning all the cosmic realms... and the intention of man's creation is for the sake
of Torah and the commandments...[However,] on the part of
the essence of the infinite light there is no possibility at all
for the desire for Torah and the commandments. As our sages
say, 'What does it matter to the Holy One if you slaughter [an
animal] from the nape or from the throat?'...Accordingly, the
meaning of "my will is made" (naseh retsoni) is that we make
and draw forth the infinite revelation, which transcends such
desire, that it shall have such a desire...Accordingly we can
understand the power of physical mitzvah performance specifically... that through the compelling force of the action we
cause the primal tsimtsum (tsimtsum harishon), that the infinite
revelation should be contracted to enter the specific desires
expressed in Torah and the commandments.[53]

This is a conception that places the single human being, and each
human being, at the center of the entire cosmic enterprise. Crucially,
it also frames the relationship between man and God as fundamentally
reciprocal. Man's action, putting selfishness aside and acting upon the
divine command, elicits the initiation of the entire cosmic project that
allows for the existence of man in the first place. The ritual performance
of a mitzvah awakens the transcendent essence of divine being, inspiring
the divine act of self-contraction (tsimtsum) that is primal to all existence.

Schneerson wanted to share this sense of cosmic purpose, power,
and responsibility; he wanted to inculcate it not only in card-carrying
members of Chabad, but in all people, including non-Jews. In pointing
to the example of Adam—the first human being—as testimony to the
cosmic nature of each individual, he often emphasized that this lesson
applies equally to all people. Rosh Hashanah, however, is primarily celebrated as a Jewish holiday rather than a universal one. Among
Jews, moreover, it is celebrated collectively by the community. This
togetherness can serve to counterbalance the emphasis on the unique
capacities of each person in particular. An even more opportune day
for the celebration of individuality is the day of one's birth. In this respect, Schneerson emphasized, non-Jews are no different from Jews.
Indeed, he noted, the very first appearance of the Hebrew term for
birthday appears in the Bible with regard to Pharaoh, king of Egypt,

and the same term is used to indicate the birthdays of Jews and non-Jews alike.[54]

From the very beginning of his leadership, and even before he became Rebbe, Schneerson emphasized the spiritual significance of celebrating one's birthday.[55] Initially he did not speak of this publicly, but in private advised people that this was a day when an extra measure of introspection, prayer, Torah study, and charity was in order. In later years he began to speak of this in public as well. This progression came to a climax following the passing of his wife in 1988: On her birthday, just over a month later, he launched a "birthday campaign," encouraging people to celebrate their birthday as a personal festival, and as an opportunity to inspire themselves and others as well with an increased sense of one's capacity and mission as an individual to transform self and world for the better:

> On one's birthday one should add in Torah, prayer, and charity, the three pillars "upon which the world stands,"[56] beginning with "the small world which is man,"[57] and accept upon oneself good resolutions...
>
> In addition: 1) It is very fitting and worthy that each person shall convene a joyous gathering on their birthday together with their family, or also their acquaintances and friends etc. in order that one shall accept these good resolutions in a *joyous* manner, which will extend to the fulfillment of the good resolutions with joy and alacrity. 2) This is relevant to each individual, men and women, and also children—initially via their parents, and especially when they attain understanding and sincerity, for then it is possible to explain to them (in a manner that is understandable and relevant to them) that on one's birthday there must be innovation in all matters of goodness and holiness, and in a manner that they too shall celebrate their birthday via a joyous gathering, together with their friends. All of this is more strongly emphasized in the case of children, who by their nature are receptive to everything with feeling and with excitement...[58]

While previously Schneerson had emphasized only the more serious dimension of the birthday, focusing especially on introspection and recommitment, the new campaign added the intertwined dimensions of joy and sharing. The personal occasion was to be enhanced through the power of the collective. Nor was it something to be reserved for a select few. Every individual, including the youngest of children, deserves a day where their unique existence and the unique cosmic contribution that is theirs to make is celebrated with due seriousness and with due excitement.

On one occasion, Schneerson commented that "the connection between the descent of the soul into the body...to Rosh Hashanah is self understood, for it was on Rosh Hashanah that He [God] breathed into his [Adam's] nostrils the spirit of life, connecting the soul with the body."[59] In light of this comment it seems quite clear that Schneerson intended the birthday as a personalized Rosh Hashanah—a personal day of annual renewal and growth. The microcosm ("the small world that is man") mirrors the macrocosm. From a sociological perspective this can be further seen as a means by which the secular is sacralized, such that the sacred transcends the regimented bounds of normative religious practice and ritualized festivity. Any day of the year—indeed every day of the year—acquires something of the status of Rosh Hashanah, simply by dint of it being someone's birthday. The sacred celebration of the cosmic power of each individual is thereby made both more personal and more universal. By means of the sacralized birthday celebration, the theory of man as the fulcrum of the cosmos is given a concrete and practical method via which it can be realized by everyone.

Notes

1. For classical and contemporary conceptions of reciprocity see Kazutaka Inamura, *Justice and Reciprocity in Aristotle's Political Philosophy* (Cambridge: Cambridge University Press, 2015); Serge-Christophe Kolm, *Reciprocity: An Economics of Social Relations* (Cambridge: Cambridge University Press, 2008).

2. Menachem Mendel Schneerson, *Sichot Kodesh 5731*, Vol. 2 (Brooklyn, NY: Vaad Hanachot Hatemimim, 1987), 339-340. This translation was amended according to the recording of the original audio, available at *Chabad.org*, <chabad.org/551649>.

3. See Menachem Mendel Schneerson, *Torat menachem hitvaduyot*, Vol. 14 [5715, II] (Brooklyn, NY: Kehot Publication Society, 2007), 300: "When the gift is not accepted by the recipient...he [the giver] is thereby pained; from this it is clear that the acceptance of the gift touches an even deeper place [in the psyche of the giver] than the giving itself."

4. Marcin Wodziński, "The Socio-Economic Profile of a Religious Movement: The Case of Hasidism," *European History Quarterly* 46, no. 4 (September, 2016): 684.

5. See Schneerson, *Torat menachem hitvaduyot, Vol. 20* [5717, III] (Brooklyn, NY: Kehot Publication Society, 2007), 27: "In order to be a receptacle for a gift...there needs to be self-contraction (*tsimtsum*) on the part of the recipient, that one puts all that one already has aside. This is the preciousness and ascent of *malkhut*...that it shall be a fitting receptacle for the gift of *ze'ir anpin*...and the second ascent of *malkhut* is that...*malkhut* and *ze'ir anpin* are equal..." The association between *malkhut*, receptivity and reciprocity will be returned to at the end of the present chapter. See also Schneerson, *Ibid.*, Vol. 14, 300: "The recipient is rooted in the essence of the [ultimate] giver [i.e. the essence of God]...this is due to the [cosmic] advantage of the recipient, which transcends the general category of thought (and extraneous manifestation)." Without unpacking the full significance of this passage, it is sufficient to note the clear suggestion that the capacity to receive is actually deeper and more essential than the capacity to give. Elsewhere Schneerson explicitly connected the advantage of receptivity to the messianic ascent of the female above the male. See for example *ibid.*, Vol. 4 [5712, I] (Brooklyn, NY: Kehot Publication Society, 1995), 118: "Of the messianic future it is written 'the female shall transcend the male' (Cf. Jeremiah, 31:21), for then the advantage of receptivity will be revealed...this was manifest in the case of our forefathers, that the matriarchs were greater than the patriarchs..." In this context it is important to note that Schneerson would often emphasize that men and women alike incorporate both the masculine and feminine capacities to give and to receive, though men are generally associated with *ze'ir anpin* and women with *malkhut*. See for example *ibid.*, Vol. 20 [5717, III], 271.

6. Menachem Mendel Schneerson, *Igrot kodesh*, Vol. 13 (Brooklyn, NY: Kehot Publication Society, 1989), 234. Cf. Meir Ibn Gabai, *Avodat hakodesh*, Shaar ha'avodah, 1.

7. Cf. *Talmud bavli*, Ketubot, 68a; *ibid.*, Nedarim, 41a; Zohar, III, 273b. This phraseology is invoked countless times by Schneerson. See for example, Menachem Mendel Schneerson, *Torat menachem hitvaduyot*, Vol. 7 [5713, I] (Brooklyn, NY: Kehot Publication Society, 2007), 78; *ibid.*, Vol. 8 [5713, II], 56-57.

8. Menachem Mendel Schneerson, *Sichot kodesh 5740*, Vol. 3 (Brooklyn, NY: Vaad Hanachot Hatemimim, 1986), 587-589. The phrase "something that will be revealed" is Talmudic in origin. Cf. *Talmud bavli*, Bechorot, 36a; Maimonides, *Mishneh torah*, Gerushin, 13:29. Also see the relevant discussion in Menachem Mendel Schneerson, *Likutei sichot*, Vol. 19 (Brooklyn, NY: Kehot Publication Society, 2000), 189-190.

9. Schneerson, *Sichot kodesh 5740, Vol. 3*, 588.

10. *Ibid.*, 589. Cf. Yosef Yitzchak Schneersohn, *Sefer hasichot kayitz 5700* (Brooklyn, NY: Kehot Publication Society, 1986), 11: "The Baal Shem Tov says that each thing that a Jew hears and sees is a lesson in the service of God...one must derive a lesson in Torah and service." For further discussion of this teaching see Jacob I. Schochet (ed.), *Keter shem tov hashalom* (Brooklyn, NY: Kehot Publication Society, 2016), 386-388 (*hosafot*, #223).

11. Schneerson, *Sichot kodesh 5740, Vol. 3*, 589-590.

12. Schneur Zalman of Liadi, *Likutei amarim tanya*, Chapter 21, 26b [52].

13. Schneerson, *Sichot kodesh 5740*, Vol. 3, 588.

14. For a wider perspective on the classical conception of the elements and their contemporary relevance see David Macauley, *Elemental Philosophy: Earth, Air, Fire, and Water as Environmental Ideas* (Albany: SUNY Press, 2010).

15. Gloss of Rabbi Moshe Iserlis, *Shluchan arukh*, Orach chaim, 6:1.

16. Schneerson, *Sichot kodesh 5740*, Vol. 3, 588-589.

17. Menachem Mendel Schneerson, *Igrot kodesh*, Vol. 4 (Brooklyn, NY: Kehot Publication Society, 1987), 480-481. The same idea, supported by the same sources, can be found throughout Schnnerson's talks and letters. For some examples see, *idem.*, *Torat menachem hitvaduyot*, Vol. 1 [5710] (Brooklyn, NY: Kehot Publication Society, 2002), 44; *ibid.*, Vol. 15 [5716, I] (Brooklyn, NY: Kehot Publication Society, 2013), 89. We should also note that the phrase, "one's heart and mind are made a thousand times more refined" is from a passage in Schneur Zalman of Liadi's *Torah or* that relates to the role of the tsadik, and which was discussed in Chapter 3 of the present book. This provides an example of the way that Schneerson often applied teachings regarding the unique role of the tsadik to all individuals, who have the capacity to sublimate the quality of the tsadik and share it with all who they encounter. For further examples of Schneerson's invocations of this phrase to the same end see *idem.*, *Torat menachem hitvaduyot*, Vol. 8 [5713, II] (Brooklyn, NY: Kehot Publication Society, 2014), 31; *idem.*, *Igrot kodesh*, Vol. 13 (Brooklyn, NY: Kehot Publication Society, 2005), 61-62.

18. Cf. Yosef Yitzchak Schneerson, *Sefer hamamarim 5710* (Brooklyn, NY: Kehot Publication Society, 1986), 117. For some instances in which Schneerson cited this Talmudic dictum see Menachem Mendel Schneerson, *Igrot kodesh*, Vol. 8 (Brooklyn, NY: Kehot Publication Society: 1998), 211; *ibid.*, Vol. 10 (Brooklyn, NY: Kehot Publication Society, 1999), 80; *ibid.*, Vol. 11 (Brooklyn, NY: Kehot Publication Society, 1999), 98-99.

19. Menachem Mendel Schneerson, *Torat menachem hitvaduyot*, Vol. 13 [5715, I] (Brooklyn, NY: Kehot Publication Society, 1999), 207.

20. Menachem Mendel Schneerson, *Likutei sichot*, Vol. 38 (Brooklyn, NY: Kehot Publication Society, 2000), 188.

21. For a selection of videos recording such encounters see Jewish Educational Media's "Living Torah Archive," hosted by *Chabad.org*, available at <https://www.chabad.org/therebbe/livingtorah/default.aspx?searchword=&day=&month=&year=&discAID=&ClipTypeID=1387&x=19&y=10>.

22. For the video footage of this exchange, see "To Benefit a Third Jew," *Chabad.org*, <chabad.org/247481>.

23. Tzvi Freeman, "The Rebbe's Investment: My Thoughts on the Rebbe's Modality of Leadership," *Chabad.org*, <chabad.org/402599>.

24. For biographical information see the entry in David Tidhar, *Entsiklopedyah lehalutse hayishuv uvonav*, Vol. 7, 2857-2858, <http://www.tidhar.tourolib.org/tidhar/view/7/2857>.

25. Menachem Mendel Schneerson, *Igrot kodesh*, Vol. 23 (Brooklyn, NY: Kehot Publication Society, 1994), 264.

26. *Ibid.*, 264-265.

27. Elizabeth S. Anderson, "What Is the Point of Equality?" *Ethics* 109, no. 2 (Jan. 1999): 287-337, esp. 315.

28. Menachem Mendel Schneerson, *Igrot kodesh*, Vol. 23, 265-266.

29. A facsimile of the original letter was available to the authors; for the text of the letter, see "A Letter from the Lubavitcher Rebbe," *myjli.com*, <http://myjli.com/faith/index.php/lesson-3/a-letter-from-the-lubavitcher-rebbe-2/>.

30. *Talmud bavli*, Bava Metziah, 108a.

31. Menachem Mendel Schneerson, *Sichot kodesh 5714* (Brooklyn, NY: Vaad Hanachot Hatemimim, 1985), 369; idem., *Likutei sichot*, Vol. 19 (Brooklyn, NY: Kehot Publication Society, 1982), 55-66.

32. Witness the long history of scholarly debate over the relationship between suicide and modernity, beginning with Émile Durkheim's book *Suicide*, first published in 1897. For a recent review of relevant literature, see Allison Milner, "Globalization and Suicide: An Ecological Study across Five Regions of the Worl," *Archives of Suicide Research* 16, no. 3 (2012): 238-249.

33. Menachem Mendel Schneerson, *Hayom yom*, entry for the 13th Shevat.

34. Menachem Mendel Schneerson, *Igrot kodesh*, Vol. 23, 269.

35. Cf. *Vayikrah rabbah*, 29:1; Tosfot to *Talmud bavli*, Rosh Hashanah, 8a: "According to Rabbi Elazar…man was created on the sixth."

36. From *Talmud bavli*, Rosh Hashanah, 27a.

37. Menachem Mendel Schneerson, *Torat menachem sefer hamamarim melukat*, Vol. 1 (Brooklyn, NY: Kehot Publication Society, 2012), 29.

38. *Ibid.*, 31.

39. Cf. Chaim Vital, *Pri ets chaim*, 24:1 (*Shaar rosh hashanah*); Schneur Zalman of Liadi, *Seder tefilot mikol hashanah im pirush hamilot al pi dach* (Brooklyn, NY: Kehot Publication Society, 1965), 234a-238a.

40. Cf. Shalom DovBer Schneersohn of Lubavitch, *Kuntras hicholtsu* (New York: Kehot Publication Society: New York, 1948), section 7: "True interinclusion and solidarity is when multifarious elements unite with one another, and support one another, to the degree that no beginning and end is found…for they each receive from one another…" For a discussion of this passage and its context see Eli Rubin, "Purging Divisiveness, Embracing Difference: Rabbi Shalom DovBer Schneersohn's Manifesto against Self-Righteousness in Interpersonal Discourse," *Chabad.org*, <chabad.org/3800391>.

41. Menachem Mendel Schneerson, *Igrot kodesh*, Vol. 23, 267-268.

42. *Ibid.*, Vol. 23, 268-269.

43. For a full development of this idea see Menachem Mendel Schneerson, *Likutei sichot*, Vol. 19 (Brooklyn, NY: Kehot Publication Society, 2000), 291-297.

44. Menachem Mendel Schneerson, *Torat menachem hitvaduyot 5744*, Vol. 4 (Brooklyn, NY: Kehot Publication Society, 1990), 2160-2161.

45. *Ibid.*, 2161-2162.

46. See, for one example, the relevant citations and discussion in Menachem Mendel Schneerson, *Likutei sichot*, Vol. 8 (Brooklyn, NY: Kehot Publication Society, 1974), 212.

47. See Chaim Vital, *Pri ets chaim*, 24:2 (*Shaar rosh hashanah*).

48. Yosef Yitzchak Schneerson, *Sefer hamamarim 5710*, 170 and 190.

49. Menachem Mendel Schneerson, *Sichot kodesh 5740*, Vol. 2 (Brooklyn, NY: Vaad Hanachot Hatemimim, 1986), 4-8.

50. For a video recording of Lapin's testimony see "Atomic Energy," *Chabad.org*, <chabad.org/3033241>.

51. Schneerson, *Igrot kodesh*, Vol. 23, 269-270.

52. Shalom DovBer Levine and Yehoshua Mondshine (eds.), *Igrot kodesh admor hazaken* (New York: Kehot Publication Society, 2012), 427-428.

53. Shmuel Schneersohn, *Likutei torah—torat shmuel, shaar revi'ei, ve'kakhah—5637* (Brooklyn, NY: Kehot Publication Society, 1945), 16-18; *Likutei torah—torat shmuel, shaar teshah asar, sefer 5637*, Vol. 2, *ve'kakhah—5637* (Brooklyn, NY: Kehot Publication Society, 2013). The newer addition includes the pagination of the original format.

54. Menachem Mendel Schneerson, *Torat menachem hitvaduyot 5742*, Vol. 4 (Brooklyn, NY: Kehot Publication Society, 1990), 2179.

55. Schneerson, *Hayom yom*, entry for 11th of Nissan.

56. Avot, 1:2.

57. Cf. *Midrash tanchuma*, Pikudei 3; Zohar, III, 33b

58. Menachem Mendel Schneerson, *Torat menachem hitvaduyot 5748*, Vol. 2 (Brooklyn, NY: Kehot Publication Society, 1990), 461.

59. Menachem Mendel Schneerson, *Torat menachem hitvaduyot 5742*, Vol. 4 (Brooklyn, NY: Kehot Publication Society, 1990), 2294.

CHAPTER 5

❦

LEARNING HOW TO LIVE:
PUBLIC EDUCATION AS SOCIAL REPAIR

5.1—Expanding the Scope of Education

IF THERE IS one thing that stands at the center of Schneerson's policy agenda it is his expansive concept of education. Education had been one of the identifying preoccupations of the Chabad movement from the outset. At the end of the 18th century and the beginning of the 19th century it was Schneur Zalman of Liadi's pedagogical project to make the mystical teachings of the Baal Shem Tov accessible to ordinary people that came to distinguish Chabad from other streams of Hasidism.[1] From the beginning of the 20th century Chabad's leaders prioritized Jewish education as the only means by which young people could be empowered and motivated to perpetuate Jewish life and learning in the new urban, and overwhelmingly secular, contexts that relegated traditional Shtetl life to the realm of nostalgia.[2] In this context too, the socio-mystical insight that is native to Chabad was given new expression in a formal philosophy of education.[3] For Schneerson, however, Chabad's theorization of education was to be expanded and applied in far more universal terms. Rightly conceived, he argued, education would provide the foundation for an all-encompassing

revision of social policy and social life in the United States and beyond. In his own words:

> Education, in general, should not be limited to the acquisi-
> tion of knowledge and preparation for a career, or, in common
> parlance, "to make a better living." We must think in terms of
> a "better living" not only for the individual, but also for the
> society as a whole.[4]

Schneerson's universalization of Chabad's educational ethos came
to the fore in 1978, when President Jimmy Carter acted upon a congressional resolution to declare Schneerson's 76th birthday "Education
Day, U.S.A."[5] The text of the resolution noted that "the Lubavitch
Movement...conducts educational activities at more than sixty centers
in twenty-eight States as well as around the world, [and] is especially committed to the advancement of education"; that "the head of the
worldwide Lubavitch Movement, Rabbi Menachem Mendel Schneerson," had a year earlier "proclaimed...a 'Year of Education'"; and that
in order to mark the year's conclusion, "be it resolved...to issue a proclamation designating April 18, 1978, as "Education Day, U.S.A."[6]

This declaration paid tribute to more than three decades of educational activism on Schneerson's part. But it also marked something of a
turning point, a shift in emphasis from the particular to the universal.

Ostensibly, the "Year of Education," and the "Education Campaign"
proclaimed by Schneerson in 1976, might be conceived as focusing on
the specific concerns of *Jewish* education—that is, as a merely quantitative intensification of the kind of activities that had most strongly
defined his agenda since his arrival in New York in 1941. At that time
his father-in-law had established the Center for Educational Affairs
(Merkos L'Inyonei Chinuch), appointing Schneerson its executive
director.[7] The latter would retain that post throughout his tenure
as Rebbe, and used the organization as the main vehicle through
which Chabad's institutional network was expanded across America
and internationally. Its publication division, Kehot Publication Society, produced everything from children's books and periodicals, to
scholarly editions on complex issues of Jewish law, to multi-volume
editions of the kabbalistic-Hasidic teachings of the successive Chabad
rebbes. Chabad's educational programs likewise went all the way

from preschool, through adulthood, to old age. For Schneerson, Jewish education was multitiered; extending from *aleph-bet*—the Jewish ABCs—to the most esoteric dimensions of Torah study.[8]

Yet, already in the 1940s the broader scope of his vision began to exhibit itself in Jewish Released Time, a program that allowed public school students to receive religious instruction during school hours, though not on school premises. This signaled Schneerson's interest in the role that religious education could—and, in his view, should—play in the American public sphere. In 1960 he dispatched a four-person delegation to the White House Conference on Children and Youth, where their recommendation that "children and youth be granted greater opportunities for specific religious education...including released time or dismissed time from public school" was endorsed.[9] A second proposal called for the proclamation of an "Annual Children and Youth Week, with a view to keeping alive the spirit, enthusiasm and sense of dedication to the high ideals and goals of the conference," and further "that the theme of such annual observance be 'Our Children Today—Our Nation Tomorrow.'" This recommendation was subsequently entered into the *Congressional Record* by Senator Kenneth Keating of New York, where it was further noted that:

> The proposal met with general acclaim. A number of leading national organizations have offered to cosponsor this recommendation. This proposal was submitted by...delegates of the Chabad (Lubavitch) movement headed by the world famous Rabbi Menachem M. Schneerson, known as the Lubavitcher Rebbe.[10]

Here we already see that Schneerson was not merely concerned with Jewish education, specifically, but also with the educational agenda of the American nation broadly conceived. The proposed theme, "Our Children Today—Our Nation Tomorrow," also hints at his underlying conception of the nature of education and its national purpose; it should be seen as a long-term investment and designed to fundamentally shape society as a whole. A decade later, when the Conference was next convened, a fuller memorandum of Lubavitch policy proposals was entered into the *Congressional Record* by Robert Giaimo, the Democratic Representative from Connecticut. It seems likely that his point of contact was one of Schneerson's emissaries to New Haven, Rivkah (Ruth) Hecht, or her husband, Moshe (Maurice), who came to Washington D.C. as members of the Lubavitch delegation.[11] In this memorandum we are given a sweeping overview of the movement's educational activities, and Schneerson's educational vision comes into sharper perspective:

> Lubavitch...operates schools for boys and girls (non-coed) and maintains youth activities and summer camps in various parts of the country, as well as in Canada and many other countries in Europe, North Africa, Israel, Australia, and South America...The Lubavitch delegates focused attention...on the need to foster moral, ethical, and spiritual values in child education. An educational system must have a soul. Children are not computers to be fed a mass of informational data, without regard for their human needs for higher goals and ideals in life.[12]

This reiterates the general principle that education is not simply about providing students with information and the tools to process it. Moreover, the specific items included in this memorandum further underscore Schneerson's expansive view of education as the provision of all the resources necessary for a child to develop as a healthy human being, both physically and psychologically, which can equally be understood to fall into the category of "human needs." Thus, education does not begin at the age when literary skills can be taught and learned, but rather from the first moments of infancy, and even earlier.[13] Likewise, it should not end with graduation from school or college, but must rather continue through every stage of life.[14] A further dimension of this is that children be provided with a sense of purpose and direction about *how to live*, that is, with the knowledge and means by which to direct themselves to "higher goals and ideals in life."[15]

As we have already seen, Schneerson wanted educational policy to be informed by the elemental insight that school does not merely equip children with the technical resources by which to successfully craft professional careers in adulthood. Much more importantly, school is the context in which children forge a concept of self; educators must therefore equip pupils with the requisite resources for the formation of a healthy identity. As has been argued elsewhere, when education does not attend to the provision of these needs a sense of alienation develops between one student and the next, and more so, between students and educators. Under such circumstances identity is not positively constructed, but emerges as a negative response that rushes in to fill the void. Under such circumstances identity becomes something that individuals must carve out for themselves; it is emptied of collectivity, indeed it sets the individual against society.[16] This is precisely the trend that Schneerson set himself to upend.

It is certainly easier and less complicated for policymakers and educators to ignore the fraught challenge of nurturing the identity and the spirit of individuals and of the collective, a challenge that requires a brave negotiation of the fault lines between diverse communities and philosophies, and, unavoidably, between the dogmas of science and religion more generally.[17] Yet, as we shall see, Schneerson took it for granted that to avoid this challenge is to abdicate an obligation that is automatically thrust upon anyone who takes up the mantle of educational responsibility.

In line with this more expansive conception of education, the proposals advanced by the Lubavitch delegation pay little attention to curricular matters. Instead they shift the emphasis to broader considerations, such as civic education (an understanding of the balance between upholding personal rights and those of others), family life (the right of a child to parental devotion and security), and teacher qualifications (to be determined not only based on professionalism but on the basis of personal moral attitudes and behavior as well). Moreover, from the holistic perspective advocated by Schneerson, education is not only for the young, but for adults as well. Keeping the focus on children, however, in this case a proposal was included for "adult education on the local community level, with emphasis on these values which would make adults better models for children."[18] This reflects Schneerson's assertion that pedagogs and adult authority figures don't merely teach in the formal sense, and that young people actually learn far more from observing and imitating the unconscious behaviors of those they look up to. Educational policy must therefore ensure that educators are not merely competent in their relevant subject areas, but also provide a living model to the young people in their sphere of influence.[19]

Aryeh Solomon, a scholar who has devoted a monograph to Schneerson's educational philosophy, wrote that Schneerson considered "education as critical to all aspects of life, to the universe as a whole and its perfection, as well as to facilitating the individual's fullest self-realization."[20] Solomon provides us with a near encyclopedic account of Schneerson's contributions to educational theory and his recommendations for pedagogical practice. Our purpose here, however, is at once broader and less ambitious. We want to place Schneerson's educational vision within the context of his larger intellectual and activist project for a revision of social policy in its totality. One of the most salient themes of the above memorandum, and a theme which Schneerson articulated on a constant basis, is that what is taught inside the classroom is but one aspect of education. In considering educational policy it is equally important to craft strategies that will transform the home, the streets, and the entire social context into an optimal environment for human development. Given these considerations, it is easy to see why Schneerson's concern with education is positioned as the underlying platform of his social policy outlook more generally.

As we have construed it, Schneerson's educational intervention is an essential dimension of the paradigmatic replacement of the secularized Protestant ethic with the new ethos of Hasidism. According to Weber, in "the rational and bureaucratic (modern) structure of domination" the "end" of education is simply "to impart specialized training."[21] From the new vantage point that is seen to arise in the case of Hasidism a compelling alternative is presented; pedagogy can be seen as initiatory and awakening, not simply for personal charisma (as it would be on the other side of the Weberian equation), but for interactive, imaginative divinization and as a method of social re-empowerment.[22] Put simply, education need not be a selfish endeavor; it can rather be directed to the greater betterment and re-enchantment of society and the world in the most inclusive sense. Schneerson sensed that the underlying religious principles of American democracy opened the United States to the possibility that such a model could succeed on a national scale. This brings us first to the still contentious question of how the collective fabric of civic society can be strengthened via the integration of spiritual and religious ideals into public education.

5.2—Non-Denominational Prayer and the Civic Utility of Religion

IN THE SECOND decade of Schneerson's tenure his concern with the role of religion in the education of the American nation was given concrete expression in his advocacy for non-denominational prayer in public school classrooms, a proposition that was ruled unconstitutional by the Supreme Court in the 1962 case of *Engel v. Vitale.* The case triggered a national debate that bears directly on the question of if and how religion can positively contribute to the construction of a shared sense of meaningful and aspirational nationhood without risking the exclusion of minorities and the oppression of outsiders. Other Jewish groups applauded the decision to declare government encouragement of non-denominational prayer illegal.[23] But Schneerson's secretariat publicized a letter in which he set out a systematic argument that such a response was gravely mistaken, not only from a Jewish perspective but from a constitutional one as well. In a word, he felt that this was a decision that ran contrary to the spirit of the American nation, contrary to the spirit of liberty and religious freedom that made America the secure bastion of hope against the global encroachment of atheistic and totalitarian communism. His framing of the issue distinctly conjures the spirit of the time:

> In our present day and age of rising tension and insecurity under the threat of a nuclear war; of the steadily growing might of communism...America has been blessed with hundreds of thousands of children, boys and girls, Jewish and gentile, throughout the width and breadth of these United States, who daily raise their youthful voices in prayer to God...With this image in mind, can anyone raise his hand to silence this vast body of American youth, saying: "Stop praising God! Stop praying to Him! It is forbidden to do so in the American Public School!"[24]

As we shall see below, what set Schneerson apart from the Jewish institutional establishment was his sense that the opportunity had arisen for the presiding Christian hegemony to be replaced by a more inclusive religious ethos with which Jewish, Muslim, and Christian

Americans could all identify.[25] But his approach to the issues also
intersects with the much larger question of the sway held by the Constitution over American political discourse. Schneerson was initially
unfazed by the Supreme Court declaration that the encouragement of
non-denominational prayer was unconstitutional:

> It is surprising to see that there are some people who are un-
> der the impression that inasmuch as the Supreme Court is
> the highest court in the land, its decision is final and there is
> nothing that should be done about it. Needless to say, this is
> not so, for the Constitution provides the ways and means of
> enacting or repealing laws, and of amending the Constitution
> itself. Constitutional ways and means can be found, should
> public opinion demand it, to rectify a situation. Indeed, this
> is one of the basic foundations of the democratic system of
> which this country is so justly proud.[26]

In a 1964 letter he would phrase the argument more pointedly:

> To oppose non-denominational prayer "on constitutional
> grounds" is, in my opinion, altogether a misunderstanding
> or misrepresentation of the problem. The issue is: Wheth-
> er a non-denominational prayer wherewith to inaugurate the
> school day is, or is not, in the best interests of the children. If
> the answer is "yes," then obviously it should be made consti-
> tutional, for there can be no difference of opinion as to the
> fact that the Constitution has been created to serve the peo-
> ple, not vice versa.[27]

Aside from its application to the specific question at hand, Schneerson's
comments here have a broader bearing on the question of how the Constitution is mediated by history and how it mediates debates about public
policy on an ongoing basis.[28] As has already been discussed, Schneerson
had high regard for the founding ideals of the United States, particularly emphasizing the central principle of religious freedom. Crucially, he
argued, interpreters of the Constitution must be attentive to the spirit in
which it was written, a spirit intended to encourage and enable—rather
than discourage and inhibit—the free practice of religion. It was their

conviction as to the centrality of religion in personal and public life that motivated them to protect it.[29] Schneerson certainly believed that the guiding spirit of the Constitution, in this case and in others, was to be embraced rather than ignored. He therefore warned that over-attentiveness to the specific wording of the law could sometimes run counter to its spirit. In the very same breath he also insisted that the Constitution was not immutable. In a case where statistics show that its laws result in a situation that is detrimental to the welfare of citizens constitutional principle itself demands that it be amended.[30]

Schneerson's view was essentially a pragmatic one; the Constitution was designed to serve the best interests of the people, and—as with all things—historical change has a way of introducing new situations and challenges that could not previously be anticipated. In this context Schneerson presented a simple illustration: "Suppose a person was ill at one time and doctors prescribed certain medication and treatment. Suppose that years later the same person became ill again, but with an entirely different, in fact quite contrary, malady. Would it be reasonable to recommend the same medication and treatment as formerly?"[31] The Constitution itself therefore provides (in Article Five) the ways and means by which it can be amended to better serve the people, providing new antidotes to new problems. In Schneerson's view this should not be seen as something that runs against the foundational spirit of the Constitution, but rather as an inbuilt mechanism by which its original religious, democratic, and pragmatic principles can best be upheld.

To date, the 1962 ruling against non-denominational prayer remains in place, and the Constitution has not been amended. Accordingly, during the 1980s Schneerson would begin a campaign to institute a daily moment of silence instead. What interests us for the moment, however, is his understanding of the relevance of prayer, and of religion more generally, to education and to the general betterment of society. To put it more straightforwardly, why indeed did he believe non-denominational prayer to be in the best interests of America's children?

This is precisely the question he addressed in the 1964 letter already cited:

> Non-denominational prayer, acknowledging the existence of a Creator and Master of the Universe, and our dependence upon Him…is absolutely necessary in order to impress upon

the minds of our growing-up generation that the world in
which they live is not a jungle, where brute force, cunning
and unbridled passion rule supreme, but that it has a Master
Who is not an abstraction, but a personal God; that this Supreme Being takes a "personal interest" in the affairs of each
and every individual, and to Him everyone is accountable for
one's daily conduct.[32]

Here we encounter the seminal principle that has already been
elaborated in the earlier chapters of this book, namely that the social
and spiritual realms cannot be bifurcated. Just as mystical experience
is fundamentally social in its constitution, so society itself can only
attain proper cohesion via the cultivation of a common sense that is
fundamentally mystical in its orientation. So long as our concept of the
social is limited to its horizontal dimension, its cohesion can only be
enforced superficially, from without. Only when the vertical dimension—an awareness of the divine dynamic at play within society—is
brought to the fore, can social cohesion flourish inherently and organ-
ically. Schneerson went on to argue that the social problems of the
day—among which he designated "juvenile delinquency" as "the tragic symptom of the disillusionment, insecurity, and confusion of the
young generation"—could not be remedied by means of merely superficial interventions, such as the deterrents provided by the police and
law-enforcing agencies. Instead, he argued:

> The remedy lies in removing the cause... It will not suffice to
> tell the juvenile delinquent that crime does not pay, and that
> he will eventually land in jail (if he is not smart enough). Nor
> will he be particularly impressed if he is admonished that
> law-breaking is an offense against society. It is necessary to
> engrave upon the child's mind the idea that any wrongdoing
> is an offense against the Divine authority and order... The
> crux of the problem lies in the success or failure of bringing
> up the children to an awareness of a Supreme Authority, who
> is not only to be feared, but also loved. Under existing con-
> ditions in this country, a daily prayer in the public schools is
> for a vast number of boys and girls the only opportunity of
> cultivating such an awareness.[33]

As we have already argued in earlier chapters, Schneerson did not seek to impose a particular religious creed, but to encourage the free cultivation of a personal and collective sense of beholdenness to God, and moreso a sense of partnership *with* God. Here we see that Schneerson viewed this as the most fundamental antidote to the social ills that continue to plague human societies the world over. In his view, criminal behavior should not be attributed primarily to secular economic factors or to the logistical problems associated with the enforcement of law and order. Criminality was rather to be seen as symptomatic of a deeper socio-spiritual problem, namely the "disillusionment, insecurity and confusion" to which young people in particular are prone. This was the root cause that needed to be addressed. For this reason, he believed, a responsible educational policy—one which indeed prioritized what was in the best interests of young people—would seek to implement strategies that would implant within them a sense of hope, security, and clarity. Given that the antonym of disillusionment is enchantment, we may posit that it was precisely a reenchantment of society that he wished to cultivate and inspire.[34]

For Schneerson, the most direct route by which such an antidote could be achieved was the provision of a daily opportunity for an encounter with God that was at once personal and collective. In making a short non-denominational prayer a part of the school day, rather than leaving it within the purview of the private sphere, children would be impressed with an axiomatic sense that the cultivation of a relationship with God should not be seen as a merely personal concern, but rather as integral to our collective success as a civic society. Schneerson re-enforced this argument with an appeal to the particular qualities of sincerity and receptivity with which children are endowed to a greater degree than adults. As he put it the same letter:

> The argument that a short non-denominational prayer would have no effect on the child reciting it could not be considered as a serious argument by anyone who has knowledge or experience in child education. On the contrary, the fact that prayer will be recited in the school and classroom, and day after day, will inevitably become an integral part of the child's thinking and is bound to be a factor which could be further cultivated to the child's advantage in terms of spiritual and psychological

development...Certainly a non-denominational prayer in the
public schools will not, in itself, provide an adequate basis for
the right and complete world-outlook, but it is an indispensable first step in this direction...[35]

Setting aside the question of whether or not it is possible to construct
a strong and unifying moral vision devoid of any theistic belief, from
an educational standpoint the more important question is whether a
non-theistic moral vision can easily be instilled in young people. While
some might view the theistic declaration of the non-denominational
prayer as overly simplistic, even naive, it is precisely that simplicity
that makes it so attractive from an educational perspective. It allows
for the cultivation of a basic sense of personal and collective moral beholdenness without recourse to complicated philosophical arguments
and investigations. Schneerson further argued that even though it is
indeed possible to arrive at a purely rational conclusion that murder
or theft, for example, are morally unacceptable, reason alone often
remains a purely cerebral exercise. For most people, well-reasoned argumentation is simply not compelling enough to entrench such moral
principles as axiomatic and inexorable convictions. The vice of self-
love, or of social pressure, can often prove more compelling. According
to Schneerson, a firm moral sensibility, along with a firm sense of identity, cohesion, and purpose, could best be cultivated through building
a much more basic socio-spiritual sense of our personal and collective
relation to God.[36]

To the very same degree that Schneerson argued for the civic util-
ity of religion, and that it be accorded its rightful place in the public
sphere, he also insisted that the principle of non-denominationalism be
rigorously upheld:

> As I have emphasized on more than one occasion, only a
> strictly non-denominational prayer, and no other, should
> be introduced into the public schools. Any denominational
> prayer or religious exercise in the public schools must be res-
> olutely opposed on various grounds, including also the fact
> that these would create divisiveness and ill-feeling. Likewise
> must Bible reading in the public schools be resolutely op-
> posed for various reasons, including the obvious reason that

the reading of the Koran and the New Testament will arouse dissension and strife.[37]

Schneerson's concern was to alleviate the problems of social disharmony, and he well understood that religious differences had the capacity to incite the very opposite effect. He wanted the American public sphere to transcend religious divisiveness without emptying it of religious content, cultivating instead the opportunity for children and adults of different faiths to comfortably share a collective sense of togetherness in the presence of God. A shared civic religiosity, he believed, would provide a firm basis for the amelioration of "disillusionment, insecurity, and confusion," and for the construction of a deeper sense of civic belonging, solidarity, and aspirationalism. In other words, he sought a non-denominational resacralization of society.

5.3—The Battle for an Independent Department of Education

As we have seen, Schneerson and his representatives were already pursuing a national policy agenda during the first decades of his leadership. Nevertheless, it was in 1978 that his more general theorization of the meaning and purpose of education began to come to its full articulation and realization, both in his own public talks and on the policymaking stage of Washington D.C. By the mid-to-late 1970s Schneerson had a more or less permanent representative in Washington, namely Abraham Shemtov, a Chabad rabbi based in Philadelphia who acted on behalf of Chabad institutions and of Schneerson personally in a variety of different ways. When he founded American Friends of Lubavitch in 1975 President Gerald Ford attended the ceremony.[38]

As Shemtov tells it, Senator Hubert Humphrey initiated the proposal to mark Schneerson's birthday with a national day dedicated to education. Another figure close to Shemtov was Stuart Eizenstat, then Carter's chief domestic policy adviser.[39] Eizenstat was deeply invested in an effort to raise the profile of education on the national agenda through the establishment of an independent Department of Education at the cabinet level.[40] Humphrey had long been one of the lone voices supporting the initiative in the Senate.[41] This was by no means a popular proposition. *The New York Times* led other mainstream newspapers in opposing it with an editorial titled "The High Price of Cheapening the Cabinet."[42] But it seems that Schneerson was recognized as an ally and an inspiration in this cause, and "Education Day, U.S.A." was one way to advance their shared agenda in the public eye. Indeed, it was precisely in April 1978 that the crucial decision on this question needed to be made by Carter. On the morning of the 14th he took the bold and unexpected step of endorsing the more transformative and ambitious of two options placed before him.[43] On the 17th he signed Proclamation 4562, which called on "all Americans" to observe the following day "in such manner as reflects their commitment to education and their recognition of its importance to the welfare of this Nation."[44]

In his Brooklyn synagogue Schneerson held a farbrengen to mark the occasion. Paying homage to the president's call he enjoined his listeners to treat it with the greatest seriousness and to think about their responsibility, both as individuals and as members of society, to advance the cause of education in the broadest terms. In doing so he set forth a theorization of educational responsibility according to which civic duty and religious duty are fundamentally intertwined due to the Jewish legal principle that "the law of the land is the law" (*Talmud bavli*, Gitin, 10b), and also by dint of the universal code delineated by Maimonides, which has the full weight of Jewish law.[45] Though education is not explicitly mentioned in that code, Schneerson is clear that one of its obvious implications is a mandate that "children should be educated to conduct themselves…to 'enact justice and law' (Genesis, 18:19) through just and good behavior, upon which the civilization of the world depends."[46] According to Schneerson, Torah law requires Jews to pay due attention to the nation's educational concerns, not merely in order to ensure that their own educational needs are met, but by dint of the religious obligation to uphold the law of the land and to advance the general cause of civilization.[47]

Schneerson went on to speak at length of the central role that education should play in U.S. policy, both in domestic affairs and in foreign affairs. As has already been noted, an abridged English version of this talk was published as an ad in *The Washington Post*, where it was read by President Carter. Several months later, Schneerson's words would be cited by Senator William Proxmire in support of his ongoing campaign for the ratification of the Genocide Convention:

Less than 5 months ago the U.S. Senate by unanimous vote proclaimed April 18 "Education Day-U.S.A." in honor of Rabbi Menachem M. Schneerson. At that time Rabbi Schneerson said:

> *Education must put greater emphasis on the promotion of fundamental human rights. Education, not to earn more money, but education for a better society. Education that builds character, that teaches moral and ethical values.*

Mr. President, I could not agree with Rabbi Schneerson more. For over 30 years this body has failed to ratify an important human rights treaty—the Genocide Convention—which seeks to guarantee the most basic of rights: the right to live...

Have we forgotten the context in which this treaty was drafted? Over 6 million Jews lie dead. The world, stunned by these brutal atrocities, resolved to take action. And they have. More than 80 countries across the world have ratified this human rights convention, including nearly all our allies. But what about the U.S. Senate? Why were we not in the forefront of this effort? Perhaps we need some re-education ourselves. We have prided ourselves on our prowess in science, technology, and business. But what about moral and ethical values?

Have they been sacrificed in the educational process?

I certainly hope not.

But Rabbi Schneerson has called attention to our need for constant vigilance. The type of vigilance that will continue our fine domestic record of respect for human rights. The type of vigilance that may someday give respect for human rights the primacy it deserves in our foreign affairs.

The type of vigilance, Mr. President, which demands the ratification of the Genocide Convention.[48]

On the domestic policy front Schneerson now threw his weight behind the effort to establish an independent Department of Education. We have already noted his agenda to raise the national status of education, and to expand the curriculum to include a greater emphasis on morality, ethics, and character building. In a memorandum circulated at the time Schneerson developed a far broader vision of the transformative impact that a new department could have, far beyond what happened inside the classroom. A central plank in Schneerson's platform, that we have failed to mention so far, was the call for the provision of more adequate salaries for teachers on a national scale. In his view this would lead to a whole raft of general improvements that would greatly enhance all aspects of the educational experience, and go a long way to rectifying many social ills that are not normally associated with education specifically:

> The quality of teaching—by qualified, dedicated and motivated teachers…requires the upgrading of teachers' salaries on par with comparable professions in other fields of science and relieving them, as far as possible, of other frustrations and stresses.
>
> The upgrading of the Nation's educational system will, of course, require considerable Federal spending. But this is one area where spending has built-in return, not only in the long term, but also in almost immediate gains, in terms of diminishing expenditures in the penal system, crime prevention, reduction in vandalism, drug abuse, etc. In the longer term it would also bring savings in expenditure on health and welfare, and—one may venture to say—even in the defense budget, since a morally healthy, strong and united nation is in itself a strong deterrent against any enemy.[49]

This is perhaps Schneerson's clearest and most definitive statement on how and why the federal government should prioritize education. In terms of "how," there is clear focus on ensuring that educators are given both the professional and financial resources necessary for them to dedicate themselves wholeheartedly to their students. In terms of "why," Schneerson argued that education is the transformative gateway through which many broader challenges can be overcome. Rather than patching the holes that appear as isolated ruptures in the fabric of society, a new focus on education would weave a stronger fabric that would be less likely to be eroded, whether from within or from without.

Schneerson also emphasized that such change could not be left in the hands of private groups, nor even to local officials. Of course, he acknowledged the need for "legislative safeguards to ensure the traditional primacy of States and localities in education affairs not be jeopardized," but argued that this did not undermine the fundamental value of raising the status of education on the national stage: "Such an enormous effort...can come only from the Federal government with the fullest cooperation of State, County and City." In his view, it should be emphasized, the need to create a separate Cabinet-level Department of Education was not merely due to technical reasons of administrative efficiency or coordination; the larger and more significant goal was "to breathe new life into the whole educational system of this Nation, and to involve the whole Nation, through its Federal government, in this massive and concerted effort."[50]

The stance taken by Schneerson stands in stark contrast to that taken by Christian organizations, which increasingly consolidated around a politically conservative platform. In April 1978 Carter had told the press that issuing tuition tax credits to parents who chose to send their children to private school would be "very detrimental to the future of education in our country," which went a long way to weakening his support among evangelicals and religious conservatives.[51] They likewise voiced concern that a Federal Department of Education would lead to increased governmental interference in the arena of religious education. In 1979 hard battles were fought in the Senate and House to introduce amendments aimed at upholding conservative values and undermining the anti-segregation and affirmative-action policies that were so important to Democratic legislators such as U.S. Representative Shirley Chisholm. It was clear, however, that their real purpose was to destroy the proposal entirely. Ultimately none of these amendments made it into the final version of the legislation that was voted into law in September 1979.[52]

In a public talk delivered in February 1979 Schneerson took note of these concerns, but dismissed them. He pointed out that Carter's plan, as reflected by the proposed legislation, placed primary responsibility for education on parents, and that "States, localities, and private institutions have the primary responsibility for supporting that parental role."[53] It was clear, in his view, that the function of the new department would not be to supplant those personal and local responsibilities but to better support public and private education alike, and he called upon his listeners to support the president's proposal in the strongest possible terms. Talking explicitly of recent deliberations in Congress and statements by the president, Schneerson, emphasized that:

It is also included in the proposals that…educational aid
and support should be provided not only to educational institutions that are connected to the Federal government, or
to local government at the State, County, or City level, but
also to private educational institutions…This also includes
education that is connected to religion, including Judaism,
Torah and mitzvot, in which it is forbidden for the government to interfere. In such affairs the only legislators are the
experts in religious matters, not merely experts in knowledge,
but rather people for whom religion defines their life and the
length of their days…Interfering therein is against the law.
But the law does allow that aid should be given to each individual who lives in this country, such that every Jew, from the
youngest to the oldest, should be able to live according to our
holy Torah—which is our life and the length of our days—
with the greatest scope, without any difficulties, and on the
contrary, with abundant provision…

Certainly one should advocate that the proposal…will be
brought into actual effect, and with greatest possible haste,
that additional aid shall be extended to the institutions of
education etc. One should not be intimidated by those who
immediately want to hinder. They want to cloak themselves
in a gown of piety, and argue that if aid will be provided by
the government this will hinder religious concerns, because
they will interfere in educational affairs. This is an old argument advanced by elders who have no relationship to wisdom;
not elders in the sense of "an elder who has acquired wisdom"
(*Talmud bavli*, Kidushin, 32b), but rather the kind of elders who
have the opposite of wisdom. Indeed, we see the actual reality
that we do receive aid from the government, and this does not
bring to interference in matters of religious education.[54]

How are we to understand Schneerson's claim that greater government involvement in the support and advancement of the nation's
educational needs will not lead to any interference in matters of
religious education? As we have already seen, his entire concept of education was that it should primarily serve to cultivate ethical and moral
character, indeed a personal and collective sense of beholdenness in

the presence of God. Equally, however, we have also seen that he was well aware of the conflicts that naturally arise between religion and state in the American public sphere. It is hard to imagine that someone as insightful and politically engaged as he could be blind to the real challenges that Jewish religious schools might later face if greater priority would be given to education at the federal level. Yet his comments on the issue are unequivocal. He did not merely argue that the minority concerns of religious groups should be set aside for the greater good of the nation as a whole. He argued that such concerns are old-fashioned, foolish, and simply erroneous.

It seems, however, that there are two basic considerations that inform Schneerson's position, both of which we have already encountered in more theoretical form. The first is his deep sense of the fundamentally religious character of the democratic institutions of the United States. Whatever tensions might ultimately arise between religion and democracy, their shared roots in the formative substance of the nation and its institutions ensure that one will never cancel the other out. The second is his equally deep conviction that when individuals or minority groups put the interest of the greater whole before their own they will never suffer as a result. If the nation as a whole is strengthened, its constituent groups will all be better provided with the resources and freedoms that they need to thrive. As Jan Feldman has put it, "it was his strong conviction that the Torah could not be at odds with the public good."[55] In other words, Schneerson's position on educational policy may well be an instantiation of his broader concept of reciprocity between self and community, as described in the previous chapter. Feldman adds that, as a result, "Lubavitch, which might otherwise be described in terms of special interest group politics, falls through the cracks of this model, at least at the national level."[56]

Be this as it may, the scope of Schneerson's educational activism certainly puts him in a class of his own. It would be difficult to find another public figure who advocated with equal passion both for non-denominational prayer and for the establishment of an independent Department of Education. This demonstrates that Schneerson's religious vision was not a narrow one, nor was it merely inclusive. Schneerson's religious vision was a fundamentally universal one, and a fundamentally educational one. Moreover, he believed that America was gifted with a combination of spiritual and material resources that could provide the requisite tools for collective spiritual enlightenment and collective social repair not only within its own borders, but throughout the world. Education, he argued, should be seen as the chief vehicle for all aspects of social and geopolitical progress. As he put it in his February 1979 talk:

> In every place where the influence of this nation reaches…the significance of education should be emphasized…Thereby…the entire world can become a place of civilization, and thereby are preempted all the undesirable occurrences that require wars to be waged, and instead energies are invested in good things.[57]

5.4—A Moment of Silence and Pedagogy's Post-Secular Horizon

IN 1981, WITH the election of Ronald Reagan to the presidency, the debate over the place of prayer in the public school system once again became an issue of national controversy. Reagan had long opposed the expansion of federal involvement in education, and had made a campaign promise to abolish the recently established Department of Education. On this issue, clearly, Schneerson and Reagan did not see eye-to-eye. But they did see eye-to-eye on the need to carve out a place for religion and the promotion of moral values in the public school system. For both this was a matter of religious freedom that went to the heart of what it meant to be "one Nation under God." For Schneerson, we must emphasize, this was equally a matter of educational principle as well.[58]

As has already been noted, Schneerson was never one to allow his policy positions to translate into partisan affiliation. In the period between the election and the inauguration Schneerson had explicitly called on the triumphant critics of Carter to recognize and be grateful for the good things he had done, and on the country as a whole to rally behind a shared national agenda under the leadership of the incoming president. At the same time he called on the president-elect to rise above his own partisan inclinations and take stock of what would be good for the nation as a whole.[59]

In May 1982 Reagan proposed an amendment to the Constitution that read "Nothing in this Constitution shall be construed to prohibit individual or group prayer in public schools or other public institutions. No person shall be required by the United States or by any state to participate in prayer." This amendment, it was hoped, would satisfy people on both sides of the issue, guaranteeing both freedom *of* religion and freedom *from* religion. Reagan's statement closely echoed the position set out by Schneerson in the 1960s:

> Just as Benjamin Franklin believed it was beneficial for the Constitutional Convention to begin each day's work with a prayer, I believe that it would be beneficial for our children to have an opportunity to begin each school day in the same manner. Since the law has been construed to prohibit this, I believe that the law should be changed. It is time for the people, through their Congress and the state legislatures, to act, using the means afforded them by the Constitution.[60]

While Schneerson vocally supported this amendment, he understood that it would be subject to much political debate, and might never be adopted. In the meantime he argued for the promotion of a daily moment of silence instead. Such a practice—bereft as it was of any content, religious or otherwise—had the potential to accrue support from a far wider cross-section of America's population. But Schneerson also argued that from an educational perspective it was in some respects *more* desirable than non-denominational prayer.

In a talk delivered in January 1983 Schneerson forcefully expressed his view that the introduction of a moment of silence had the capacity to open a whole new conversation not only about the nature and purpose of education, but also about the need for parents to engage themselves more deeply in educational activity and discourse. He lamented that the entire notion of education, and of parental responsibility, had by now been reduced to purely material concerns. This in turn was fueling an increased sense of selfishness and entitlement among young people, with obviously detrimental consequences for the future of society. The introduction of a moment of silence, he argued, had the potential to entirely change the face of America's educational ethos. From a broader vantage point this can be read as an implicit

argument that an injection of quasi Hasidic practices into public education could provide a much needed antidote to the consumerist culture
of the late capitalist era. For Schneerson, we will further argue, the
moment of silence initiative created an opening for a post-secular turn
in education.

What follows is his diagnosis of the problem:

> The actual situation in this country is that parents have no
> time—and even those who have the time do not have the
> patience—to invest themselves in the education of their chil-
> dren. They send the children off to public school, and along
> with them they send a good sandwich, or two sandwiches, and
> they even give them pocket money to buy whatever else they
> desire in addition to the sandwich…They sacrifice and bor-
> row money to buy their daughter another outfit, or to buy their
> son another toy, and they believe that thereby they have com-
> pletely fulfilled their parental obligation to their children…
>
> Meanwhile the child grows up indoctrinated with the na-
> tional ethos that "my own strength and the might of my hand
> have brought me this success"—that everyone is a "pioneer,"
> that everyone can turn the wilderness into a civilized city—
> with proof brought from the nation itself and from its history,
> the conclusion being that the child should also know that there
> is no one greater than he! Since he is a smart boy, and she is a
> smart girl, they will each use the knowledge taught to them
> in public school to achieve whatever they personally desire.[61]

What is striking here is the hairsbreadth of difference that so profoundly divides Schneerson's own view of the immense potential of
each individual from the one that he so bitingly decries. As we saw in
the previous chapter, Schneerson strongly encouraged and validated
the promotion of self-worth, of an entrenched faith that "in whatever
place and situation one might be found, one has the full capacity…to
strive and to attain the highest degree of completion, and also to
achieve the same for the entire world."[62] In his view, education absolutely should empower the student with the confidence to change the
world from a jungle, or wilderness, into a civilized and harmonious garden.[63] The problem he sees, however, is one of profound materialism,

entitlement, and self-centeredness, which is expressed in an utter lack of gratitude for the gifts and opportunities that one has been afforded; in a self-interest that subordinates everything to the all consuming impulses of "personal desire"; and in an utter disregard for the wants and needs of others, whether in one's immediate circle or in the wider strata of society. What Schneerson is diagnosing here is the social petrification predicted by Weber when he wrote of the increasing reduction of the American ethos to a mundane and competitive consumerism embellished with "convulsive self-importance."[64]

But Schneerson doesn't stop at a phenomenological description of the malady. He proposes a practical antidote as well:

> The solution is one that does not stand in contradiction to anything: If at the beginning of each day in public school, each and every child is told, "we will soon learn arithmetic, geography, and all other good things, indeed important things, which will enable you to succeed in the world and make a living, but first and foremost we give you a moment to be silent, and during that silence you should think about whatever your father and mother, or grandfather or grandmother, have instructed. They will tell you what to think about." This will provide a true beginning to the day, a beginning with blessing, so that afterwards the child will be blessed with the ability to utilize what he learns throughout the day in the best possible way, for himself, and at the same time in a manner that is good for the world. Indeed the priority will be reversed: First he will think about what is good for those around him, for the world, and only afterwards about what is good for him, to the point that his decisions reflect what is best for the world...
>
> The only thing that the principal or the teacher is allowed to say, and indeed should say, is that...this is not in order to let a moment go by and be wasted—one mustn't teach a child to let time go by to no end. The child must be taught to make full use of his time and his abilities. It must be explained to him that this silence is also a part of his education, and that it should therefore be used for a good thought, and that if he wants to know what the content of that good thought should be he should ask his father and mother. Additionally, this

> will awaken fathers and mothers around the country to be-
> come cognizant of their vital and foremost mission to raise
> a generation that is upright and blessed. This cannot be ful-
> ly accomplished by anyone else, nor does it simply require
> a helping hand [on the parents' part], rather it demands the
> heart and mind, the effort and the time...[65]

This excerpt from a much longer talk constitutes a withering critique of an American ethos that Schneerson felt had been emptied not
only of religious content, but of any sense of introspection or greater purpose. The intervention he proposed wasn't merely designed to
afford religious children an opportunity for silent prayer. More significantly, it was designed to engage the hearts and minds of children and
parents alike in a more reflective and considered approach to the entire educational endeavor. Irrespective of religious inclination, parents
would be awakened to the fact that they could not simply discharge
their responsibility by providing for the physical needs of their children. It was their primary duty, in fact, to nourish the moral and ethical
character of their children. They couldn't make do with the provision of sandwiches, clothes, and toys; they needed to provide food for
thought as well. The moment of silence initiative, in Schneerson's view,
had the capacity to transform the entire culture of American society,
beginning with a reframing of the way parents and children considered
and reconsidered the meaning and purpose of education.

Since the 1980s the moment of silence initiative has not been left
without controversy. But courts have ultimately upheld its constitu-
tionality on the grounds that there is no "excessive entanglement with
religion" since "students may think as they wish—and this thinking
can be purely religious in nature or purely secular in nature."[66]

Indeed, rather than thinking of Schneerson's moment of silence
advocacy as an expression of a conservative religious orientation, we
might to do better to think of it as heralding a progressive post-secular
turn. This does not simply mean that society must "adjust itself to the
continued presence of religious communities in an increasingly secularized environment," as Jürgen Habermas has put it.[67] In identifying
a post-secular turn we mean that the social environment is moving
beyond the axiomatic assumption of a secular, disenchanted status
quo. Instead, contemporary culture is increasingly open to processes

of reenchantment, particularly in the multifarious forms of "new-age" spirituality. Though in Schneerson's case "progressive religion" might be a more apt term, we would nevertheless argue that it anticipates the broader post-secular phenomenon.[68] Oren Ergas, a theorist of education and mindfulness, has written that post-secular society "is reflected in a continuous blurring of dualistic categories" such as "science/religion, spirituality/secularity, body/mind, self/society." He further posits that "contemplative practices incorporated in education" can be seen as "bearing the potential of healing these traditional rivalries and hierarchies."[69] Indeed, the very notion that a personal moment of silence can become both a collective social practice and a vehicle for far-reaching social healing is an overcoming of the old assumption that to take the road of contemplation is to retreat from society.[70]

Among the features that separate old forms of religious conservatism from new-age spirituality is the replacement of hierarchical dogmatism with a more pragmatic emphasis on personal practice and conviction. As discussed earlier, in Chapter 3, Naftali Loewenthal has described the Chabad tradition of education and communication as taking the radical step of questioning all the axioms of religion, albeit in order to uphold them.[71] Above we paid particular attention to the farbrengen as a communicative practice that—at least in its more radical forms—encourages the fullest degree of openness and interaction, granting complete agency and empowerment to the student. Here we add that it is precisely this kind of openness that the moment of silence provides. The teacher's role here, as described by Schneerson, is not to fill the silence with educational information, but rather to empower the students to go beyond all the normative axioms of education and find their own ways to make good use of an educational opportunity of an entirely different sort.

Loewenthal has argued elsewhere that Schneerson's advocacy for a moment of silence can also be interpreted as a universalization of the practice of contemplative prayer, which has been a central plank of Chabad worship and pedagogy since the movement's earliest period.[72] This is a suggestion that aligns well with our broader argument that Hasidism advances a system of socially embodied practices that can provide a compelling alternative to the iron cage of capitalism.

The prescience of Schneerson's vision is demonstrated in the explosion of interest in the incorporation of mindfulness and meditation practices within educational curricula, including within U.S. public schools. Ergas has documented and analyzed this phenomenon, and observes that the discourse around justifying such innovation draws on the traditional scientific axis of the "economic-rational-secular" conception of education, but also seeks to advance a new concept of education that looks to ancient wisdom-traditions (whether Buddhist, Native American, Monotheistic, etc.) as a critical source for rethinking what education is meant to achieve. In Ergas' term these two approaches are respectively labeled "in-the-box" and "out-of-the-box." The former entails a secularization of contemplative praxis, the later a resacralization of education. He also shows that in many cases the rhetoric attempts to walk between both approaches, which "creates a novel situation in which science and wisdom-traditions...those notorious historical rivals, find themselves peculiarly collaborating...towards a shared mission of rejuvenating education."[73] This echoes Schneerson's own words in a 1984 talk advocating for the moment of silence initiative: "It can be implemented without any bitter feelings because it will not mean that one side of society has been victorious and the other has lost; this is something that everyone can agree to."[74] Following Ergas, this itself is an instantiation of the blurring of the secular and the sacred in post-secular society.

"The main thing about schools," it has been noted elsewhere, "is that they are one of a very few remaining public interactional spaces in which people are still engaged with each other in the reciprocal, though organizationally patterned, labor of producing meaning—indeed, the core meaning of self identity."[75] In other words, it is first and foremost in the public schools that cultural meaning and self-identity can most effectively be cultivated on a national scale. As we have seen, this was something that Schneerson recognized from the earliest period of his tenure, and this explains why he campaigned with such tenacity against the utter secularization of these institutions and the utter commodification of their pedagogical agendas. He understood that in the unyielding quest to fill the minds of children with "useful" knowledge we run the risk of emptying their lives of moral aspirations and meaning. In advocating for a moment of silence, he was advocating for a radical shift in the basic conception of educational purpose and pedagogical technique. In a word, education should not be about learning how to make money. Education should be about learning how to live, how to orientate oneself in the world, and how to orientate oneself toward others. Such is the post-secular horizon of pedagogy.

Notes

1. See Naftali Loewenthal, *Communicating the Infinite: The Emergence of the Habad School* (Chicago: Chicago University Press, 1990), esp. 4-6; Immanuel Etkes, *Rabbi Shneur Zalman of Liady: The Origins of Chabad Hasidism* (Waltham, MA: Brandeis University Press, 2015), 27-38, 59-60, 93-96.

2. See Naftali Brawer, *Resistance and Response to Change: The Leadership of Rabbi Shalom DovBer Schneersohn (1860-1920)* (PhD thesis, University College London, 2004), 182-284. Also see the relevant discussion in Eli Rubin, "A Linguistic Bridge Between Alienation and Intimacy: Habad's Theorization of Yiddish in Historical and Cultural Perspective," *In Geveb: A Journal of Yiddish Studies* (forthcoming).

3. See Shalom DovBer Schneersohn, Kuntras ets hachayim (Brooklyn, NY: Kehot Publication Society, 1946); Yosef Yitzchak Schneersohn, "Klalai hachinukh vehahadrakhah," appendix to idem., *Sefer hasichot 5703* (Brooklyn, NY: Kehot Publication Society, 1986), 205-230.

4. "Excerpts from Address by Rabbi Menachem M. Schneerson, The Lubavitcher Rebbe, שליט"א, Nissan 11, 5738—April 18, 1978" in *Report on "Education Day—U.S.A." Legislation* (Brooklyn, NY: Merkos L'Inyonei Chinuch, 1979), 11.

5. Proclamation 4562, April 17, 1978, <https://www.govinfo.gov/content/pkg/STATUTE-92/pdf/STATUTE-92-Pg3923.pdf>.

6. H.J. Res. 770, Public Law 95-262, 95th Congress, <https://www.govinfo.gov/content/pkg/STATUTE-92/pdf/STATUTE-92-Pg200.pdf>. A facsimile of the original resolution—complete with the signatures of the Speaker of the House, the vice president, and the president—was published in *Report on "Education Day—U.S.A." Legislation*, 7.

7. See Shalom DovBer Levine, *Toldot chabad be'artsot habrit* (Brooklyn, NY: Kehot Publication Society, 1988), 271.

8. *Ibid.*, 271-319; Zushe Wolf, *Hotsa'at seforim kehot: toldot hotsa'at hasefarim hachabadit* (Brooklyn, NY: Kehot Publication Society, 2013).

9. *Conference Proceedings: Golden Anniversary White House Conference on Children and Youth*, March 27–April 2, 1960, Washington D.C. (Golden Anniversary White House Conference on Children and Youth, Inc., 1960), 194. For an internal report on their activities by the Lubavitch delegates see <https://www.collive.com/show_news.rtx?id=49984>.

10. *Congressional Record*, Volume 106, Part 6, April 4, 1960, 7198-7199.

11. On Rivkah Hecht, her life, and her educational career, see David Zaklikowski, "Northeastern Matriarch of Jewish Education Passes Away at 91," *Chabad.org*, <chabad.org/1251764>.

12. Cong. Rec. - Volume 116, Part 33, December 28, 1970, 43738.

13. For one articulation of this position see Menachem Mendel Schneerson, *Sichot Kodesh 5738*, Vol. 2 (Brooklyn, NY: Vaad Hanachot Hatemimim, 1986), 127: "Education of boys and girls—which is ultimately reflected in the private home…and in the collective 'home'—…begins in the earliest phase of a child's life…"

14. For one articulation of this view of Schneerson's see *Sichot kodesh 5739*, Vol. 2, 20: "We should not in any way neglect the education of adults, nor even that of people who have acquired great knowledge, for no one is complete, except One [i.e. God]. However much one has grown in quantitative terms one must always grow closer to true completeness."

15. See *Report on "Education Day—U.S.A." Legislation* (Brooklyn, NY: Merkos L'Inyonei Chinuch, 1979), 4: "It is insufficient that education merely impart knowledge, for it must also teach mankind *how to live*." Emphasis in the original.

16. Philip Wexler, et al., *Becoming Somebody: Toward a Social Psychology of School* (London and Washington D.C.: The Falmer Press, 1992).

17. For a relevant case study and an extensive theorization of how these fault lines might be negotiated, see Shlomo Fischer, Yotam Hotam, and Philip Wexler, "Democracy and Education in Postsecular Society," *Review of Research in Education* 36, no. 1 (2012): 261-281. Schneerson's American project, as described below, provides a rather different case study, demonstrating the elasticity of the post-secular phenomenon and its various manifestations. With particular reference to the case of Lubavitchers in the United States and Canada, and for a more ethnographic perspective, see Jan Feldman, *Lubavitchers as Citizens: A Paradox of Liberal Democracy* (Ithaca and London: Cornell University Press, 2003).

18. *Congressional Record*, Volume 106, Part 6, April 4, 1960, 7198-7199.

19. For one example of Schneerson's articulation of this point see Menachem Mendel Schneerson, *Sichot kodesh 5738*, Vol. 2 (Brooklyn, NY: Vaad Hanachot Hatemimim, 1986), 120: "The greatest impression of a child is not when one suffices with speech alone…the main effect is when the child sees an action practiced by the instructor or guide that demonstrates how one must act in actuality." For a fuller discussion of the theory and practice of such an approach to education as informed by the teachings of Schneerson and his predecessors see Rivkah Slonim, "Education as Life: Reflections from the Field by a Chabad Shlucha on a College Campus," in *Jewish Spirituality and Social Transformation*, edited by Philip Wexler (New York: Herder and Herder, 2019), 113-124.

20. Aryeh Solomon, *Spiritual Education: The Educational Theory and Practice of the Lubavitcher Rebbe Rabbi Menachem M. Schneerson* (New York: Herder and Herder, 2019).

21. Max Weber, *Essays in Sociology*, trans. H.H. Gerth and C. Wright Mills (New York: Oxford University Press, 1946), 426.

22. Fischer, Hotam, and Wexler, "Democracy and Education," esp. 276-27.

23. Indeed two of the plaintiffs, Steven I. Engel and Lawrence Roth, who brought the case against school board president William J. Vitale, Jr., were Jewish. See Susan D. Gold, *Engel v. Vitale: Prayer in the Schools* (Tarrytown, NY: Marshall Cavendish Benchmark, 2006). The American Jewish Committee, B'nai B'rith, and the Synagogue Council of America, among other organizations, filed briefs in support of the plaintiffs.

24. "Excerpt from the Lubavitcher Rabbi's שליט״א Letter on the Question of the Regents Prayer," *Chabad.org*, <chabad.org/1274011>.

25. Relatedly, Ari Goldman, a journalism professor at Columbia University and a former religion reporter for *The New York Times,* recalled that Schneerson once read an article of his in which he used the term "Judeo-Christian values" and asked his secretary to call Goldman and relay some critical feedback: "Why do you only write about Jews and Christians? It's really Judeo-Christian-Muslim values." See Ari Goldman, "Message for the World," *Chabad.org*, <chabad.org/3482592>.

26. *Ibid.*

27. "Prayer in Public Schools and Separation of Church and State," *Chabad.org*, <chabad.org/2051611>.

28. See Jack N. Rakove (ed.), *Interpreting the Constitution: The Debate over Original Intent* (Boston: Northeastern University Press, 1990).

29. This is a view that Schneerson would reiterate many times throughout the decades of his leadership. See, for example, Menachem Mendel Schneerson, *Sichot Kodesh 5735*, Vol. 1, 330 (quoted above, in Chapter 2). For a review of the vast literature on the tension in the Constitution between the establishment clause and the free exercise clause see Alan Schwarz, "No Imposition of Religion: The Establishment Clause Value," *The Yale Law Journal* 77, no. 4 (1968): 692-737.

30. This point was more fully elaborated in a talk delivered on January 24, 1983, viewable at "A Moment to Save the World—Part 3," *Chabad.org*, <chabad.org/443372>.

31. "Prayer in Public Schools and Separation of Church and State," *Chabad.org*, <chabad.org/2051611>.

32. *Ibid.*

33. *Ibid.*

34. The idea that Schneerson's approach to education and social transformation can be seen as heralding the post-secular turn in society will be returned to, and more fully developed, at the end of the present chapter.

35. "Prayer in Public Schools and Separation of Church and State," *Chabad.org*, <chabad.org/2051611>. Also see the relevant comments in "Excerpt from the Lubavitcher Rabbi's שליט״א Letter on the Question of the Regents Prayer."

36. These points were more fully elaborated in a talk delivered on January 24, 1983, viewable at "A Moment to Save the World—Part 1," *Chabad.org*, <chabad .org/433702>.

37. "Prayer in Public Schools and Separation of Church and State," *Chabad.org*, <chabad.org/2051611>.

38. For his remarks on that occasion, at which Senator Hugh Scott was honored, see *Public Papers of the Presidents of the United States: Gerald R. Ford, 1975—January 1 to July 20, 1975* (Washington D.C.: United States Government Printing Office, 1977), 684-685. Also see Dovid Zaklikowski, "The Rebbe and President Ford," *Chabad.org*, <chabad.org/461848>.

39. On Shemtov and his relationship with Humphrey and Eizenstat, as well as other leading political figures, see Sue Fishkoff, *The Rebbe's Army: Inside the World of Chabad-Lubavitch* (New York: Schocken Books, 2003), 193. An audio recording of

Shemtov's account to a gathering organized by Chabad Youth Organization in New York in the Autumn of 1978 was made available to the authors.

40. For a full account of this effort, from inception to implementation, see Beryl A. Radin and Willis D. Hawley, *The Politics of Federal Reorganization: Creating the U.S. Department of Education* (New York: Pergamon Press, 1988).

41. *Ibid.*, 24.

42. *The New York Times*, Jan. 16, 1978.

43. *Ibid.*, 109: "At 7:30 a.m. the morning of the 14th...high level PRP (President's Reorganization Project) staff met with Carter...they were told to...present an argument for the broader department of education...Not surprisingly, the entire PRP...was flabbergasted. Speculation abounded about the reasons for the Carter decision—a decision that appears to have been his..."

44. Proclamation 4562, April 17, 1978, <https://www.govinfo.gov/content/pkg/STATUTE-92/pdf/STATUTE-92-Pg3923.pdf>.

45. Maimonides, *Mishneh torah*, Hilkhot malakhim, 8:11, 9.

46. Menachem Mendel Schneerson, *Sichot kodesh 5738*, Vol. 2 (Brooklyn, NY: Vaad Hanachot Hatemimim, 1986), 119-120.

47. *Ibid.*, 126-127.

48. *Congressional Record*, Volume 124, Part 22, Sept. 13, 1978, 29092.

49. "Excerpt from a Letter by the Rebbe שליט״א on the Proposed Creation of a Special Department of Education," in *Report on "Education Day—U.S.A." Legislation*, 18-19.

50. *Ibid.*

51. "Tuition Tax Credits: Reality and Illusion," April 22, 1978, *The Washington Post*, retrieved from <https://search.proquest.com/docview/146858868?accountid=14511>.

52. For a full account of the legislative battles see Logan Michael Scisco, *Vanguard of the Right: The Department of Education Battle, 1978-1979* (master's thesis, Western Kentucky University, 2014), 56-57 and 91-99.

53. *Department of Education Organization Act* [Public Law 96–88, Approved Oct. 17, 1979, 93 Stat 669], Sec. 101.

54. Menachem Mendel Schneerson, *Sichot kodesh 5739*, Vol. 2 (Brooklyn, NY: Vaad Hanachot Hatemimim, 1986), 13-18.

55. Feldman, *Lubavitchers as Citizens*, 47.

56. *Ibid.*

57. Menachem Mendel Schneerson, *Sichot kodesh 5739*, Vol. 2, 16-17.

58. On Reagan's opposition to the Carter innovations see Gareth Davis, *See Government Grow: Education Politics from Johnson to Reagan* (Lawrence: University Press of Kansas, 2007), esp. 247.

59. Menachem Mendel Schneerson, *Sichot kodesh 5741*, Vol. 2 (Brooklyn, NY: Vaad Hanachot Hatemimim, 1986), 168 and on: "In contrast to the opinion of the erroneous people who, when they see that someone has been brought down from their office take advantage of the opportunity to pour additional pain upon them, to the extent that they even overlook that person's merits and the good things that

they said and did—this is the opposite of the teaching of the Torah: 'When you judge a person there you must mention the good things he has done.' [Cf. Rashi's gloss to *Talmud bavli*, 78b, following Zephaniah, 2:3.]…Thereby one fulfils the mission God has given you in the world to add good in the world…though some might say that it isn't politically expedient to extend thanks to someone who has descended from office with someone else taking their place…" We should further note that in the very same talk Schneerson also made it clear that he did not regret his disagreements with Carter on certain policy issues, and went so far as to reiterate his criticism in order that no mistake should be made.

60. *Congressional Record*, Volume 128, Part 8, May 17, 1982, 10230.

61. Menachem Mendel Schneerson, "A Moment to Save the World—Part 2: 10 Shevat, 5743 • January 24, 1983," *Chabad.org*, <chabad.org/433707>.

62. Menachem Mendel Schneerson, *Igrot kodesh*, Vol. 23 (Brooklyn, NY: Kehot Publication Society: 1994), 268-269. Cited above, Chapter 4.

63. Menachem Mendel Schneerson, ""I Have Come to My Garden"—Part 1: 10 Shevat, 5746 · January 20, 1986," *Chabad.org*, <chabad.org/618969>; *idem.*, "This World Is Not a Jungle: Farbrengen, 12 Tammuz, 5743 • July 23, 1983," *Chabad.org*, <chabad.org/217047>.

64. Max Weber, *The Protestant Ethic and the Spirit of Capitalism*, translated by Talcott Parsons (New York and London: Charles Scribner's Sons / George Allen & Unwin Ltd., 1950), 182.

65. "A Moment to Save the World—Part 2: 10 Shevat, 5743 • January 24, 1983," Chabad.org, <chabad.org/433707>.

66. See Dennis Kurzon, "A Pragmatic Analysis of Silence in an American Constitutional Issue," *Lodz Papers in Pragmatics* 6, no. 1 (2010): 63. Also see Mary Ellen Quinn Johnson, "School Prayer and the Constitution: Silence Is Golden," *Maryland Law Review* 48, no. 6 (1989): 1018-1044.

67. Jürgen Habermas, *Glauben und Wissen* (Frankfurt: Suhrkamp, 2001), 13.

68. For a fuller elaboration of what we mean when we refer to the post-secular turn see Philip Wexler and Yotam Hotam, "Introduction" to *New Social Foundations for Education: Education in "Post Secular" Society*, edited by Wexler and Hotam (New York: Peter Lang, 2015), 6-8.

69. Oren Ergas, "The Post-Secular Rhetoric of Contemplative Practice in the Public Curriculum," in Wexler and Hotam, *New Social Foundations for Education*, 107-108.

70. See the relevant discussion above, Chapter 3.

71. Naftali Loewenthal, "Hasidism and Modernity: The Case of Habad," *Proceedings of the World Congress of Jewish Studies* 11C(2) (1993): 111-113.

72. Naftali Loewenthal, "Chassidic Prayer and Society," in *Jewish Spirituality and Social Transformation*, edited by Philip Wexler (New York: Herder and Herder, 2019), 81-98.

73. Oren Ergas, "Post-Secular Rhetoric," 107-128.

74. Menachem Mendel Schneerson, "Food for Thought: A Moment of Silence," *Chabad.org*, <chabad.org/3961926>.

75. Wexler, *Becoming Somebody*, 10.

CHAPTER 6

⚬〰〰⚬

SOCIO-MYSTICAL JUSTICE, HUMANISM, AND ECOLOGY

6.1—Affluence, Crime, and the Possibility of an Educational Antidote

Just two months after Ronald Reagan's January 1981 inuguration as the 40th president of the United States, he was struck by the bullet of a would-be assassin. By the 15th of April he had been released from George Washington University Hospital and was convalescing in the White House residence. From there a telegram communicated the president's wishes of "a very Happy Seventy-Ninth Birthday" to Rabbi Menachem Mendel Schneerson, together with "deep-felt respect and admiration." Reagan described the Chabad leader's "dedication and devotion to the spiritual and intellectual well-being of the Jewish people" as "an inspiration to all Americans."[1] That evening, at a public farbrengen, Schneerson spoke of the extraordinary reciprocal obligation imposed by the unique circumstances under which this telegram was sent and received:

> If there is a requirement to extend gratitude to everyone, it is all
> the more so appropriate to reciprocate the blessings extended
> by the President of the United States, and even more so when

179

we bear in mind his personal situation, and the condition of
his health in the most literal sense... This [attempt on his life]
is something that should never have occurred, something that
is entirely incomprehensible... But, nevertheless it did occur,
and with supernal kindness he will be entirely healed, speed-
ily and completely. Yet, even before that complete recovery he
expressed his good wishes... Certainly the obligation of reciprocal appreciation is, therefore, many times greater. He is a
person upon whom the public relies, and because "the hearts
of kings and princes are in the hands of God" (cf. Proverbs,
21:1), through him God's will is fulfilled for the public good, including the good of the country's Jewish citizens as well as all
the others who live here. He therefore especially deserves... a
blessing of superlative greatness... which is hereby extended
enthusiastically and wholeheartedly.[2]

Yet Schneerson was not content to offer good wishes, however ef-
fusive. Characteristically, he emphasized the need to use this negative
episode as an opportunity for constructive reflection that would lead to
positive action. Specifically, Schneerson dwelled on the responsibility
incumbent on the new occupant of the presidential office to consider the
welfare of the nation as a diverse whole, and also to take a hard look at
the cultural mores and social circumstances that might have inspired so
criminal and deranged an act as an attempt on the life of the president.

Much of the talk that follows reads as a thinly veiled critique of
Reagan's economic and social agenda, which sought to scale down government investment in healthcare and welfare programs while cutting
taxes for the wealthy. Reacting against the legacy of the Great Society
project of the 1960s, Reagan and his allies saw the social safety net as
well-intentioned but utterly misguided. Rather than ameliorating the
problems of poverty and crime, they argued, it actually encouraged
irresponsibility and prevented the poor from bettering their financial and moral situation. In their eyes, government would do better by
contributing less to the collective, thus allowing individuals to more
freely prosper both materially and morally.[3] Schneerson, by contrast,
emphasized that individual and collective welfare should not be seen
as standing in competition with one another, and that the presidential
mandate is not based solely on the interests of those who voted for him,

but must rather represent the interests of the entire spectrum of individuals and peoples who make up the nation as a whole. This critique, however, is offered in the gentlest of terms, fully in harmony with a sincere expression of prayerful hope and blessing for Reagan's speedy and complete recovery:

> A speedy and complete recovery leads to something that is not only also important, but actually comes hand in hand with it, namely the possibility to use the opportunities, capacities, and powers given to an individual elected by the entire nation. This is especially so in the case of a nation in which there are many peoples who all come together in accord with the majority opinion, such that the minority accept the democratic result and accept him as their President and representative in all their affairs, whether internationally or domestically. He should use this mandate to its full for the benefit of the collective and for the benefit of the individual. As emphasized in the Torah: While "the ruling follows the majority" (Exodus, 23:2; *Mishnah*, Sanhedrin, 1:6) each individual nevertheless remains "in place" and is not effaced[4]... This can be achieved in such a manner such that—not only will there be no contradiction between the benefit of the collective and the benefit of the individual, but on the contrary—each of these complement the other, achieving wholeness both for the individual and for the collective, a wholeness that also impacts the wholeness of the entire world...[5]

The basic message here is certainly characteristic of Schneerson's rhetoric. Yet given the specificity of the context it is difficult to dismiss this as anything less than a call for Reagan to use his convalescence as an opportunity to reconsider some of the most salient elements of the policy platform on which he had been elected. Watching and listening to the video recording of the talk, this impression is sharpened as Schneerson launches into a passionate analysis of the root social problems that led John Hinckley Jr. to attempt such a reckless crime.[6]

In the immediate aftermath of the shooting, *The New York Times* reported that Hinckley was "the youngest of the three children of a prosperous oilman," who "had grown up in a luxurious home and

attended perhaps the most elite public high school in Dallas." This
privileged background, however, did not set him up for success. He
never completed college or held a job. Having read Hitler's *Mein Kampf*
he tried to join the American Nazi Party. Infatuated with a teenage ac-
tress, he sought to win her respect by what he termed "this historical
deed" of killing the president.[7] His defense team would successfully
argue that this infatuation was symptomatic of insanity.[8] In the days
and weeks following the shooting, the entire nation struggled to come
to terms with how it had happened and what it said about the state of
American society. On April 5th a headline in the *Times* editorial section
read: "The Symptoms Surround Us, But What Is the Malady?"[9]

Schneerson's analysis cut through the confused din of the media
discourse like a knife:

> It is very painful that while all kinds of issues are considered
> concerning how to prevent such an occurrence from transpir-
> ing in the future, these considerations are all concerned with
> how to address the consequences—or, in English, "the symp-
> toms." No one is considering how to correct the fundamental
> ethos, the approach that resulted in these consequences.[10]

For Schneerson, as we have already seen, America's social malady
was a materialistic purposelessness rooted in the secularization of education. In this talk, in addition to focusing on the centrality of education,
Schneerson also offered a forceful argument that such materialistic purposelessness is especially encouraged by prosperity and the entitlement
it breeds. The children of the wealthy, he said, are not only raised without faith in God and without a sense of social purpose, they are also
pampered and applauded by parents who have otherwise abdicated all
educational responsibility. The only thing that is nourished is their egotistical sense of entitlement. Hinckley was a case in point. Accordingly,
Schneerson framed the attempt on Reagan's life as a resounding rebut-
tal of the still popular narrative that blames social problems on the lazy
and embittered inclinations of the poorer sectors of society:

> The normative argument, that the root of undesirable actions
> is related to poverty, is well known. Since he is poor [the argu-
> ment goes] he becomes embittered, and embitterment brings

vengefulness, which ultimately leads to undesirable actions. But we see in actuality that this perpetrator [i.e. Hinckley] was not born to a poor family. On the contrary, he grew up the son of a wealthy man, "never did his father rebuke him" (Kings I, 1:6), and it seem like nothing was ever withheld from him.

If you think that undesirable actions are related to poverty, this event emphasizes that we need to seek the root of such conduct not in poverty, but somewhere else entirely. This only reinforces the fact that—entirely independent of this event—the claim that the root of undesirable actions is related to poverty is entirely contrary to what the Torah tells us... The Torah tells us, "take care of the sons of paupers, as it is from them that the Torah will issue forth" (*Talmud bavli*, Nedarim, 81a)... When the sons of paupers receive a fit education, on the contrary, the very fact that they are poor and find themselves in an underprivileged situation... inspires them to invest greater effort and to strive. Thereby they ultimately stand higher in all aspects of goodness, kindness and justice when compared to those who find themselves in... an intermediate situation, or even in a prosperous situation...

For children of the poor to obtain the means to commit a crime they must first go through all kinds of steps to obtain money, and to attain the brazenness to act just as they desire without any inhibition. Whereas for children of the wealthy, whose parents have thrown away the entire responsibility of building up the faith of their children... [and who] give their children whatever they desire, always patting them on the back... the result is precisely what occurred [in the case of Hinckley]... He wasn't lacking any money. He was able to buy weapons, and his education was corrupted; corrupted because it was built on the foundation that "my own strength and the might of my own hand brought me this success" (Deuteronomy, 8:17).[11]

These passages present a clear critique of the Reaganesque social paradigm. The poor, Schneerson argued, are not inclined to abuse the aid they are given. On the contrary, they are motivated to utilize any opportunity to better their situation to the fullest degree. Therefore—if only they are given due care—they are actually likely to outpace the achievements of wealthier peers "in all aspects of goodness, kindness and justice." This argument is particularly noteworthy when set within the debates that were ongoing at that time among sociologists, economists, criminologists, and political scientists, and which are still ongoing in popular discourse.

In 1979 Lawrence E. Cohen and Marcus Felson coauthored an article in the *American Sociological Review* that fundamentally changed the way scholars have since thought about the causes of crime. Cohen and Felson showed that even as income levels rose throughout the 1960s and '70s, crime rates continued to rise. Poverty could no longer be seen as a direct correlate, much less a direct cause, of criminal activity. Instead a more complex theory was proposed: Crime was largely situational, or opportunistic, resulting from the convergence of "three minimal elements: (1) motivated offenders, (2) suitable targets, and (3) the absence of capable guardians against a violation." Cohen and Felson concluded their initial paper on what is now termed "routine activity theory" with the suggestion that "the very factors that increase the opportunity to enjoy the benefits of life may increase the opportunity for predatory violations. For example, automobiles provide freedom of movement to offenders as well as average citizens." Affluence, in other words, increases all forms of opportunity, including criminal opportunities.[12]

Tangentially, an antecedent to the routine activity theory of crime can be discerned in Schneur Zalman of Liadi's pronouncement that the reason we are enjoined, "do not judge your fellow until you reach his place" (*Mishnah*, Avot, 2:4) is because it is a person's "place," meaning the particular circumstances within which they alone find themselves, "that causes them to sin."[13] In modern criminological terms: "Variations in individuals' routines of life—traveling to and from work, school, or religious institutions; shopping; recreating; communicating via various electronic technologies; and so forth—determine the likelihood of when and where criminal events occur."[14] What is notable, however, is that the formalization of this theory in 1979 met the need to explain the correlation between affluence and crime, which is precisely the issue highlighted by Schneerson in his 1981 talk.

The assumption that crime should be blamed on poverty, or worse, on the poor, has now been further undermined as scholars are increasingly aware of the inherent bias ensconced in a conception of crime that

is confined to violence, property theft or vandalism, and delinquency (street crime). Domestic and financial crimes, conversely, as well
as abuses of power by police and elected officials, are underreported,
understudied, and usually ignored in statistical surveys. Consequently,
researchers have overwhelmingly overlooked the ways in which affluence contributes to criminal behavior.[15] Moreover—unlike in the case
of the poor—in those instances where "behavioral problems" are attributed to affluence, such attribution is often twisted into a defense
of the perpetrators; it is argued that they are pathological victims of
their financial circumstances and should not, therefore, be treated as
criminals.[16] Scholarly discourse on crime, whether implicitly or explicitly, generally assumes that the poor are "likely offenders" and that the
wealthy are targets of victimization. In more recent literature on the
negative effects of affluence the normative language of criminology is
generally avoided in favor of discussions of "well-being" and "risk."[17] It
should also be noted that routine activity theory tends to focus on the
opportune circumstances under which violations occur, and to skirt
the question of what turns a person into a motivated offender.

Schneerson's theorization, by contrast, (1) inverts the assumed relationship between economic status and crime, and (2) focuses directly
on the relationship between opportunity and the motivation to offend.
He distinguishes between those born into affluence and those born into
poverty; the former are more likely to take opportunities for granted,
and are therefore more likely to abuse opportunities for criminal ends,
while the latter are more likely to appreciate the responsibilities that
come along with any opportunities obtained and are more motivated
to use such opportunities for the advancement of themselves and others, morally as well as materially.[18] Implicit in Schneerson's theorization
is a more expansive conception of crime, which neither privileges the
wealthy nor apologizes for their pathologies. Moreover it inverts the
standard assumptions of criminology so that the more affluent classes
are seen as more liable to produce likely offenders. This both anticipates
and goes beyond the recent findings of Suniyah S. Luthar and others,
according to which "the high degree of autonomy implied by personal
wealth leads many to believe that they can live exactly the kind of lives
they want" and that, among affluent youth, "early trajectories of 'gaming
the system' often end up in serious crime later in life."[19] What Luthar
calls "the culture of affluence" provides optimal conditions for a culture

of delinquency to fester; entitlement breeds criminality. Schneerson not only diagnosed this cultural malady, but forcefully argued that it could only be healed through the educational inculcation of a basic sense of responsibility toward God and humanity:

> Axiomatic faith in the Creator and Orchestrator of the world, who pays attention to each individual, negates the assumption that "each person is free to do whatever is right in their own eyes" (cf. Judges, 21:25). It negates the assumption that one need only be sufficiently "smart"—I won't say "wise," for this in fact is foolishness; to use the opportunities one has been given in order to cause harm to someone else. Indeed, this is also harmful for the perpetrator, and perhaps to an even greater degree than to the victim. The victim is harmed physically, but the perpetrator is harmed both physically and spiritually [morally]...
>
> When an educational system is established on the basis that the requirement of education is satisfied merely by the accumulation of knowledge...if the student excels academically, or doesn't excel etc., he can also embellish his accumulation of knowledge with knowledge of how to use firearms, even to the point of mastery. But since the accumulation of knowledge is not connected to the purpose of manifesting good—for the self, true good, and good for society—but rather to the purpose of proving that "I exist, and besides me there is nothing" (Zephaniah, 2:15), it follows that he does not need take into account the opinions of anyone else, and certainly that he does not need to obey anyone else...Certainly he can outsmart the authorities and find a way to avoid punishment. And, on the contrary, how can he best demonstrate his greatness? By inflicting pain and damage, which demonstrates that he has no need to take anyone else into account...To these ends he utilizes his wealth, and the freedoms granted by this nation, rather than exercising the freedom that "all peoples shall each go in the way of their God" (Micah, 4:5)...[20]

Schneerson went on to say that if schools would instead prioritize the need to "fashion, build up and construct the inclination of the

person's heart," endowing pupils with good character and an axiomatic
sense of God's providential investment in human life, then

> from the outset it will never occur to him that he needs to
> seek out weapons, even for self protection, because he lives
> with the knowledge and the security that there is "an eye that
> sees and an ear that listens" (*Mishnah*, Avot, 2:1). It will certain-
> ly never occur to him to use weapons in a criminal fashion.[21]

While the attempt on Reagan's life renewed the call for gun-control
legislation (to which Reagan would remain opposed), Schneerson did
not address this legislative question directly. Yet he was emphatic that
the American obsession with guns was fundamentally at odds with sincere faith in God, and utterly inconsistent with the socio-mystical ideal
that he called all people to strive for. He saw the impulse to obtain
a weapon—"even for self protection"—as symptomatic of a perva-
sive cultural malady that leads people to abuse the opportunities of
freedom and affluence, seeking only to satisfy their own egotistical ap-
petites rather than to serve the divine cause of social solidarity and
progress. In a talk delivered in 1972 Schneerson had similarly criticized
the practice of hunting animals for sport and the cultural valorization
of gun training, describing both as expressions of boredom and destructive inhumanity.[22]

Luthar has described the psychological and behavioral problems found
among upper-middle-class youths in suburban settings as "the costs of affluence," and noted that the rates of delinquency among this demographic
are significantly higher than average rates among poorer demographics
across America.[23] Studies have also shown that "multiple-victim shootings by adolescents in the United States" occur in suburbia, "not in areas
of concentrated poverty and social isolation, nor in areas of dense population or high crime rates," suggesting that this phenomenon too is a
product of the "culture of affluence."[24] An important caveat noted by
Luthar is that these social problems should not be attributed to the "possession of wealth in itself," but rather to "the overemphasis on status and
wealth."[25] This is an assessment that Schneerson would likely agree with.
Indeed, his call for a shift in educational priorities for the poor and the
affluent alike is echoed in Luthar's recommendations for educational
interventions designed to help schools find "balance in their goals for

students" and foster "curiosity, creativity, and character development."[26] Schneerson, however, would likely have put character development first on the list, rather than last. He consistently argued that the most effective and far-reaching intervention of this kind is the educational cultivation of a socio-mystical value system in which a sincere faith in God is axiomatically intertwined with civic responsibility.

6.2—Jewish Humanism and the Inhumanity of Incarceration

ON SUNDAY, DECEMBER 17th, 1989, Schneerson was visited by Judge Jack B. Weinstein of the United States District Court for the Eastern District of New York. Their brief exchange was captured on video: Weinstein tells Schneerson that he would soon be meeting with the Federal Sentencing Commission, "and I am going to tell them your views on imprisonment." After securing assurance that Weinstein will not only communicate his views but also support them, Schneerson responds with a blessing that also reads as a succinct manifesto on crime prevention through education:

> May God Almighty bless you to go from strength to strength, and to reach the time when there will be no prisons, only preventative education to prevent people from going astray from the right way.[27]

This short exchange reflects a dialogue between Schneerson and Weinstein going back at least to 1981. It was in that year that the latter was instrumental in the establishment of the Aleph Institute, under the leadership of Chabad's Rabbi Shalom Lipsker. The non-profit is dedicated to "assisting and caring for the wellbeing of members of specific populations that are isolated from the regular community: U.S. military personnel, prisoners, and people institutionalized or at risk of incarceration due to mental illness or addictions." In addition to providing visitation and chaplaincy services for Jews in the above categories, Aleph provides services to their family members, and advocates for their civil and religious rights. Aleph also advances a criminal justice reform and recidivism reduction agenda that is fundamentally

rooted in a critique of incarceration that Schneerson developed and ex-
pounded from 1950 on.[28]

His theorization of the Torah concept of justice was anchored in
the fact that the Torah never prescribes incarceration as a punishment.
Some crimes carry a death sentence, others carry fines. The closest
thing to a prison are the "cities of refuge" or "sanctuary cities" that the
Israelites were commanded to designate so that "a murderer who killed
a person unintentionally shall flee there" (Numbers, 35:11). First and
foremost, these cities—which were populated by the priestly caste—
provided protection from the vigilante instincts of the slain person's
family. But confinement was imposed, regardless of such risks, on anyone guilty of manslaughter.[29] Significantly, the Talmud establishes that
such confinement should not be understood as a punishment (*onesh*) but
rather as part of a process of atonement (*kaparah*).[30] Schneerson argued
that such a distinction only applies from a purely legalistic perspective. From the deeper mystical perspective that underlies Torah law all
punishments should actually be construed as corrective, or reparational,
rather than retributive or punitive in the ordinary sense. One undergoes
punishment *only* as part of the process of atonement and repair (*tikun*).[31]

Schneerson applies this conception even in cases where Torah law
mandates the death penalty; this is interpreted as a form of spiritual repair through which the subject's life mission is not merely ended
but actually completed. In one talk Schneerson anchored this claim in
a Midrashic gloss that proclaims of those sentenced to death: "On *this*
day you are vilified but you are not vilified in the world-to-come (*olam
haba*), in which you have a portion."[32] Physical death, in other words,
serves as spiritual atonement. Even in such cases, the rabbis emphasized, the individual must always be treated with dignity, as a human
being endowed with the divine form (*tselem elokim*).[33] What is untenable,
however, is that an individual who yet lives shall be deprived of the capacity to live meaningfully.[34]

In what might be Schneerson's earliest discussion of the topic, he suggested that the whole notion of modern incarceration is only tenable if
one accepts a utilitarian view of justice that is fundamentally materialistic in its assumptions. The materialistic view assumes that nothing exists
beyond the physical universe, that there is only "this world" (*olam hazeh*)
and no world-to-come (*olam haba*). From this perspective, questions that
relate to social welfare are reduced to a material conception of society,

and individuals are judged only in terms of their relationship with other people in this world. To borrow Anthony Steinbock's term, there is
no "vertical dimension," nothing that anchors the inherent worth of the
individual in an absolute that transcends the terms of their horizontal
contract with society.[35] Accordingly, once that contract is broken their
individuality is forfeit; through incarceration, society divests criminals
of the freedom to fashion their own contributions to the world.

Schneerson describes this materialistic-utilitarian stance as follows:

> They know of only one world, [namely] this world that we
> presently inhabit…As a result, when a person sins, infring-
> ing and straying from the path, and causes damage and
> spoilage to the world—the only world that exists—they ar-
> rest him and incarcerate him, isolated in prison, so that he
> can no longer damage and spoil the world. And even though
> the freedom that is required for him to fulfill his purpose is
> thereby withdrawn—such that thereby…he becomes dehu-
> manized—nevertheless this is [considered] inexorable, with
> no alternative way to prevent damage and spoilage being
> caused to the majority…The majority supersedes the indi-
> vidual and the individual is inexorably forfeit for the good of
> the majority.
>
> But according to Torah, in contrast—which is called "To-
> rah of life" (in the daily prayer liturgy) and "Torah of kindness"
> (Proverbs, 31:26), which is "good for heaven and good for crea-
> tures" (cf. *Talmud bavli*, Kidushin, 40a)—it is impossible…to
> forfeit the individual and cause him damage in order to pre-
> vent damage to the majority…Torah does not cause damage,
> and even the punishments prescribed by Torah are not sim-
> ply for the sake of punishment, but are rather for the sake of
> repairing the sin. Therefore the punishment of incarceration
> cannot be entertained, because we thereby deny the perpe-
> trator the possibility of fulfilling his purpose and mission.[36]

On this reading, crime is not simply understood as a decontextual-
ized rupture of the law, or as a transgression of the individual against
the collective. It is not to be met with either a retributivist or consequentialist response. It is rather seen as a rupture in the fabric of the

self, a rupture in the fabric of society, and ultimately a rupture in the fabric of the cosmos. Such a rupture cannot be healed simply by isolating the perpetrator from society. Isolation alone actually preserves each of these ruptures without providing a path of repair, whether on the level of self-repair, social repair, or cosmic repair. On the contrary, thus unattended, these ruptures can actually fester and deteriorate. A more holistic approach would provide a constructive framework within which perpetrators could right their wrongs, doing whatever possible to undo the damage. Ultimately, recognition of the tremendous moral obligation they are under can provide the impetus for a reformed criminal, or sinner, to achieve and contribute something of even greater value than that to which they would have previously aspired.

Schneerson goes so far as to equate the inhumanity of punitive incarceration with the inhumanity of punitive amputation:

> Torah only legislates punishments of the sort that do not efface the divine form (*tselem elokim*), and which do not efface the obligation of a human being to be similar to his creator...Therefore Torah does not legislate any punishment that literally takes "an eye for an eye" or "a hand for a hand." (Cf. Exodus, 21:24; *Talmud bavli*, Bava kama, 84a.) Among even the best and greatest of nations at the time when the Torah was given it was the norm that they would literally take "a hand for a hand"...A thief who stole using their hand would have his hand amputated. But in the "Torah of kindness" such punishments are untenable since a person is thereby rendered incapable of achieving their life's work to the fullest degree...If he is deemed utterly unfit to continue his mission [i.e., subject to the death penalty], then he is relieved of his mission through being removed from this world (*olam hazeh*). But to remain in this world and be unable to fulfill his mission [as in the case of incarceration] is an untenable coincidence of opposites.[37]

To confine someone to a modern prison, Schneerson suggests, is to sever the individual from their very personhood, to rob them of the human dignity that Torah law protects even in death.

The normative critique of the utilitarian approach is that it can justify the punishment of innocents, as well as the guilty, so long as the cause of the greater good is advanced.[38] But Schneerson goes much further. For him, the very notion that the greater good can be used to justify the forfeiture, erasure, and dehumanization of any individual, including one who is indeed guilty of crime, should rightly be construed as tyrannical; a tyranny of the majority. But it is a tyranny that seems inexorable, and even just, so long as one's concept of society is reduced to its material dimension.[39] Schneerson contrasts this with the Talmudic assurance that "The Holy One, Blessed be He, does not deal tyrannically (*beteruneya*) with His creations."[40]

Beyond the particular application to the question of incarceration, Schneerson's critique reveals the deeper moral dimension that lies beyond secularized discussions of ethics. Anthony Steinbock has argued that the introduction of a moral absolute depends entirely on the vertical dimension: "The moral is vertical in the sense that persons are 'absolute,' unique, as finite, and not merely relative or interchangeable." He echoes Schneerson's discussion in distinguishing between "a universal ethic," which fundamentally isolates the subject from others, and "morality," which he describes as implicitly interpersonal:

> While the inter-Personal [*sic*] dimension of experience (or what I have called elsewhere religious experience) may not be explicit in the moral, it is implicitly connected to it...The moral emotions are expressive of person-to-person relations; they illuminate a creative dimension of person and an interpersonal dimension of freedom...clearly seen in emotions like hope and repentance...[41]

Appropriating Steinbock's conceptual framework we can parse Schneerson's moral conception as follows: Without the vertical dimension, a universal ethic reduces individual value—and ethical responsibility—to the transactional terms of one's relationship with society. Outside of the social contract the individual is alone, isolated, and emptied of significance. The vertical dimension—which Schneerson would identify with the divine—endows individuals with a unique moral purpose that makes their individuated personhood an irreducible absolute. But this personal purpose is also irreducibly interpersonal; it is not grounded in the self but in something that stands beyond the self, namely in the vertical nexus of socio-mystical reciprocity.

This conception of the moral verticality of personhood is the basis for Schneerson's Jewish humanism. This is a socio-mystical humanism according to which divine sanctity is enmeshed in every moment of the life of every individual, including those moments in which one's morality is compromised by crime or sin. Schneerson echoes the assertion of earlier Hasidic masters that God must ultimately be seen as a de facto accomplice in the sins of human beings.[42] This is not to absolve human beings of moral freedom or of moral responsibility. On the contrary, moral freedom and responsibility are rendered all the more weighty when it is understood that each person has the power either to turn divinity against itself or to affirm God's singular integrity. To sin is to rend the name of God asunder. To act for the good, actualizing the precepts of the Torah, is to repair the name of God through repairing self, society, and cosmos.[43] Most significantly, the enmeshment of divinity in every human action means that no sin is beyond redemption, no sin is beyond the restorative power of return (*teshuvah*), or what the mystics term "the secret of the refinements" (*sod haberurim*). On this account, the givenness of human morality can never be impaired. Whatever one may have done a moment prior, one is always called to the moral mission, to one's socio-mystical responsibility, so long as one yet lives. Punitive incarceration, it emerges, is fundamentally antithetical to the mystical ethos of rehabilitation. In Schneerson's own words:

> Whatever his standing or situation—even if he sinned, infringing and straying from the path—the obligation remains upon him to continue in the execution of his purpose and mission in life, and "what business have you with the secrets of the Merciful One?" (*Talmud bavli*, Berakhot, 10a)...We know nothing of "the secret of the refinements" (*sod haberurim*). Therefore, irrespective of his standing and situation, he must fulfill every mitzvah that comes his way, without making a calculation [and arguing] how can he fulfill this precept...while he is yet lacking in his fulfillment of others...Therefore he cannot possibly be placed in prison, thereby withholding the possibility of fulfilling his purpose and mission...[44]

The "secret of the refinements" mentioned here is a kabbalistic doctrine according to which sparks of divinity and holiness are ensconced

within all things, even the impure and unholy aspects of the world and
of human behavior. This is a secret and mysterious form of holiness
that must be discovered and "refined" through the spiritual toil of humanity in the world, much as composite minerals must be smelted in
order for precious metals to be extracted and refined. This is not an
easy process, but it cannot be evaded.[45]

Returning to the biblical example of "a murderer who killed a person unintentionally," Schneerson noted that while confinement to the
cities of refuge is indeed a form of imposed exile that cuts guilty parties off from their normative social networks—from family, friends,
etc.—at the same time the Talmud makes it clear that he must be provided "with everything that he needs to fulfill his purpose and mission
like a free person." Maimonides' ruling is illustrative:

> If a student is exiled to a city of refuge his teacher must be
> exiled along with him, as the verse says "[he shall flee to one
> of these cities], and live" (Deuteronomy, 19:5). Meaning you
> must provide him with the means to live; and for the wise,
> and for seekers of wisdom, life without Torah study is consid-
> ered like death. Similarly, if a teacher is exiled his academy is
> exiled along with him.[46]

This again underscores the centrality of education in the process of
social repair. Torah education in particular, which is understood as the
exemplar of the kind of education that arches toward the sacralization
of life, is indeed constitutive of life itself.

6.3—Criminal Justice Reform and the Rehabilitation of Humanity

IN A TALK delivered in 1976 on the festival of Purim—one of the most
joyous dates on the Jewish calendar—Schneerson grappled with the
problem of formulating a pragmatic stance considering that incarceration is sanctioned under law in the United States and elsewhere. Citing
the Jewish legal principle that "the law of the land is law" (*Talmud bavli*,
Gitin, 10b), he argued that it was the duty of those who lived by Torah
ideals to work toward the transformation of the criminal justice system

from within, and especially emphasized the obligation to alleviate the physical and spiritual suffering of incarcerated people:

> Maimonides writes at the end of the Laws of Purim that there is no joy that is greater or more splendid than "to revive the spirit of the humble and to revive the heart of the crushed" (Isaiah, 57:15), through which one is similar to the divine.[47] It is therefore understood that we must give special emphasis that the greatest efforts must be made to enable people who are in prison to fulfill the mitzvot in general, and all the more so the particular mitzvot of Purim; sending food [to one's fellows] and gifts to the poor. Indeed, this is actually part of the broader purpose of any "correctional facility" that is fit for such a name. The purpose of holding a person in prison must not merely be for the sake of punishment. But rather to provide an opportunity to contemplate the undesirable things that he perpetrated…and to make himself whole again, that he might prepare himself to be released from prison and begin to live a life of order, peace, and uprightness.[48]

Speaking with extraordinary seriousness and passion, Schneerson called for a fundamental change in the attitude of society toward incarcerated human beings, beginning with the need to militate against the systematic dehumanization of prison populations:

> To begin with it must be seen to that the individual should feel that he is [as God said] "in our form and like our image" (Genesis, 1:26), that he is a human being. That, if only he so desires, he can be a person (*adam*) in the likeness of the supernal God (*adamah le'elyon*)…But when we take away that possibility, when we persecute and pressurize him, when we don't allow him to raise his head, not only is the "correctional facility" not conducive to its own purpose, on the contrary, it actually makes him even more disposed to criminality than he was before his initial incarceration. For that reason it must be among the aims of the facility to raise the spirits of those who find themselves there, and in all possible ways they should be treated just like free people, and just like the prison

guards, and therefore they are to be given the opportunity to achieve their human potential to the most complete degree.[49]

In this talk, and in others, Schneerson called upon his listeners to do everything they could to cater to the spiritual needs of Jews and non-Jews alike, through prison visitation, counseling, and mediation with prison administrators. He was emphatic in his insistence that a massive shift was required in the governing ethos of the criminal justice system, a shift that would replace meaningless and dehumanizing punishment with purposeful education and rehabilitation. From his perspective, incarceration should not be seen merely as a means to segregate felons from society, thereby preventing further offenses and negative influence on others. Incarceration should rather be seen as a means to provide a conducive environment for self-reflection and self-improvement and for the provision of educational resources, guidance, and support. Within that framework prisoners must especially be afforded the fullest spiritual and religious opportunities, which are crucial to a nourished sense of personhood, of self-worth and responsibility, in relation to God and to society. It is specifically under such circumstances that the risk of recidivism can be reduced, leading to earlier releases and to a general reduction of the prison population. Schneerson further suggested that creative policymaking along these lines would lead to more creative sentencing protocols, and should eventually eliminate the need for prisons entirely.

What differentiates Schneerson is that he is not simply interested in social justice, but rather in socio-mystical justice. Justice must be endowed with a verticality, with a morality that transcends and overcomes the reductive and dehumanizing equations that emerge from the secularization of ethics. From this *moral* standpoint, human freedom is of ultimate value. A system of justice that is imposed, and whose basis is the power to impose, will always fall short. Justice must rather be cultivated and nourished from within society; justice must become a way of being, a free mode of living—if you will, a lifestyle. This is a concept of justice that depends upon the kind of autonomous personhood and agency that empower each individual to lead rather than to follow, to choose meaningful action over nihilistic apathy, to choose the greater good over one's own inclinations and desires. It also depends on faith, faith in the personhood and essential morality of each individual, faith in the sacred solidarity of society, and faith in God who creates all people with the capacity to live in His image. For Schneerson, autonomy and faith go hand in hand. As we have already noted, he theorized autonomous choice as the highest measure of religious value and commitment.[50]

Indeed, Schneerson's notion of autonomy as a religious value was often given particular emphasis in connection to the festival of Purim. In his 1976 talk he cited the Talmudic teaching that the Israelites initially accepted the Torah under duress, thus applying a substantial caveat to their acceptance of its laws. But following their miraculous salvation from Haman's plot to annihilate them, as recorded in the book of Esther, they renewed their covenantal commitment to the Torah out of their own volition, embracing God's law out of love.[51] In Schneerson's paraphrase:

> Purim achieves that all aspects of one's engagement in Torah and its mitzvot should not be performed merely in a manner of accepting the yoke of obligation (*kabbalat ol*)...but also in fulfillment of the verse "you shall serve God with joy" (Psalms, 100:2)...The Talmud says that this is not just one element of Purim, but rather one of its most salient themes...The innovation of Purim is that "they upheld what they had previously [only] accepted."[52] It was the same Torah, but now they precluded the possibility of anyone claiming that there was any duress involved. This means, as mentioned above, that the innovation of Purim is that Torah and its mitzvot should not merely be approached with toil and acceptance...but must also be embraced with joy.[53]

In this spirit, Schneerson urged incarcerated individuals to use whatever degree of freedom they are afforded to joyously embrace the Torah and its mitzvot, beginning with the enthusiastic celebrations of Purim, and with Passover, the festival of freedom, which follows shortly thereafter. Just as the messianic future is built out of the destructive pain of exile, incarceration too can be transformed into the crucible of freedom, so long as the individual is given the impetus and support to overcome the crushing weight of the system, the spiritual wherewithal to reclaim the internal and eternal freedom with which each person is endowed. Moreover, Schneerson said, the rehabilitation of the individual leads to the collective rehabilitation and redemption of all humanity from what Weber would have called the "iron cage":

> This hastens the "end made to darkness" (cf. Job, 28:3), the end to the double and redoubled darkness of the collective prison, namely the exile, and inaugurates an era of true freedom "from blackness to great light, from enslavement to redemption,"... a redemption after which there will be no further exile, through our righteous messiah. And may that advent be very soon.[54]

It is this synthesis of pragmatic policy and prophetic hope that Schneerson encapsulated in his wish—articulated to Judge Weinstein in 1989—for "the time when there will be no prisons, only preventative education to prevent people from going astray from the right way."[55] As of this writing, Weinstein is still active on the federal bench in the Eastern District of New York, and has acquired a national reputation as a "judicial entrepreneur."[56] A prolific writer and scholar, he is also an activist who has pioneered alternative sentencing practices, innovative techniques, and interventions, all emanating from a set of priorities that "orbits steadfastly around a moral sun: individual dignity and moral worth."[57] On June 14, 2018, *The New York Times* ran a story with the headline, "The 96-Year-Old Brooklyn Judge Standing Up to the Supreme Court." In a "spirited decision" denying immunity to four Brooklyn police officers accused of assault, Weinstein had declared that "the Supreme Court's recent emphasis on shielding public officials and federal and local law enforcement means many individuals who suffer a constitutional deprivation will have no redress."[58]

This is only one of many controversial headlines that his decades-long career has generated. Many law-review articles and tributes have been devoted to his work, as well as a full-length biography, *Leadership on the Federal Bench: The Craft and Activism of Jack Weinstein.*[59] While his biographer did pay some attention to his involvement in Jewish life, he failed to note Weinstein's relationship with Schneerson or with Lipsker and the Aleph Institute. Nevertheless Weinstein's compassionate attitude toward defendants, and especially toward prisoners, is clearly in step with the ideals espoused by Schneerson.

Weinstein...has said: "You have humanity coming into court. You have people in trouble. The judge acts in a compassionate human way to show that the law isn't all that rigid and cruel." He has a deep concern for others and the ability to put himself in their shoes..."Many people coming to our building [the courthouse] are tense, concerned, and confused. They need our reassurance and help."...Of cases brought by prisoners, he says, "We ought to in some way touch them and say, 'Look, we know you're a human being. We know you're there, we feel we would like to help you...keep trying and we respect you as a person.'"[60]

In close resonance with the line of thought articulated by Schneerson, Weinstein's longest-running battle is the one he continues to wage against sentencing guidelines that favor incarceration and enforce mandatory minimums that, in his view, are not only disproportionate but detrimental. In an article published in 1988 he wrote:

The aims of the sentencing guidelines—to rationalize sentencing, avoid some of the hypocrisy of the past, provide for more uniformity, and require explanations by the court for its sentences—are legitimate. Nevertheless, the soundest policy considerations can, when applied rigidly and without exception to individual human beings, be unnecessarily cruel. Many times I have had brought before me defendants who have the brains, ambition, and character to rehabilitate themselves through our alternative programs. Some would be destroyed by a term in prison. There are defendants for whom prison incarceration makes no sense.[61]

In the decades since, Weinstein has continued his efforts to change and creatively stretch the law in order to provide more rehabilitative responses to crime. His preference is for supervised release rather than the more punitive options of probation, as the more effective means to prevent recidivism.[62]

In March 2016, the Aleph Institute convened the first Alternative Sentencing Key Stakeholders (ASKS) Summit at Georgetown Law School in Washington, D.C. Chaired by Charles Renfrew, who served as deputy attorney general in the Carter administration, the summit brought together a strongly bipartisan group of legislators, justices, NGOs and activists from across the nation and beyond. Representatives of the Heritage Foundation and American Civil Liberties Union, for example, appeared side by side on a panel discussing the possibility of passing federal criminal justice reform. At the time, Senator Chuck Grassley (R-Iowa), who also participated in the summit, was leading an effort to introduce the Sentencing Reform and Corrections Act (SRCA). This ultimately failed in the face of opposition from Senator Tom Cotton (R-Ark.), then-senator Jeff Sessions (R-Ala.), and others.[63]

It would be another two years before some of the provisions of the SRCA were incorporated into the FIRST STEP Act, which was finally signed into law on December 21, 2018. According to a report by the Brennan Center for Justice at New York University Law School the FIRST STEP Act goes a long way to changing the conversation on mass incarceration, not only because "it's the largest step the federal government has taken to reduce the number of people in federal custody" but also because it "has elevated criminal justice reform as a rare space for bipartisan consensus and cooperation in a fractured national political environment."[64] But most activists, including leaders at the Aleph Institute, insist that this is merely the first step toward much further-reaching reforms both at the federal and state levels.[65]

At the ASKS Summit in 2016 Shalom Lipsker used his opening remarks to underscore the social repercussions of incarceration in the broadest terms. Beyond the damage to the lives of the individuals who are imprisoned, he emphasized, further damage is done to their families and to their communities. He reminded the audience that 29 percent of the global female prison population are in American prisons, and 7 percent of American children have had a parent incarcerated.[66]

From this perspective, the problem of incarceration should rightly be seen as a feminist issue, and also as an educational issue in the broadest terms. Incarceration is not only traumatic for those convicted of crimes, or for populations who suffer from institutional and structural racial discrimination within the criminal justice system. Incarceration also inflicts a collective trauma, albeit a less recognizable one, upon society as a whole. Though it especially dehumanizes the families, children, and communities of incarcerated individuals, it fundamentally undermines the personhood of all citizens. All members of society are implicated in structural injustices such as these. The national conversation around criminal justice reform cannot be reduced to an abstract theorization of ethics when the welfare of entire populations, and of millions of innocent children, is at stake.[67]

The result of incarceration, Lipsker said, is "enormous cost, wasted lives, destroyed families, and the most effective environment for the perpetual promulgation of criminal conduct." Invoking Schneerson's explanation of why incarceration is not mentioned in the Torah, Lipsker offered the caveat that "this is not a theological discussion." For many of his interlocutors that may have been true. But for him it plainly *is* a theological discussion; it is the vertical dimension that endows him with the faith and confidence, the moral conviction and authority, to speak and to act.

6.4—Solar Energy, Geopolitics, and the Sacralization of Science

FROM SCHNEERSON'S SOCIO-MYSTICAL justice and socio-mystical humanism, we turn to his socio-mystical ecology. As Weber wrote, what distinguishes the prophetic visionary is the cosmic breadth of his message: "To the prophet, both the life of man and the world, both social and cosmic events, have a certain systematic and coherent meaning." It should not be surprising, therefore, that Schneerson did not merely address himself to the political, economic, and social debates of his era, nor did he only speak of the relationship between the individual and the cosmos in a purely spiritual or mystical sense. Some of his earliest correspondence, dating from the 1920s, demonstrates his long-standing fascination with the intersection of Torah's timeless wisdom, as he regarded it, and the new discoveries of science.[68] Indeed, an entire monograph could be devoted to his engagement with this intersection over the course of his lifetime.[69] But what concerns us here is the particular attention he gave to the development of alternative energy sources, especially solar energy. Not coincidentally, his fullest treatment of this issue is found in a talk delivered in 1981, on the same evening as the talks with which this chapter began, which directly address Ronald Reagan, the newly inaugurated president.[70]

It was in the aftermath of the Santa Barbara oil spill in 1969 that environmental awareness first began to intrude on the collective American consciousness.[71] Over the course of the following decade the United States was also beset by two major oil crises, or "shocks." The first was sparked when the Organization of the Petroleum Exporting Countries (OPEC) announced an oil embargo designed to quash Western support for Israel during the Yom Kippur war. The Iranian Revolution of 1979 triggered a second crisis, which intensified following the outbreak of the Iran-Iraq war. These events highlighted the degree to which the global reach and influence of the United States were handicapped by its dependence on oil. To make matters worse, in 1974 the Soviet Union replaced the United States as the world's biggest producer of petroleum. Well into the 21st century, oil production and supply continue to be a key factor in the international struggle for power and dominance. Though the Iron Curtain has fallen, the oil-rich Middle East remains an arena of increasingly disastrous proxy wars between the United States, Russia, and others. Likewise, Russia's dominance as a supplier of energy is a significant strategic problem in Europe.[72]

Should human beings merely conceive of themselves as passive inhabitants of the earth, or as standing in some kind of relationship with the earth? Should they merely reap the bounty of the earth and its assets, or do they need to figure out how the earth can potentially be improved or ruined through the utilization, distribution, and development of material resources? In the aftermath of the oil crises of the 1970s, Schneerson argued, these questions were given a geopolitical edge—and indeed a moral edge—that made them much harder to ignore. Concerns about the impact of human activities on ecological environments often seem to be at odds with commercial, economic, and geopolitical concerns. Indeed, under the administrations of Nixon and Carter there had been much discussion about the need to strike a balance between the dueling priorities of environmental security and energy security.[73] But in Schneerson's view these debates were futile and self-serving. Both of these agendas could be prioritized through concerted investments in alternative energy solutions. While warning against the dangers of nuclear energy plants, he heralded solar technology and the abundant energy resource provided by the sun as an especially attractive opportunity.[74]

Characteristically, Schneerson rooted his ecological approach in a Midrashic teaching that he had cited many times before:

> Everything created in the six days of creation needs work. Mustard seeds need to be sweetened, lupin beans need to be sweetened, wheat needs to be milled. Even man needs to be perfected.[75]

Indeed, this principle is hinted at in the text of the Torah itself. We are told that on the seventh day God "rested from all His work, which God created to do" (Genesis, 2:3). This formulation might seem grammatically clumsy. But it provides a crucial hermeneutical suggestion: It is not written that God's work was "created and done" (*bara elokim ve'asah*)—i.e., completed—but that God's work was "created to do" (*bara elokim la'asot*), meaning that it was created to be completed by humanity. On the one hand, "God saw everything He had made, and behold it was very good" (Genesis, 1:31). On the other hand, "Everything needs *tikun*." Everything needs to be perfected, fixed, and completed.[76] Thereby the opening is made for humanity to become "partners with God in the work of genesis," partners in creation.[77]

The ecological example provided in the above teaching from the Midrash is that of food. "Mustard seeds need to be sweetened... wheat needs to be milled." The rabbinic authors of the Midrash invoke this to explain why God did not create man already circumcised; the commandment of circumcision signifies the empowerment of humankind to take raw matter and improve it. Moreover, it is specifically through the contributions of humankind that the material world—beginning with the human body—is sacralized. This indicates that holiness is not simply the gift of God, but rather the product of humanity's partnership with God. Schneerson extends this conception to our relationship with food as well. A human being should not merely transform raw foodstuffs into food fit for human consumption, but is also enjoined to sacralize the food through uttering a blessing before eating and afterward, as the Torah instructs, "and you shall eat, and you shall be satisfied, and you shall bless the Lord your God" (Deuteronomy, 8:10). "Thereby," said Schneerson, "it becomes the food of Supernal Man as well."[78]

As he introduces the topic of solar energy, this brief comment is a clear articulation of the vertical dimension that is the foundation of

Schneerson's ecological conception. To enter into an ecological relationship with the earth and its resources is to enter into a sacred and
reciprocal partnership with God. It is not only the human beings who
are nurtured by the bread they eat, but the being of God is thereby
nurtured too. As Schneerson put it earlier on the same evening, "In
initiating praise of God it is as if one becomes a giver and a provider
in relation to God."[79] Moreover, the blessing links this local act, this
seemingly insignificant act, to the larger purpose of the entire cosmos:
"When a small child drinks a small glass of water, and first blesses the
One 'whom all is created by His word,' that bit of water is thereby connected with all the manifold things that are created by God's word, for
they all depend on being used for blessing."[80]

With the above in mind it should not surprise us that Schneerson
linked his promotion of solar energy to a blessing as well. The Talmud
states:

> One who sees the sun in its cycle...recites "Blessed [are
> You]...Maker of creation." And when is it? Abaye said: Every
> twenty-eight years when the cycle is complete and returns
> [to its genesis] and the vernal equinox (*tekufat nisan*) falls
> within the constellation of Saturn, on the night of the third
> (Tuesday) and eve of the fourth (Wednesday).[81]

This fairly rare event on the Jewish calendar occurred twice
during Schneerson's tenure as leader; in 1953 and in 1981, just a few
days before he delivered the talk under discussion. On both occasions
Schneerson displayed profound interest in the significance of this
blessing, delivering lengthy talks exploring its literary legacy in the
Jewish legal codes, and establishing an authorized Chabad version of
the accompanying liturgy. In 1981 his conclusions were codified and
published in a short pamphlet.[82] At his behest, a large crowd—including men, women, and children—gathered to recite the liturgy
together with him, and the ceremony took the form of an outdoor
farbrengen, which he led from a raised platform under a brilliant blue
sky and a shining sun.[83] Citing the verse from Psalms, "the heavens
proclaim the glory of God" (Psalms, 19:2), he emphasized that to see
"the great luminary" "in its cycle" is to answer the call of the prophet
Isaiah, "Lift up your eyes on high and see who created these" (Isaiah,

40:26), such that this visionary experience would ultimately be manifest in practical action.[84]

One week later, as he broached the supreme practicality of a national solar energy agenda, he explicated the thematic connection:

> The "blessing of the sun" reminds us again, and with additional emphasis, that we have an open and clear path...precisely that which has already been initiated in other countries—and in this country too, albeit in the smallest possible mode— to utilize the sun, of which it is written "nothing is hidden from its heat" (Psalms, 19:7), that it should become the driving force for the supply of requisite energy and power...This is a resource that this nation in particular, in its southern regions, has in very great abundance; the heat of the sun. And it would indeed be very easy to transfer the energy produced there...throughout all the other regions of the nation...This can all be achieved if it is based on the foundation of God's help, and on faith in God. Then we will not reckon with the challenges that will come from people who might stand to profit personally by not allowing this. In a relatively short time this will free the entire nation from being servile to those small fiefdoms who have oil in their territories.[85]

In this passage Schneerson briefly touches on a number of factors that play into policy considerations associated with energy production. First, he mentions financial and commercial interests that stand in the way of the full development and commercialization of solar energy technologies and systems. Second, he mentions the interests of the "small fiefdoms," namely the Arab states, who dominate international oil markets and thereby hold Western democracies in their thrall.

Elsewhere in this talk Schneerson also discussed the role played by the Soviet Union in the fraught dynamics of American energy security and foreign policy. The United States, he said, was established by God as the nation that could provide a check to the influence of "that nation," and even pressure them (the Soviets) to act with charity and justice toward their own citizens. On this score, Schneerson emphasized freedom of religion, that each shall "go in the way of their God" (Micah, 4:5), and "especially that Jews should be able to conduct themselves Jewishly."[86]

This discussion obviously reflects something of Schneerson's deep involvement in covert Jewish activism behind the Iron Curtain.[87] But it also exemplifies the degree to which he consistently placed the moral and religious dimension, what we have called the socio-mystical dimension, at the center of every issue. The question of energy independence was not a narrow national security issue, but rather an expression of Schneerson's anti-isolationist stance and his socio-mystical intervention in geopolitical discourse. The imperative for the United States to secure energy independence, he emphasized, could not be reduced to the material dynamics of geopolitics as they are usually conceived. "The foundation," he said, "must not come from [the desire to bolster] 'my own strength and the might of my own hand,' and in order to augment imagined glory."[88] Instead, he explicitly equated the ability to stand up to the Soviet Union with "the ability to stop the spread of atheism [kefirah], which is in turn commensurate to the ability to spread true peace throughout the world."[89]

In a similar vein Schneerson also highlighted the responsibility of the United States to stand firm in its support of Israel's existence. The Yom Kippur war of 1973 began as a surprise attack led by Egypt, whose military was supplied by the Soviet Union, and supported by Syria. The Arab nations then used the oil weapon to coerce the United States into supporting the achievement of their strategic aims. Israel counterattacked, but the strategic weakness and isolation of the Jewish state was exposed, severely undermining the sense of security and confidence that had prevailed since the victories of the Six Day War in 1967.[90] From Schneerson's perspective this only heightened the moral imperative of energy independence for America, and for other democratic nations.[91]

Schneerson's consideration of the moral and religious dimensions of the geopolitical situation was also intertwined with a consideration of the mystical significance of scientific progress in the modern era. In this connection Schneerson quoted the Zoharic prediction that

> In the sixth hundredth year of the sixth millennium [5600 in the Jewish calendar, corresponding to 1840 C.E.] the gates of wisdom will be opened above and the wellsprings of wisdom below and the world will prepare to ascend into the seventh millennium. This is analogous to one who prepares on Friday, as the sun gets lower in the sky, to ascend into Shabbat.[92]

As the scholar Arie Morgenstern has discussed, this passage inspired Jews the world over to ascribe some kind of messianic significance to the year 5600 (1840).[93] Schneerson developed his own retrospective interpretation of this passage on several different occasions. For him, the reference to "the gates of wisdom *above* and the wellsprings of wisdom *below*" predicted the duel development and discovery of Jewish esoteric wisdom (the opening "above") and of secular scientific wisdom (the opening "below"). He noted that it was around the year 1840 that the great compendia of Schneur Zalman of Liadi's oral discourses, *Torah or* (1837) and *Likutei torah* (1848), were published by the third rebbe of Chabad. These publications made Schneur Zalman's elaborate elucidations of kabbalistic wisdom— designated as the "inner" dimension of the Torah—much more widely accessible. In the Chabad tradition they were hailed as a new spiritual revelation of the kind that would indeed prepare the world to ascend into the messianic age.[94] Likewise, Schneerson pointed out, the year 1840 marked the culmination of the scientific and industrial revolutions, which set the stage for the modern era of scientific discovery and technology.[95] This historical alignment, in his view, was indicative of a messianic significance that is shared in the dual advancement of scientific and Torah knowledge:

> Since the Zohar connects the development of worldly wisdom with the revelation of the inner dimension of Torah, and with the ascent into the seventh millennium, this itself signifies that this is the entire purpose of their development...to use them to reveal and disseminate the inner dimension of Torah.[96]

Schneerson emphasized that the application of scientific discoveries for the furtherance of the Torah's messianic agenda was not simply a secondary result, or a welcome opportunity. In his view, the advancement of Torah and the advancement of science are fundamentally intertwined, and it is the secular applications of science that are secondary opportunities. Indeed, for Schneerson, the distinction between the secular and sacred realms was ultimately a false construction. Just as he argued for the resacralization of society generally—and for the resacralization of ethics and education in particular—so he argued for the resacralization of science.

The seriousness of Schneerson's engagement with new developments in science, and with their practical applications in the construction of

a better world, is especially exemplified by his advocacy for solar energy solutions. Two prominent Chabad scientists, Jack (Yaakov) Hanoka
and Herman (Yirmiyahu) Branover, were pioneers in this arena. The
former first encountered Chabad as a physics student at Pennsylvania
State University, circa 1962. After a long spell at the Chabad rabbinic
academy (yeshiva) in Brooklyn, Schneerson told him to enroll in graduate school and continue his studies. He even offered him a loan to
help him cover tuition expenses.[97] After completing his PhD, Hanoka accepted a job with Mobil Solar Energy Corporation. In 1994 he
co-founded Evergreen Solar, which, according to *The New York Times*,
became the third-largest maker of solar panels in the United States.[98]
Hanoka left the company in 2007 and joined 7AC Tech, where he used
solar technology in the development of energy-efficient air condition-
ing systems.[99] In 2011 Evergreen Solar moved its operations to China.[100]

In his 1981 talk Schneerson had bemoaned the fact that by allowing
narrow financial interests to take precedence over national security interests the United States was forfeiting its chance to become a world
leader in energy production and supply through renewable technologies.
Writing of energy policy more generally Richard Vietor similarly concluded that Congress "was unwilling to provide adequate, unfettered
incentives" to get industry to develop alternative energy resources: "In
fact, to avoid political opposition from the oil industry, or criticisms of a
giveaway to Big Oil, government initiatives were explicitly restricted so
as not to impinge on the domain of 'private enterprise.'"[101] According to
a report issued in 1983, solar energy was subject to particular neglect in
favor of nuclear research and development until 1979 when Carter called
for the creation of the Solar Energy Development Bank, to be funded
with one hundred million dollars. "This victory," they predicted, "may
have come too late. Ronald Reagan's defeat of Carter in the November, 1980, Presidential election may result in the defeat of solar energy
promotion."[102] It seems likely that it was precisely this possibility that
Schneerson sought to ward off with his public call for the United States
to prioritize solar energy and to ignore the financial concerns of "private enterprise" as determined by the free market. But Evergreen Solar's
move to China showed that, as of 2011, optimal conditions did not yet
exist for the renewable resources industry to thrive in the United States.

Herman Branover, a former refusenik, was allowed to leave the Soviet Union in 1972, and he set up the Joint Israeli-Russian Laboratory

for Energy Research at Ben Gurion University in Beersheba, Israel. His association with Chabad had begun during his refusenik years, and he enjoyed a particularly close relationship with Schneerson, who had himself trained as an electrical engineer in pre-war Paris.[103] In an early journal entry discovered after his death, Schneerson had also discussed the spiritual corollaries of Pascal's law, a principle that governs the transmission of fluid pressure.[104] These two disciplinary areas, electrical engineering and fluid mechanics, intersected in Branover's field of expertise, magnetohydrodynamics (MHD), with a particular focus on its application in solar energy conversion.[105] In a tribute written to mark Schneerson's thirtieth year as leader of Chabad, Branover testified that Schneerson would often interrogate him about his work, getting deep into the specific technicalities and problems of his research:

> If someone decided to secretly listen in on our conversation, they certainly would not believe their ears. From the room of the Rebbe—the tsadik, the embodiment of Torah, the leader of the hasidim, the teacher and advisor to thousands of Jews—would be heard half sentences and expressions like "the advantages of heat transfer through direct contact via liquids...", "resolution of a system of differential equations using empirical formulas for Reynolds number..."...All of this in Yiddish, with the scientific terms partly in English, partly in Russian...The result of such conversations has often been the publication of several scientific papers, the initiation of new research, or fundamental changes in the direction of ongoing projects.[106]

By the early 1980s Branover had developed a prototype for solar-assisted liquid metal MHD power generation that showed some commercial promise.[107] In the end, however, it wasn't deemed economically viable for the American market.[108] Nevertheless, the underlying technology has continued to be studied by researchers around the world in an effort to increase efficiency and demonstrate its practical feasibility.[109] In a 1998 article Branover argued that it is now scientifically possible to devise a solution for every ecological problem. Yet these scientific possibilities are frustrated by short-sighted economic and political interests, and by the psychological and educational challenge of motivating individuals to overcome the sort of egocentric entitlement and consumerism that leads to ecological misconduct.[110] From the socio-mystical ecological perspective articulated by Schneerson in his 1981 talk, God provides the material resources that are necessary for humanity to successfully execute its mission. Given that the resources exist and the United States has not yet achieved energy independence, he reasoned, "we must conclude that what is missing in this situation is the contribution of humanity."[111]

Branover pointed out that Schneerson's ultimate interest did not lie in the specifics of one scientific problem or another, but rather in the fulfillment of the Torah's charge, "Know God in all your ways" (Proverbs, 3:6). In one example recounted by Branover, Schneerson drew a direct line between their shared interest in solar energy and the imperative to ensure that religious life is socio-mystically constituted:

> What is the characteristic—the Rebbe asked—that determines more than any other that people consider the sun to be a blessing? Obviously it is its ability to radiate, "to shine upon the earth" (Genesis, 1:15). What would happen if the sun was just as hot, and had the same amount of energy, but did not radiate? Indeed, there are stars of that sort, which are known as "black holes," whose gravitational pull is so intense that not a single ray of light can escape. Who then would be interested in the sun? What purpose would it have? The same applies to a Jew. One's main purpose is to shine, to radiate, to do good for the other…Otherwise one turns into a black hole, while one was actually created with the mission to be a sun.[112]

Notes

1. For a copy of this telegram, and for Schneerson's written reply, see Dovid Zaklikowski, "Recovering Reagan Writes to the Rebbe," *Chabad.org*, <chabad.org/979502>.

2. For the transcript of this talk see Menachem Mendel Schneerson, *Sichot kodesh 5741*, Vol. 3 (Brooklyn, NY: Vaad Hanachot Hatemimim, 1986), 104-5. All translations have been amended based on the audio recording, "11 Nissan 5741: Sicha 2," *Chabad.org*, <chabad.org/553208>.

3. See Gil Troy, *Morning in America: How Ronald Reagan Invented the 1980's* (Princeton: Princeton University Press, 2005), 50-69; Marisa Chappell, *The War on Welfare:*

Family, Poverty, and Politics in Modern America (Philadelphia: University of Pennsylvania Press, 2011), 199-241.

4.   This is a reference to the halachic principle of *kavu'a*. See *Talmud bavli*, Kesubot, 15a.

5.   Schneerson, *Sichot kodesh 5741*, Vol. 3, 105-106.

6.   For a video of this talk see, "Pre-Passover Farbrengen: A 1981 Satellite Feed of a Gathering with the Rebbe," *Chabad.org*, <chabad.org/1809252>.

7.   Joseph B. Treaster, "A Life That Started Out with Much Promise Took Reclusive and Hostile Path," *New York Times*, April 1, 1981: 19; Special to *The New York Times*, "Agents Tracing Hinckley's Path Find a Shift to Violent Emotion," *ibid.*, April 5, 1981: 1.

8.   Stuart Taylor Jr., "Hinckley Cleared but Is Held Insane in Reagan Attack," *New York Times*, June 22, 1982: 1. Also see Louis S. Gallart, *The Crossroads of Mental Disorder and Criminal Responsibility* (PhD dissertation, Drew University, 2011), esp. 1-4.

9.   David E. Rosenbaum, "The Symptoms Surround Us, But What Is the Malady?" *New York Times*, April 5, 1981, section 4: 1. Also see Douglas E. Kneeland, "Young Drifters in America: Who, Where and Why," *New York Times*, April 15, 1981: 28.

10.   Schneerson, *Sichot kodesh 5741*, Vol. 3, 111.

11.   *Ibid.*, 107-111.

12.   Lawrence E. Cohen and Marcus Felson, "Social Change and Crime Rate Trends: A Routine Activity Approach," *American Sociological Review* 44, no. 4 (Aug., 1979): 588-608. Also see Arelys Madero-Hernandez and Bonnie S. Fisher, "Routine Activity Theory," in *The Oxford Handbook of Criminological Theory*, edited by Francis T. Cullen and Pamela Wilcox (Oxford: Oxford University Press, 2013), 513-530.

13.   Schneur Zalman of Liadi, *Likutei amarim tanya*, Chapter 30, 38a-b [75-76].

14.   Madero-Hernandez and Fisher, "Routine Activity Theory," 513.

15.   Patrick Sharkey, Max Besbris, and Michael Friedson, "Poverty and Crime," in *The Oxford Handbook of the Social Science of Poverty*, edited by David Brady and Linda M. Burton (Oxford: Oxford University Press, 2016), 623-633.

16.   The most well known example of this is the successful deployment of the so-called "affluenza defense" in the case of Ethan Couch, a sixteen year old who stole beer from a store and then struck and killed four pedestrians with his father's pickup truck while drunk. The ruling provoked popular outrage and has also been invoked to demonstrate that—irrespective of legal guidelines—wealth is actually a factor in sentencing considerations in the US criminal justice system. See Danielle Eckenroth, "Wealthy 'Justice': The Role Wealth Plays in Sentencing and in the Affluenza Defense," *New England Journal on Criminal and Civil Confinement* 41 (2015): 443-461; Anne S. Douds, Daniel Howard, Don Hummer and Shaun L. Gabbidon, "Public Opinion on the Afluenza Defense, Race, and Sentencing Decisions: Results from a Statewide Poll," *Journal of Crime and Justice* 39, no. 1 (2016): 230-242.

17.   This is exemplified in the development and psychopathology literature cited below.

18.   Indeed, studies in which returning offenders were randomly assigned different levels of unemployment benefits upon leaving prison have shown that even modest supplements of income reduce subsequent recidivism. Sharkey, et. al., "Poverty and Crime," 626.

19. Suniya S. Luthar, Samuel S. Barkin, and Elizabeth J. Crossman, ""I Can, Therefore I Must": Fragility in the Upper-Middle Classes" *Development and Psychopathology* 25 (2013): 1529–1549.

20. Schneerson, *Sichot kodesh 5741*, Vol. 3, 108-112.

21. *Ibid.*, 114.

22. Menachem Mendel Schneerson, *Sichot kodesh 5732*, Vol. 1 (Brooklyn, NY: Vaad Hanachot Hatemimim, 1986), 438-439.

23. Suniya S. Luthar and Shawn J. Latendresse, "Adolescent Risk: The Costs of Affluence," *New Directions for Student Leadership* 2002, no. 95, *Special Issue: Pathways to Positive Development among Diverse Youth* (Autumn, 2002): 101-122; Suniya S. Luthar and Karen D'Avanzo, "Contextual Factors in Substance Use: A Study of Suburban and Inner-City Adolescents," *Development and Psychopathology*, 11 (1999): 845–867. Studies have also shown that this demographic is more likely to be involved in multiple-victim shootings.

24. Deanna L. Wilkinson and Jeffrey Fagan, "What We Know about Gun Use among Adolescents," *Clinical Child and Family Psychology Review* 4, no. 2 (June, 2001): 125.

25. Luthar et. al., ""I can,'" 1536.

26. *Ibid.*, 1541.

27. For the video record of this exchange see "Crime Prevention: 19 Kislev, 5750 • December 17, 1989," *Chabad.org*, <chabad.org/471235>.

28. "Mission Statement," *Aleph Institute*, <https://aleph-institute.org/wp/about/>. On the Aleph Institute, its history, and its activities, see also Shalom D. Lipsker, "A Little Light Dispels a Lot of Darkness," *American Jails* 32, no. 6 (Jan.-Feb., 2019): 77-79.

29. See Maimonides, *Mishneh torah*, Hilkhot rotsei'ach, 5:1.

30. *Talmud bavli*, Makot, 2b.

31. Menachem Mendel Schneerson, *Torat menachem hitvaduyot*, Vol. 1 [5710] (Brooklyn, NY: Kehot Publication Society, 1992), 195-196.

32. *Bamidbar rabbah*, 23:6, glossing Joshua, 7:25.

33. Cf. Genesis, 1:26. Schneerson supports this with the parable related by Rabbi Meir in the *Talmud bavli*, Sanhedrin, 46b, in which the king's twin brother is hung for banditry; "anyone who sees him says, 'the king has been hung.' The king issued a command and they took him down [i.e. they did not leave the corpse hanging there for all to see]." Rabbi Meir's point is that the punishment must be carried out, but even a criminal is in the image of God and must be treated accordingly.

34. Menachem Mendel Schneerson, *Sichot kodesh 5736*, Vol. 1 (Brooklyn, NY: Vaad Hanachot Hatemimim, 1986), 613-614.

35. Anthony J. Steinbock, Phenomenology and Mysticism: The Verticality of Religious Experience (Bloomington: Indiana University Press, 2009). See also above, 87, 89 and 106.

36. Schneerson, *Torat menachem hitvaduyot*, Vol. 1, 195.

37. Schneerson, *Sichot kodesh 5736*, Vol. 1, 613-615.

38. See Emmanuel Melissaris, "Theories of Crime and Punishment," in *The Oxford Handbook of Criminal Law*, edited by Markus D. Dubber and Tatjana Hörnle (Oxford, UK: Oxford University Press, 2014), 375-378.

39. Immanuel Kant criticized the consequentialist theory of punishment on the grounds that it violated the subject's personhood, but argued that crime itself retributively condemns him to forfeit such personhood: "A human being can never be treated merely as a means to the purposes of another or be put among the objects of rights to things: his innate personality protects him from this, even though he can be condemned to lose his civil personality." John Rawls argued that such a retributive condemnation itself derives from a system of laws that can ultimately be justified only in utilitarian terms. For a fuller discussion of these competing and intersecting arguments see David Dolinko, "Punishment," in *The Oxford Handbook of Philosophy of Criminal Law*, edited by John Deigh and David Dolinko (Oxford, UK: Oxford University Press, 2011), 403-440.

40. *Talmud bavli*, Avodah zarah, 2a.

41. Anthony J. Steinbock, *Moral Emotions: Reclaiming the Evidence of the Heart* (Evanston, IL: Northwestern University Press, 2014), 13-14.

42. See Yaakov Yosef of Polonne, *Toldot yaakov yosef*, Vayakhel, 23, in the name of the Baal Shem Tov; Schneur Zalman of Liadi, *Likutei amarim tanya*, 14b [28]. Both of these sources refer to *Zohar II*, 163a. Also see the relevant discussion in Menachem Mendel Schneerson, *Sefer hamamarim melukat*, Vol. 2 (Brooklyn, NY: Kehot Publication Society, 2012), 355-357.

43. On turning divinity against itself see Schneur Zalman of Liadi, *Likutei amarim tanya*, Chapter 24, 29b-31a [58-61]. On the rupture and repair of the divine name see *idem.*, *Likutei torah*, Re'eh, 19a, and Derushim lerosh hashanah, 61b-d. The centrality of this conception in Chabad thought is alluded to in the opening discourse of Shalom DovBer Schneersohn, where he comments on the meaning of the *leshem yichud* prayer. See Shalom DovBer Schneersohn, *Yom tov shel rosh hashanah 5666* (Brooklyn, NY: Kehot Publication Society, 1991), 3. Also see Gershom Scholem, *Major Trends in Jewish Mysticism* (New York: Schocken Books, 1941), 275: "To unify the name of God...restores the unity of God's name which was destroyed by the original defect...and every true religious act is directed towards the same aim."

44. Schneerson, *Torat menachem hitvaduyot*, Vol. 1, 196.

45. See Scholem, *Major Trends*, 265-268, 273-275. Also see Philip Wexler, *Holy Sparks: Social Theory, Education and Religion* (New York: St. Martin's Press, 1996).

46. Maimonides, *Mishneh torah*, Hilkhot rotsei'ach, 7:1.

47. Maimonides, *Mishneh torah*, Hilkhot megilah vechanukah, 2:17.

48. Schneerson, *Sichot kodesh 5736*, Vol. 1, 616.

49. *Ibid.*.

50. Above, 63.

51. *Talmud bavli*, Shabbat, 88a.

52. *Ibid.*, paraphrase of Esther, 9:27.

53. Schneerson, *Sichot kodesh 5736*, Vol. 1, 618-619.

54. *Ibid.*, 617. The phrase "from blackness to great light, from enslavement to redemption" is from the Haggadah liturgy read at the Passover seder.

55. "Crime Prevention," *Chabad.org*, <chabad.org/471235>; "Mission Statement," Aleph Institute, <https://aleph-institute.org/wp/about/>.

56. Jeffrey B. Morris, "Jack B. Weinstein: Judicial Entrepreneur," *University of Miami Law Review* 69, no. 2 (Winter, 2015): 393-428.

57. David Luban, "Heroic Judging in an Antiheroic Age," *Columbia Law Review* 97, no. 7 ("A Special Issue Dedicated to Judge Jack B. Weinstein," Nov., 1997): 2070.

58. Alan Feuer, "The 96-Year-Old Brooklyn Judge Standing Up to the Supreme Court," *New York Times*, June 14, 2018, <https://www.nytimes.com/2018/06/14/nyregion/the-96-year-old-brooklyn-judge-standing-up-to-the-supreme-court.html>.

59. Jeffrey B. Morris, *Leadership on the Federal Bench: The Craft and Activism of Jack Weinstein* (Oxford: Oxford University Press, 2011).

60. *Ibid.*, 62-63.

61. Jack B. Weinstein, "Alternative Punishments under the New Federal Sentencing Guidelines," *Federal Sentencing Reporter* 1, no. 2 (Jul.-Aug., 1988): 97.

62. See Jack B. Weinstein, "A Trial Judge's Reflections on Departures from the Federal Sentencing Guidelines," *Federal Sentencing Reporter* 10, no. 1 (Jul.—Aug., 1997): 9-12.; Morris, *Leadership*, 243-279.

63. "Nearly 200 Judges, Prosecutors, Lawyers and Practitioners Attend Aleph's Alternative Sentencing Summit at Georgetown," *Aleph Institute*, <https://aleph-institute.org/wp/nearly-200-judges-prosecutors-lawyers-and-practitioners-attend-alephs-alternative-sentencing-summit-at-georgetown/>. Videos of all of the summit proceedings are available at *AsksSummit.com*.

64. Ames Grawert and Tim Lau, "How the FIRST STEP Act Became Law — and What Happens Next," *BrennanCenter.org*, January 4, 2019, <https://www.brennancenter.org/blog/how-first-step-act-became-law-and-what-happens-next>.

65. See Dovid Margolin, "The Backstory of the Chassidim Who Got Criminal Justice Reform Done," *Chabad.org/News*, December 27, 2018, <chabad.org/4246392>.

66. The Aleph Institute, "Day 1 Rabbi Sholom Lipskar v2," <https://vimeo.com/163606986>. Accessed via *AsksSummit.com*.

67. On the need to take race into account when addressing more general criminal justice issues see Anna R. Haskins and Hedwig Lee, "Reexamining Race When Studying the Consequences of Criminal Justice Contact for Families," *ANNALS of the American Academy of Political and Social Science* 665, no. 1 (May 2016): 224–230.

68. Menachem Mendel Schneerson, *Igrot kodesh*, Vol. 1 (Brooklyn, NY: Kehot Publication Society, 1997), 1-2.; *ibid.*, Vol. 21 (Brooklyn, NY: Kehot Publication Society, 1998), 1-6.

69. For some relevant discussions of Schneerson's approach to science see Elliot R. Wolfson, *Open Secret: Postmessianic Messianism and the Mystical Revision of Menahem Mendel Schneerson* (New York: Columbia University Press, 2009), 301-302, n. 3; Meir Klein, *In Search of the Center of the Circle: The Rhetoric of Science and Technology in the Writings of Rabbi Menachem Mendel Schneerson* (masters thesis, Bar Ilan University,

2014) [Hebrew with English Abstract]; Eli Rubin, "Studies in Berlin: Science, Torah & Quantum Theory," *Chabad.org*, <chabad.org/2619782>.

70. Schneerson, *Sichot kodesh 5741*, Vol. 3, 120-124.

71. See Teresa Sabol Spezio, *Rising Tide: The Santa Barbara Oil Spill and Its Aftermath* (PhD dissertation, University of California, Davis, 2011); Paul Sabin, "Crisis and Continuity in U.S. Oil Politics, 1965–1980," *Journal of American History* 99, no. 1 (June 2012): 177-186.

72. See James D. Hamilton, "Historical Oil Shocks," in *Routledge Handbook of Major Events in Economic History*, edited by Randall E. Parker and Robert Whaples (New York: Routledge, 2013), 239-265; Tyler Priest, "The Dilemmas of Oil Empire," *Journal of American History* 99, no. 1 (June 2012): 236-251. On Russia in particular see Rafael Kandiyoti, *Powering Europe: Russia, Ukraine, and the Energy Squeeze* (New York: Palgrave Macmillan, 2015).

73. See Emily Martens, *The Discourses of Energy and Environmental Security in the Debate over Offshore Oil Drilling Policy in Florida* (MA thesis, The University of Miami, 2011).

74. *Sichot kodesh 5741*, Vol. 3, 123: "Work has already begun with atomic technologies, but this is clearly connected with various dangers, and this is not the place for a long digression on this point." The inherent risks of the nuclear option had already been made clear by the Three Mile Island incident in 1979, and would be even more catastrophically demonstrated by the Chernobyl disaster in 1986. On Chabad's humanitarian relief effort in the aftermath of the Chernobyl explosion see Dovid Margolin, "30 Years since Chernobyl: How 3,000 Children Were Airlifted out of Nuclear Disaster," *Chabad.org*, <chabad.org/3377542>.

75. *Bereishit rabbah*, 11:6. Also see Schneur Zalman of Liadi, *Torah or*, 12a.

76. *Ibid.*, following the "Rashi" commentary. Schneerson was particularly fond of citing the formulation "to do, to perfect" (*la'asot, letaken*). Also see Schneur Zalman of Liadi, *Torah or*, 3b; 17b; 18a; 70a; 77d.

77. *Talmud bavli*, Shabbat, 119b.

78. Schneerson, *Sichot kodesh 5741*, Vol. 3, 121.

79. *Ibid.*, 101. The relevant passage was quoted more fully above, pages 97-98.

80. For the fuller context of this remark see the relevant discussion and citations above, page 101.

81. *Talmud bavli*, Berakhot, 59b.

82. *Seder birchat hachamah al pi minhag chabad*, (Brooklyn, NY: 1981)

83. For video footage of this occasion, including snippets from Schneerson's talks, see "Birchas Hachama: Blessing of the Sun: 4 Nissan, 5741 · April 8, 1981," *Chabad.org*, <chabad.org/858592>; "Birchas Hachama: 4 Nissan, 5741 · April 8, 1981," *Chabad. org*, <chabad.org/858593>; "Reb Levik's Nigun—Blessing of the Sun: 4 Nissan, 5741 • April 8, 1981," *Chabad.org*, <chabad.org/302768>.

84. See *Seder birchat hachamah al pi minhag chabad*, (Brooklyn, NY: 2009), 35.

85. Schneerson, *Sichot kodesh 5741*, Vol. 3, 123-124.

86. *Ibid.*, 121.

87. See Dovid Margolin, "The Roots of Today's Revival of Russian Judaism Lies Deep in the Soviet Past," *Mosaic Magazine*, <https://mosaicmagazine.com/ response/2017/03/the-roots-of-todays-revival-of-russian-judaism-lie-deep-in-the-soviet-past/>; Eli Rubin, "Soviet Jewry: Quiet Diplomacy, Covert Activity," *Chabad.org*, <chabad.org/2619818>. Also see Hillel Zaltzman, *Samarkand: The Underground with a Far-Reaching Impact* (New York: Chamah, 2015).

88. Schneerson, *Sichot kodesh 5741*, Vol. 3, 123.

89. *Ibid.*, 121.

90. See Douglas Little, The Cold War in the Middle East: Suez Crisis to Camp David Accords," in *The Cambridge History of the Cold War*, edited by Melvyn P. Leffler and Odd Arne Westad (Cambridge, UK: Cambridge University Press, 2010), 319-322; James W. Bean and Craig S. Girard, *Anwar Al-Sadat's Grand Strategy in the Yom Kippur War*, (Long Paper, National War College, Washington D.C., 2001).

91. Schneerson, *Sichot kodesh 5741*, Vol. 3, 122.

92. *Zohar* I, 116b-117a. Cited in Schneerson, *Sichot kodesh 5741*, Vol. 3, 122.

93. Arie Morgenstern, *Hastening Redemption: Messianism and the Resettlement of the Land of Israel* (Oxford: Oxford University Press, 2006), 24-50.

94. Shalom DovBer Schneersohn, *Torat shalom*, (Brooklyn, NY: Kehot Publication Society, 1983) 237. See further relevant discussion and citations in Eli Rubin, "The Idealistic Realism of Jewish Messianism," *Chabad.org*, <chabad.org/2766417>.

95. See Menachem Mendel Schneerson, *Likutei sichot*, Vol. 15 (Brooklyn, NY: Kehot Publication Society, 1999), 42-48.

96. *Ibid.*, 46.

97. For Hanoka's own account of his relationship with Schneerson see Yaakov Hanoka, "Returning to Torah—Part 1," *Chabad.org*, <chabad.org/675639>, and *idem.*, "Returning to Torah—Part 2," *Chabad.org*, <chabad.org/675644>.

98. Keith Bradsher, "Solar Panel Maker Moves Work to China," *New York Times*, January 14, 2011, <https://www.nytimes.com/2011/01/15/business/energy-environment/15solar.html>.

99. See Kyle Alspach, "7AC Technologies Head Peter Vandermeulen Says Solar Plans Leave Investors Chilled," *MassLive.com*, January 30, 2011, <https://www.masslive.com/business-news/index.ssf/2011/01/7ac_technologies_head_peter_vandermeulen.html>.

100. Bradsher, "Solar Panel Maker."

101. Richard H. K. Vietor , *Energy Policy in America since 1945: A Study of Business-Government Relations* (New York: Cambridge University Press, 1984), 345-346.

102. Harvey Strum and Fred Strum, "Solar Energy Policy, 1952-1982," *Environmental Review* 7, no. 2 (Summer, 1983): 135-154

103. Schneerson enrolled in the École Spéciale des Travaux Publics (ESTP) in 1933, and graduated as a mechanical and electrical engineer in March 1938. Records show that in November 1937 and 1938 he was registered as a student at the Sorbonne University of Paris, where he studied differential calculus. For the

relevant documentation see, "In the Halls of the Sorbonne," *Chabad.org*, <chabad. org/604930/>.

104. Menachem Mendel Schneerson, *Reshimot*, Vol. 1 (Brooklyn, NY: Kehot Publication Society, 2012), 3-4 (Choveret 3). See Yanki Tauber, "The Fluidity of Life: Based on the Notebooks of Rabbi Menahem Mendel Schneerson," *B'or Hatorah* 10 (1997-1998): 59-67.

105. See Herman Branover, Michael Mond, and Yeshajahu Unger, *Liquid-Metal Flows: Magnetohydrodynamics and Applications* (Washington D.C.: American Institute of Aeronautics and Astronautics, 1988).

106. Herman Branover, "Al mada, madanim veha'idon hatekhnolagi," in *Harabi shloshim shenot nesi'ut*, edited by Chanoch Glitzenstein and Adin Steinsaltz (Jerusalem: Vaad Hotsa'at Sefer Hayovel, 1980), 338. With particular reference to solar energy technologies see *ibid.*, 341.

107. See Daniel Ruby, "Rooftop MHD: On Site Electricity from Low-Grade Heat," *Popular Science*, November 1982, 64-66.

108. See Matthew L. Wald, "A Race to Make an Old Power-Plant Idea Work," *The New York Times*, July 27, 1988, 7, <https://www.nytimes.com/1988/07/27/business/business-technology-a-race-to-make-an-old-power-plant-idea-work.html>.

109. See S.C. Kaushik, S.S. Verma and A. Chandra, "Solar-Assisted Liquid Metal MHD Power Generation: A State-of-the-Art Study," *Heat Recovery Systems & CHP* 15, no. 7 (October, 1995): 675-689; Eva-Marie Cosoroaba, *Multiphysics Simulation, Analysis and Design of a Permanent Magnet Excited Liquid Metal Magnetohydrodynamic Power Generator* (PhD thesis, The University of Texas at Dallas, 2017).

110. Herman Branover, "Towards Environmental Consciousness: The Need to Educate," *B'or Hatorah* 10 (1997-1998): 11-15.

111. Schneerson, *Sichot kodesh 5741*, Vol. 3, 122.

112. Herman Branover, "Al mada," 340-341.

⧟

THE DYNAMIC OF DISENCHANTMENT AND REENCHANTMENT IN THE PAST AND FUTURE

Schneerson's Temporal Dialogue with the Eternal Torah

IN 1972 MENACHEM Mendel Schneerson was interviewed for a *New York Times* profile by Israel Shenker. Shenker put it to him that his orthodoxy marked him as a conservative. But Schneerson objected:

> I don't believe that Reform Judaism is liberal and Orthodox is conservative. My explanation of conservative is some-one who is so petrified he cannot accept something new. For me, Judaism, or halacha [Jewish religious law], or Torah en-compasses all the universe, and it encompasses every new invention, every new theory, every new piece of knowledge or thought or action.[1]

This exchange does not simply highlight the tension between tra-dition and progress, but also between the eternal and the temporal. Schneerson maintains that he is unafraid of change because Torah is eternal. For him this means that Torah does not merely endure for all time, but that Torah actually ecompasses all time. The eternal and

universal reach of Torah contains every temporal moment, every new
contribution to human knowledge and activity. Here the verse from
Ecclesiastes (1:9) comes to mind, "there is nothing new under the sun."
In Ecclesiastes, however, this is a statement of pessimism, even nihilism.
For Schneerson, by contrast, it communicates a sense of security, of ex-
pectancy, of progressive openness and hope. He is unafraid of change
because the eternal Torah already anticipates change, requires change,
and calls forth change. In his view, as we have previously noted, it is
only through the progressive march of time that the eternal universality of the Torah can be fully unfolded and expressed.[2]

The full paradox of the Torah's unchanging anticipation of the ever
changing circumstances of history was articulated in one of Schneerson's edited talks:

> The service of God in its totality is founded upon the
> principle that both of these attitudes must be maintained,
> 1) "upstanding," standing strong, without change, and
> 2) "walking," progressing "from strength to strength" to the
> point that "they have no rest" (cf. *Talmud bavli*, Brakhot, 64a),
> constant change...
>
> In the unchanging nature of Torah and the command-
> ments it is underscored that the nature of the giver of the
> Torah and the commandments, the Almighty, is unchanging,
> "I God am unchanged." (Malakhi, 3:6.) But on account of Torah
> and the commandments being the service of the Jewish peo-
> ple... [and considering that] the definition of a creation entails
> being subject to change and being a progressive (*a mehalekh*)...,
> the work of Torah and the commandments is set up in such a
> manner that there is progress "from strength to strength" in
> the service of God; change (and ascent) constantly...
>
> The service of God in its totality demands both ele-
> ments...In every change...the foundation must be in the
> aspect of Torah and the commandments that is "upstanding,"
> [i.e.] in the aspect of..."I God am unchanged."[3]

For Schneerson, this tension—between the unchanging foundation
of the God given Torah, and its constantly changing application in the
transient lives of its recipients—is negotiated through the very serious

business of Torah study within the rigorous framework of the rabbinic legal tradition. This calls, on the one hand, for extreme faithfulness to the received texts and the rules that govern their interpretation. On the other hand, it calls for extreme intellectual innovation in the discovery of new lines of reasoning and new rulings that apply to new situations.

This negotiation is also regarded as a dialogue with God, as a temporal dialogue with eternity. Following the principle of reciprocity—as described above, in Chapter 3—we cannot reduce God to the role of the giver of the Torah, nor the Jewish people to the role of receivers of the Torah. On one occasion, Schneerson emphasized that the novel interpretation of Torah that is adduced by "a veteran scholar" (*talmid vatik*) is a true novelty, a product of a particular mind negotiating a particular nexus of textual and circumstantial problems.[4] Accordingly, the innovative progress made is historically and temporally situated. Even such innovation, however, is understood to be part of the very Torah that was "given to Moses at Sinai," following the exodus of the Israelites from Egypt.[5] In other words, it was "given" thousands of years before its initial innovation. This is possible because to study Torah is to enter into a temporally situated dialogue with the atemporal eternity of God's wisdom. In Schneerson's words:

> These innovations come from the Jewish people, but are nevertheless encompassed in God's thought even before they are innovated by the Jewish people, because on the part of God the past and future are one.[6]

On this score, God first received the progressive Torah innovations from the veteran students in each generation, and then gave the all-inclusive totality of Torah to the Jewish people at Sinai. As Elliot Wolfson has adduced, this "calls into question the model of aligning events chronoscopically in a sequence stretched between before and after" and replaces it with "a temporal configuration that is circular in its linearity and linear in its circularity."[7] Equally importantly, however, it signals the awesome imperative of history. The very fact of being situated in a particular nexus of historical circumstances calls the "veteran scholar" to craft the particular Torah innovation that can only be discovered at that time, thereby making a unique contribution to God's eternal wisdom.

Repeating the rabbinic dictum, "each day they shall be in your eyes like new,"[8] Schneerson often called upon his listeners to sacralize time—perhaps we could say to "enchant" time—through embracing the constant novelty of the Torah and its commandments. Based on a text by Schneur Zalman of Liadi, he would frequently add that the word "like" in the above dictum should be dropped, and that the Torah and its commandments should always be "literally new" (*chadashim mamash*).[9]

The imperative to scrutinize and sacralize the present through the constant novelty of the eternal Torah is well reflected in Schneerson's own practice as a historically situated student, interpreter and teacher of Torah. As we have already noted, Schneerson's activist leadership cannot be separated from his prolific oratory; the farbrengen was his primary medium for socio-mystical communication and interchange, and his mystical theorizations of Torah law and lore were themselves a form of activism. Applying Abraham J. Heschel's concept of "prophetic thinking" to Schneerson's speech, we have argued that he used his erudite mastery of Torah literature "to bring the world into divine focus."[10] His brand of prophetic mysticism was not at all disinterested in worldly affairs. To turn Weber's characterization of mysticism on its head, it is clear that Schneerson was very much prone to accomplish a "transformation of the mundane order on the basis of a methodical pattern of life."[11] The pattern of his practice was the methodical renewal of the unchanging Torah to illuminate the particular challenges of living in the present.

The nexus between Schneerson's methodical leadership practice and his theorization of the imperative of Torah progress is clearly visible in what we have termed his "countercultural strategy for Jewish renaissance."[12] As described above, in Chapter 2, he was unafraid of youthful energy and agitation for change. On the contrary, he welcomed it and encouraged it. He maintained that youthful revolution—"a transformation from one extreme to another"—need not stand in contradiction to the Torah, nor be perceived as a threat to the Torah. "The Torah, need not be afraid of the world; rather its role is to run the world." Schneerson accordingly sought a partnership between "the elder who has acquired [Torah] wisdom" and the rebellious youth who could take the new Torah paradigm much further than the elder himself might imagine.[13]

Schneerson's practice as an activist Torah interpreter is further demonstrated in his discussions of educational policy; of the relationship between poverty, affluence and crime; and in his critical theorizations of socio-mystical justice, humanism and ecology (above, chapters 5 and 6). In all these instances he wove new arguments through bold applications of the classical tools of rabbinic interpretation and innovation.

Ambassadorship and Sacred Interaction as Vehicles of Transformation

WE HAVE SAID a lot about the driving ethos of Chabad as articulated by Schneerson, but what are the *practical* vehicles of Chabad's success?

According to Chabad's official website, "4,900 Chabad-Lubavitch emissary families, or *shluchim*, operate 3,500 institutions, in 100 countries and territories, with activities in many more," and "Chabad on Campus serves students and faculty at 500 campuses, with 284 permanent campus centers."[14] Chabad's international reach is similarly borne out by the independent work of Marcin Wodziński in his *Historical Atlas of Hasidism*.[15]

In addition to the rhetorical power of Schneerson's Torah teachings, he developed two practical mechanisms that are the primary vehicles of Chabad's expansion into an international network that continues to grow each year: The first is *shlichut*, which is best translated as "ambassadorship." The second is Schneerson's initiation of ten distinct *mivtsa'im*, mitzvah "campaigns." These two initiatives have given rise to a global network of "Chabad houses"—as well as Chabad run schools, synagogues, and even restaurants—and given Chabad a very high degree of visibility, especially on the streets and college campuses of American cities.

The two mechanisms are closely linked: Building on the practice of his predecessors, Schneerson appointed official ambassadors (*shluchim*) to represent him, and to advance his agenda through encouraging and supporting the fundamental practices of Jewish life. While Chabad's official ambassadors have often built large and successful institutions, that has never been their primary focus; such institutions are merely mediums through which to reach individuals, facilitating, encouraging and inspiring individual engagement in Jewish life. The mitzvah

campaigns (*mivtsa'im*) provide a template of ten forms of Jewish engagement that the *shluchim*, and indeed all disciples of Schneerson, most
actively prioritise and promote.[16]

In Chapter 3 we gave an account of Schneerson's mystical theorization of the function of the Torah and its commandments as the most
essential basis for any lasting fellowship. From his perspective the perpetuation of social cohesion and progress does not depend only on the
constant renewal of the eternal Torah as a corpus of study and interpretation, but also on the constant renewal of Jewish life on the everyday
level of actual practice, actual observance of the mitzvot. Among the
ten campaigns are some mitzvot that we have already mentioned, at
least in passing; tefillin, Torah study, charity, love of one's fellow, and
education. The others are Shabbat candles (this campaign was aimed
specifically at women and girls from the age of three and older), to af-
fix *mezuzah* scrolls to the doors of Jewish homes and workplaces, to fill
one's home with Torah books, to keep the laws governing food consumption and preparation (*kashrut*), and for women to immerse in the
mikvah (a bath or immersion pool) in accord with the laws of family purity (*taharat hamishpacha*).

In a 1974 talk Schneerson responded to critics of his initiation of
these campaigns and, as part of a fuller dissertation on their significance, elaborated on the meaning of Hebrew term *mivtsa* (the singular
form of *mivtsa'im*):

> The root of the word *mivtsa* is *betsa*, which means profit or
> purpose. As in the phrase "*mah betsa*" in the story of Joseph
> (Genesis, 37:26), which means "what purpose is there in
> this?"...When we add the letter *mem* to this root the word
> *mivtsa* is formed, and it means that we share *betsa* with oth-
> ers...Just as adding a *mem* to the root for food (*okhel*) forms the
> word feed (*makhil*).[17]

For Schneerson, accordingly, the purpose of these campaigns was to
share meaning and purposefulness with others. These are practices that
would ordinarily be understood as personal lifestyle choices, observed
within the home or synagogue alongside others of one's own persua-
sion, or—alternatively—as vertical interactions between the individual
and God. But through the *mivtsa'im* they are transformed into horizontal

interactions between self and other as well. The *mivtsa'im* are a form of spiritual sharing. These practices are endowed with all the qualities of Schneerson's reciprocal paradigm, of which various examples have already been discussed, according to which hierarchies are upended through dynamic interchange. Schneerson also encouraged seasonal campaigns to promote the observance of the various Jewish festivals; *mivtsa shofar* on Rosh Hashanah, *mivtsa lulav* on Sukkot, *mivtsa chanukah*, *mivtsa purim* etc. These created further opportunity to extend festive celebrations beyond their ordinary bounds, bringing the vertical or cosmic dimension beyond the home or synagogue and into the streets.[18]

Another aspect of these campaigns and of their effectiveness, both within Chabad and beyond Chabad, is that they create a new enthusiasm for some of the most fundamental practices of traditional Jewish life. Here the move is from the pure materialization of daily life—from the increasing reduction of even religious ritual to the horizontal plane—to the restoration of the vertical dimension. We should note that such practices as the weekly lighting of Shabbat candles, following the laws of *kashrut*, or going to the *mikvah*, have the effect of reorganising mundane routines—like the weekly work cycle, what one can eat and when, and even sexual activity—on a sacred basis, reframing them as divine interactions.

These are practices that are often seen as the stale and primitive relics of the middle ages or the shtetl. But Schneerson enthused his listeners; he did not merely call upon them to hold fast to tradition, but rather to campaign for the renewal of tradition. These campaigns formed the practical basis for the reenchantment of the elemental rituals of Jewish life, even for the resacralization of the Jewish religion itself.

In Chapter 5 we noted that Schneerson's approach could be termed "progressive religion." This is not to say that he combined a progressive outlook with a religious outlook, but rather that his outlook was wholly religious, and that his religiosity was itself progressive. His progressivism cannot be conflated with the generic progressivism that is identified with left wing political attitudes. In the quote with which this epilogue begins he explicitly rejected the conservative label. But he did not go so far as to claim the mantle of liberalism. Indeed, on other occasions he invoked that label critically. Schneerson's progressivism was not defined—or borrowed—from the outside, but was rather an inherent expression of the eternal tradition of Judaism, of its messianic impulse not only to repair the world but to reenchant the world. But it was also a progressivism that could only be articulated in the post-war context of the United States. Schneerson was consciously in sync with, and in dialogue with, the spirit of his times. Yet he zealously guarded the autonomy of Jewish law and lore as the unchanging arbiter of moral standards, reframing his traditionalism as of a piece with rebellious countercultural trends.[19]

This talk of "religious progressivism" may sound grand and bold, but Schneerson understood that such a macro vision depended on grassroots micro activism and on grassroots micro interactions; it is the individual experience and the individual action that is transformative. It is the massing of individual interactions that creates a social movement, a movement in society, a wellspring of transformation that carries Judaism forward. It is the reshaping and reenchantment of lives—one individual at a time, one interaction at a time, one moment at a time, one family at a time—that reshapes and reenchants communities, creates new communities, and ultimately transforms the world.

We have already paid some attention to Schneerson's broader theory and practice of leadership (above, Chapter 3) and also to his concept of the individual as the fulcrum of macrocosmic purpose (above, Chapter 4). But taking note of the institutions of *shlichut* and *mivtsa'im* provides a deeper perception of how he applied these ideas in the practical work of reenchantment.

Universalizing the Dynamic Between the Individual and the Collective

HERE IT IS also worth noting the discussion of Chabad activism in the 2015 report of the Jewish People Policy Institute (JPPI).[20] Chabad's focus on individual engagement is cited as the key factor that sets the movement apart from other groups and organizations that seek to ensure the perpetuation of Jewish identity and peoplehood. According to the JPPI report, other groups and organizations focus on denominational membership, on the payment of dues as a measure of belonging, and on programs that are specifically designed to encourage young Jews to marry "within the tribe" and to raise Jewish families. Belonging, on this score, is marked only by the horizontal ties of institutional and family affiliation. Chabad, by contrast, does not prioritize membership, fees or long-term commitments. Instead, Chabad offers "capsules of ultimate meaning that can be consumed with other kinds of capsules of meaning (Zen, movies, literature, sculpture, shopping) on various levels."[21]

The JPPI report correctly asserts that Chabad's "individualistic approach" is rooted in its "metaphysical collectivism" (a notion that anticipates are own theorization of Chabad's socio-mystical orientation), and further that "Chabad metaphysics and activity is truly suited to…provide a path to Jewish identification in individualist, fluid 21st Century American culture." Chabad places the greatest emphasis on personal interaction, personal action, and personal meaning, and this also changes the shape of the larger interpersonal networks that inevitably coalesse around Chabad *shluchim*, and within the institutions they build. Here again the JPPI report has it right:

> The interpersonal experience Chabad offers is different from the conventional one offered by the Jewish community. Chabad religious philosophy and practice basically strips people and situations down to their metaphysical essentials. Viewed in Chabad eyes, individual Jews are not "members of the Jewish community" with social roles, status, and resources. They are basically divine Jewish souls placed in the lower material world to provide God with a dwelling place. Thus, ideally speaking, Chabad social practice and convention tends to ignore the external "garments" of money, status and sexual attraction. Rather, it tends to relate to people on the basis of their common human/Jewish essence, creating an egalitarian, open, and accepting space (for Jews) that ignores social distinctions. It resembles the concepts of "communitas" that the anthropologist, Victor Turner made famous.[22]

The JPPI report is right to note that Chabad's focus on the individual is well suited to the individualistic culture of 21st Century America. But it should be further emphasized that thereby Chabad also poses a critique, and provides an antidote, to American individualism and consumerism. For Schneerson the position of the self at the center of social action is not an expression of narcissism. It is rather an expression of personal agency and mission; the recognition that the individual has the greatest influence and responsibility over their own self, their own choices, and secondarily over the choices of their close family members, friends and colleagues. Each person is seen as a center from which collective change can emanate progressively outward. This is an individualism that seeks to liberate the self from dependencies imposed by hierarchical structures and corporate organizations. So long as religiosity, moral compunction, or identity are enforced only from without they are understood to inhibit the successful flourishing of an authentic socio-mystical pneuma.[23]

We should further note that the JPPI report's focus on Jewish identity overlooks the more universalistic dimension of the Chabad worldview, especially as espoused by Schneerson himself. There is, of course, no question that he successfully inspired a global Jewish renaissance. And it is likewise clear that this success is rooted in his bold articulation, elaboration, and application of Hasidism's socio-mystical ethos. But we have further demonstrated that Schneerson never shared the defensive mentality that places the central emphasis on the "question" of Jewish survival. Actually, for Schneerson the perpetuation of Jewish identity was never in question at all; for him the Jewish people are an eternal people, essentially bound up with the eternal Torah and the eternal God. For him the question was less "how can Judaism survive?" and more "how can Judaism repair the world?" As described above, in Chapter 2, from the very beginning of his tenure he sought to unleash the eternal and universal power of Jewish life and of Torah wisdom to transform the world for the better.

At the outset of this book we asked a simple question: What did Schneerson want?

Now, with all our cards on the table, we can give a simple answer: Schneerson wanted to reenchant the world. He wanted to reenchant and resacralize the everyday experiences, practices and interactions of all people, everywhere.

In his own words:

> So long as there is one place (even a marginalized corner) where the revelation of divinity does not shine it is a bounded revelation… "Even if one tsadik would completely reconcile with God the messiah would come in that generation." For through reconciliation (*teshuvah*) the unbounded revelation of

the infinite is drawn forth, and such a revelation would extend everywhere.[24]

In the immediate aftermath of the Holocaust Schneerson sought to
shake his people from the bleak and nihilistic sense of being in the
grip of evil, in the grip of catastrophe. America, which he referred to
as "a nation of kindness," would be the new center for a global Jewish
renaissance, and also the new fulcrum for the reenchantment of the
world. He consistently argued that America should not adopt an isola-
tionist attitude, nor should America merely see itself as an exporter of
consumerism and culture on a purely materialistic scale. He called on
the American nation and its leaders to adopt a socio-mystical view of
its privileged place in the family of nations, investing in the global proliferation of charity and justice, of education and morality, of optimism
and reciprocity, of ecological sanctity and geopolitical security.

On all the policy issues that we have looked at Schneerson went
beyond the normative modes of discourse and theorization, subverting what you might expect from a religious thinker and subverting
normative secular positions as well. He was never just checking boxes on someone else's list. On each issue he developed his approach
independently, as an extension of the Hasidic ethos and of his socio-mystical worldview.

Schneerson's vision was fundamentally optimistic, aspirational, and
global. But it rests on a foundation of concrete realism, on the fundamental need for individuals to be empowered to recognize and actualize
their agency. The divine surges up from within each individual so that
all become reciprocal wellsprings of blessing, and thereby society and
the cosmos are transformed from within. The divine infuses everyday life and permeates social interaction, horizontally (between fellow
humans) and vertically (between humanity and God), so that the transcendent essence of divine being is unfolded and realized in human
activity in the world. Schneerson's messianic aspiration was that on this
basis a new paradigm would take hold of society as a whole; a sacred
paradigm of dynamic interchange and mutuality between individuals,
communities, and nations.

Against the polarization of capitalism versus socialism—which respectively advocate for static utopias of personal completeness and
collective sameness—Schneerson envisioned a dynamic state of joyous

reciprocity. He maintained that individuality is enhanced through contribution to the collective, rather than compromised thereby. "A feeling of true happiness comes to a person when he is able to do something for the good of another...every creation, if only it acts in concert with its telos, is not merely a recipient but also a giver."[25] It is through constant imbalance and rebalance that relationships of joyous and graceful reciprocation can be cultivated and cherished. Schneerson upheld a deepset faith that without eliminating difference we can yet achieve a peaceful, harmonious, universal life, for all of humanity.

Hasidic Transformation in the Past, Present, and Future

AT THE PRESENT moment there is a palpable spirit of social and cultural transformation in the air. Some are afraid of it. Some celebrate it. It might not be too soon to say that the iron cage of capitalism is beginning to crumble. Schneerson not only anticipated this moment but also provided us with a coherent set of tools with which to chart a new future. We have noted his appreciation of the social, mystical, and cultural potentials of the 1960s American counterculture. We have noted what Ada Rapoport-Albert termed his "counter-feminism," including advocacy for women's education and his mobilization of women as agents of cultural change. We have given significant attention to his conceptions of leadership, community, and reciprocity, as well as to his engagement with questions of particular and universal love, individualism and collectivism. We have shown that his activist critique of contemporary approaches to politics, economics, education, criminal justice reform, and ecology were all expressions of his unique development of the socio-mystical ethos of Hasidism.

It is our contention that while Schneerson was born, lived, and died in the 20th century, his ideas do not belong to the past but to the future. In his own lifetime his impact was already international, and in the subsequent quarter century his influence has continued to proliferate. Yet the full universality of his vision remains to be realized in the redemptive step beyond the present.

The initial unfolding of Schneerson's vision for the dissemination of the Hasidic ethos is already well under way. This unfolding is part of a broader process of sacralization and reenchantment that extends

beyond traditional Hasidic communities into other Jewish denomina-
tions, and also into wider culture. No less an iconic cultural figure than
Bob Dylan is known to have visited Schneerson, and to have maintained relationships with various Chabad rabbis.[26] A more specific
and more developed example of this kind of process is the well-recognized and quite diffuse phenomenon that scholars have termed
"neo-hasidism." This can be regarded as a philosophical movement, a
literary movement, and a spiritual movement. Examples of neo-hasidism can be identified from the early decades of the 20th century on,
and among its better-known representatives can be counted Martin
Buber, I. L. Peretz, Hillel Zeitlin, Abraham J. Heschel, Elie Wiesel,
Zalman Schachter-Shalomi, and Shlomo Carlebach.[27] The last three,
notably, were all profoundly influenced by Schneerson.

Schachter-Shalomi and Carlebach began their Jewish leadership
careers among the first wave of Chabad *shluchim* in the United States,
but ultimately broke with Chabad to chart their own paths of reenchantment. Both went on to have a broad impact on the changing face
of American Judaism. Many contemporary proponents of "Jewish renewal" and of other new-age experiments in Jewish spirituality and
spiritual community—whether in America, Israel, or elsewhere—look
to Schachter-Shalomi and Carlebach for inspiration.[28] Recent decades
have also seen elements of the Hasidic ethos taking a firmer hold within
former bastions of traditional, or Orthodox, Judaism.[29] In 2013 a senior
official at the flagship Modern Orthodox institution, Yeshiva University (YU), commented, "Neo-Chassidus is very popular in Israel where
85 to 90 percent of our students study before YU. The administration
said that if this moves many of our students, let's give it a try."[30]

Neo-hasidism, in other words, has many forms. Some forms openly
embrace and appropriate Hasidic texts and practices. Others borrow
more selectively or more surreptitiously. But one way or another, the
spirit of the Hasidic ethos continues to disseminate outward into broader culture and echoes beyond the particular confines of Judaism in the
broader phenomena of new-age decentralized and non-denominational
religiosity or spirituality, often marked by the phrase "spiritual but not
religious," which is now well-recognized by sociologists and scholars
of religion.[31]

An illustrative example of the cultural and literary dimensions
of Hasidic reenchantment is provided by Russian-Israeli poet Zelda

Schneurson-Mishkovsky (1914-1984), a first cousin of Schneerson. Her poetry was very popular in Israel, yet the centrality of her personal and familial identification with Chabad Hasidism, along with the mystical pathos of her religiosity, has for the most part been underappreciated. This provides an example of the dynamic of secularization that can take hold as the sacred is disseminated into wider avenues of cultural expression; her poetry is enchanting and yet often speaks in the language of the disenchanted world it confronts. As Ariel Mayse has written, Zelda *whispers* "of a radical awareness that God is veiled and absent but also revealed through ordinary phenomena," and her "religious personality and literary works push beyond conventional categories such as 'secular' or 'sacred.'"[32]

This gestures toward the larger possibility for the adaption of the Hasidic ethos, beyond self-described sacred or spiritual communities and traditions. It is quite possible for Schneerson's social vision, and for more general aspects of the Hasidic ethos, to be adapted into wider culture and into the wider processes of policymaking and social change. This can happen either deliberately or through the more roundabout processes by which new ideas are disseminated, undergoing all manner of transmutation. In an essay dating from 1961 Jürgen Habermas already noted the influence of Kabbalah on German Idealism, one of the most influential philosophical movements of the modern era, and of Hasidism on German Jewish thinkers beginning with Franz Rosenzweig. Other scholars have by now illuminated these connections more rigorously.[33] But these words of Habermas are all the more worthy of citation because they register the dialectic of revelation and concealment that is often a function of the way ideas disseminate in society:

> Because the legacy of the Kabballah [*sic*] already flowed into and was absorbed by Idealism, its light seems to refract all the more richly in the spectrum of a spirit in which something of the spirit of Jewish mysticism lives on, in however hidden a way.[34]

Here we take up the broader possibility that the new ethos of Hasidism could ultimately become a new basis for social life, economics, and culture, much in the same way that the process of secularization and universalization transformed the Protestant ethic into the spirit of capitalism. We should remember, however, that such processes can span many centuries. To imagine the possibility of a new Hasidic epoch is to look beyond the deconstructive processes of postmodernity and beyond the rise of new-age phenomena. To imagine this possibility is to anticipate a new new-age, an entirely new cultural form, an entirely new social paradigm built out of the ruins of modernity. Such an adaption might well render the Hasidic ethos unrecognizable, much as the Protestant ethic was rendered unrecognizable via its secularization. But that doesn't necessarily make it any less transformative, and we would do well to imagine what such a new new-age would look like.

On the one hand, we should be alive to the possibility that, like in the case of Protestantism, such a process of dissemination could lead to secularization and disenchantment, ultimately transforming Hasidism from a "light cloak" into an "iron cage" of a different sort. Alternatively, Hasidism might simply sublimate its ethos to the reigning capitalist order. One way or another it is entirely possible that through various processes of universalization, dissemination, and assimilation the transformative power of Hasidism will be lost, congealing into an oppressive perversion of its original spirit. Of course, there is always the danger that this can happen within one corner or another of the Hasidic world, or of the Jewish world more broadly. It might easily be argued that such processes can already be diagnosed. But here we gesture to the broader possibility that the transformative success of Hasidism as the basis for a new social paradigm might lead to its own failure—to a new form of secularization and disenchantment. Such has been the dynamic of enchantment and disenchantment in the past. Who is to say that history will not repeat itself?

On the other hand, things could work out very differently this time around. The failure of the Protestant ethic might give way to the success of the Hasidic ethos, and not at the price of its congealment into a new form of social petrification and impasse. Here we are reminded of Émile Durkheim's argument that the sacred is destined to endure modernity and survive it:

> There is something eternal in religion that is destined to outlive the succession of particular symbols in which religious thought has clothed itself... The great things of the past that excited our fathers no longer suit our aspirations. Meanwhile,

no replacement for them has yet been created...We would
like one that is more rigorous but do not yet see clearly what
it should be or how it might be realized...But that state of
uncertainty and confused anxiety cannot last forever. A day
will come when our societies once again will know hours of
collective effervescence during which new ideals will again
spring forth and new formulas emerge to guide humanity for
a time...Religion seems destined to transform itself rather
than disappear.[35]

Perhaps we really are on the cusp of the new cultural paradigm
foreseen from afar by Weber, Durkheim, and Sorokin, and from up
close by Menachem Mendel Schneerson. Perhaps the Hasidic ethos
will prove to provide a new foundation for the realization of a universal socio-mystical reenchantment. Perhaps we will yet see the
repair of social relations—the establishment of a reciprocal dynamic
through which all individuals can attain dignity, joy, and fulfillment
grounded in everyday manifestations of the sacred. Perhaps Hasidism's
inner-worldly mysticism will fare differently from the inner-worldly
asceticism of the Protestant ethic. Indeed, the profound differences between their respective paradigms provides a substantive basis for such
a supposition. As noted above, in Chapter 1, the very constitution of
the Protestant ethic is such that it tends to empty good works of real
significance. In contrast, we have argued, the Hasidic ethos endows
the good works of embodied human beings with ultimate significance;
every human action is recast as a dynamic fulcrum of socio-mystical
revitalization and reciprocity between self, community, and God.

Hasidism, as inspired by the Baal Shem Tov, seeks to universalize
the mystical union of worlds, souls, and divinity in every spoken word.
Chabad articulates and elaborates the promise that this will inaugurate
the messianic promise of Judaism as foreseen by the prophets of old,
and as revisioned in the 20th century by the Lubavitcher Rebbe. For
him, we have shown, Hasidism is not merely Kabbalah become ethos,
but Kabbalah become activism. His Hasidic vision has the capacity to
replace the empty ritualisms of contemporary life, instead infusing all
interactions with divinity, wisdom, and empathy. Extending from micro activity to macro culture, this would constitute a transformative
recalibration of the most elemental paradigms that govern life in this

world, thereby bringing about the full realization and eternal renewal of social being and of human being.

Notes

1. Israel Shenker, "Lubavitch Rabbi Marks His 70th Year With Call for 'Kindness'," *The New York Times*, March 27, 1972, Page 39.

2. Menachem Mendel Schneerson, *Torat menachem—hitvaduyot*, Vol. 33 (Brooklyn, NY: Kehot Publication Society, 2006), 331. Cited above, page 23

3. Menachem Mendel Schneerson, *Likutei sichot*, Vol. 29 (Brooklyn, NY: Kehot Publication Society, 2000), 175-178.

4. Cf. *Talmud bavli*, Megillah, 19b; *Talmud yerushalmi*, Pe'ah, 2:4; *Shemot rabbah*, 47:1.

5. See sources cited in previous note.

6. Menachem Mendel Schneerson, *Torat menachem—hitvaduyot 5752*, Vol. 2 (Brooklyn, NY: Kehot Publication Society, 1994), 242.

7. Elliot R. Wolfson, *Open Secret: Postmessianic Messianism and the Mystical Revision of Menachem Mendel Schneerson* (New York: Columbia University Press, 2009), 22-3.

8. Rashi's commentary to Deuteronomy, 6:6, paraphrasing the comment of the *Sifre* ad loc..

9. Schneur Zalman of Liadi, *Likutei torah, Devarim*, 1b. For a few of the many instances in which Schneerson invoked this phrase, see Menachem Mendel Schneerson, *Torat menachem—sefer hamamrim melukat*, Vol. 1 (Brooklyn, NY: Kehot Publication Society, 2012), 52; *ibid.*, Vol. 3 (Brooklyn, NY: Kehot Publication Society, 2012), 145, 309.

10. See above, page 97; Abraham J. Heschel, *The Prophets* (New York: Jewish Publication Society of America, 1962), 24.

11. Cf. Max Weber, *Economy and Society*, edited by Guenther Roth and Claus Wittich (Berkeley: University of California Press, 1978), 550. Cited above, page xv.

12. Above, page 49.

13. Menachem Mendel Schneerson, *Torat menachem hitvaduyot*, Vol. 25 [5719, 2] (Brooklyn, NY: Kehot Publication Society, 2003), 39-41. Cited above page 53-4.

14. "Facts and Statistics," *Chabad.org*, <chabad.org/2346206> (accessed March 25, 2019).

15. Marcin Wodziński, *Historical Atlas of Hasidism* (Princeton, NJ: Princeton University Press, 2018), 190-205 and 214-219.

16. For more on *shlichut* and *mivtsa'im* see Sue Fishkoff, *The Rebbe's Army: Inside the World of Chabad-Lubavitch* (New York: Schocken Books, 2003). For a useful guide to the *mivtsa'im* produced by a Chabad rabbi, and directed to a Chabad audience, see Shmuel Bistritzky, *The Rebbe's Mivtzoyim*, trans. N. Grossman, Vol. 1 (Kfar Chabad: Sifriat Eshel, 2011).

17. Menachem Mendel Schneerson, *Sichot kodesh 5734*, Vol. 2 (Brooklyn, NY: Vaad Hanachot Hatemimim, 1986), 177.

18. See Shmuel Bistritzky, *The Rebbe's Mivtzoyim*, trans. N. Grossman, Vol. 2 (Kfar Chabad: Sifriat Eshel, 2012).

19. For a relevant discussion of Schneerson's concept of the resonance between rebellion and religiosity, see Eli Rubin, "Traveling and Traversing Chabad's Literary Paths: From Likutei torah to Khayim gravitser and Beyond," *In Geveb: A Journal of Yiddish Studies*, October 2018, <https://ingeveb.org/articles/traveling-and-traversing-chabads-literary-paths-from-likutei-torah-to-khayim-gravitser-and-beyond>, Part 3.

20. Barry Geltman and Rami Tal (eds.), *Annual Assessment: The Situation and Dynamics of the Jewish People 2014-2015* (Jerusalem: The Jewish People Policy Institute, 2015) <http://jppi.org.il/new/wp-content/uploads/2015/JPPI_AA2015E.pdf>, esp. 152-160.

21. *Ibid.*, 159.

22. *Ibid.*

23. On the supreme value of personal religious autonomy in Schneerson's thought see above, page 63.

24. Menachem Mendel Schneerson, "Mamar ve'atah tetsaveh 5741—kuntras purim katan 5752," in *Sefer hamamarim melukatim*, Vol. 3 (Brooklyn, NY: Kehot Publication Society, 2012), 39-40. Cited above, page 81.

25. Menachem Mendel Schneerson, *Igrot kodesh*, Vol. 13 (Brooklyn, NY: Kehot Publication Society, 1989), 234. Cited above, page 114.

26. See Nadine Epstein and Rebecca Frankel, "Bob Dylan: The Unauthorized Spiritual Biography," *Moment Magazine*, October 13, 2016, <https://www.momentmag.com/bob-dylan-unauthorized-spiritual-biography/>: "Dylan spent several years in the 1980s studying with the Lubavitcher Jews of Brooklyn, receiving instruction from Talmudic scholars and listening to tapes of Rebbe Menachem Schneerson. Since then he has been seen praying with Chabad in Los Angeles, Minneapolis-St. Paul and New York." In a 2010 interview with *The New York Times* (Deborah Solomon, "The Rabbi," Aug. 6, 2010, <https://www.nytimes.com/2010/08/08/magazine/08fob-q4-t.html>) Schneerson's aid Yehudah Krinsky remarked: "Bob Dylan comes to the Lubavitch outpost from time to time. Did you know that? He was at my house for dinner a couple of times." For a photograph of Dylan visiting Schneerson in Krinsky's company, see *The Living Archive*, image #222687, <http://www.thelivingarchive.org/photos/222687>.

27. For a general overview that introduces key neo-hasidic figures from the beginning of the 20th century to the present see Ariel Mayse, "The Development of Neo-Hasidism: Echoes and Repercussions" [in four parts], *The Lehrhaus*, <https://www.thelehrhaus.com/scholarship/the-development-of-neo-hasidism-echoes-and-repercussions-part-i-introduction-hillel-zeitlin-and-martin-buber/>. On Wiesel, see Arthur Green, "Wiesel in the Context of Neo-Hasidism," in *Elie Wiesel: Jewish, Literary, and Moral Perspectives*, edited by Steven T. Katz and Alan Rosen (Bloomington: Indiana University Press, 2013), 51-58.

28. On Schachter-Shalomi and Carlebach and their roots in Chabad, see Shaul Magid, *American Post-Judaism: Identity and Renewal in a Postethnic Society* (Bloomington: Indiana University Press, 2013), esp. 116 and 233. On recent developments

of new-age Jewish spirituality in Israel see Rachel Werczberger, *Jews in the Age of Authenticity: Jewish Spiritual Renewal in Israel* (New York: Peter Lang, 2017).

29. Adam S. Ferziger, *Beyond Sectarianism: The Realignment of American Orthodox Judaism* (Detroit, MI: Wayne State University Press, 2015), esp. 175-194.

30. "Rabbi Moshe Weinberger to Join RIETS Faculty as Mashigach Ruchani," *The Commentator*, February 14, 2013, <https://yucommentator.org/2013/02/rabbi-moshe-weinberger-to-join-riets-faculty-as-mashigach-ruchani/>. In 2015 YU dedicated its annual research conference to issues facing contemporary Orthodox Judaism, the Orthodox Forum, and the increasing popularity of neo-hasidism.

31. See the relevant discussions collected in William B. Parsons (ed.), *Being Spiritual but Not Religious: Past, Present, Future(s)* (New York: Routledge, 2018).

32. Ariel Mayse, "The Development of Neo-Hasidism: Echoes and Repercussions Part II: Abraham Joshua Heschel and Zelda Schneurson Mishkovsky," *The Lehrhaus*, <https://www.thelehrhaus.com/scholarship/the-development-of-neo-hasidism-echoes-and-repercussions-part-ii-abraham-joshua-heschel-and-zelda-schneurson-mishkovsky/>.

33. See Paul Franks, "Inner Anti-Semitism or Kabbalistic Legacy? German Idealism's Relationship to Judaism," in *Yearbook of German Idealism, Volume VII, Faith and Reason*, edited by Fred Rush, Jürgen Stolzenberg, and Paul Franks (Berlin: Walter de Gruyter, 2010), 254-279; Yitzhak Y. Melamed, "Spinozism, Acosmism, and Hassidism: A Closed Circle," in *The Concept of Judaism in German Idealism*, edited by Amit Kravitz and Jörg Noller (Berlin: Suhrkamp Verlag, 2018), 75-85. For an especially relevant meditation on resonances between Rosenzweig's thought and Schneerson's see Wolfson, *Open Secret*, 266-276, and esp. 394, n. 8.

34. Jürgen Habermas, "The German Idealism of the Jewish Philosophers (1961)," in idem., *Philosophical-Political Profiles*, translated by Frederick G. Lawrence (Cambridge, MA: MIT Press, 1983), 21-22.

35. Émile Durkheim, *The Elementary Forms of Religious Life*, translated by Karen E. Fields (New York: Free Press, 1995), 429-432.

BIBLIOGRAPHY

Adair-Toteff, Christopher. "Max Weber's Charismatic Prophets." *History of the Human Sciences* 27, no. 1 (February 2014): 3-20.

Aleph Institute, The. "Mission Statement." https://aleph-institute.org/wp/about/.

———. "Nearly 200 Judges, Prosecutors, Lawyers and Practitioners Attend Aleph's Alternative Sentencing Summit at Georgetown." https://aleph-institute.org/wp/nearly-200-judges-prosecutors-lawyers-and-practitioners-attend-alephs-alternative-sentencing-summit-at-georgetown/.

———. "Day 1 Rabbi Sholom Lipskar v2." https://vimeo.com/163606986.

Allen, Philip. *Pitirim A. Sorokin in Review*. Durham, NC: Duke University Press, 1963.

Anderson, Elizabeth. "What Is the Point of Equality?" *Ethics* 109, no. 2 (January 1999): 287-337.

Ashton, Dianne. *Hanukkah in America: A History*. New York: New York University Press, 2013.

Balakirsky Katz, Maya. *The Visual Culture of Chabad*. New York: Cambridge University Press, 2010.

Bean, James and Girard, Craig. "Anwar Al-Sadat's Grand Strategy in the Yom Kippur War." Long Paper, National War College, Washington D.C., 2001.

Beiner, Ronald. "Walter Benjamin's Philosophy of History." *Political Theory* 12, no. 3 (Aug., 1984): 423-434.

Benjamin, Walter. *Illuminations: Essays and Reflections*, edited by Hannah Arendt, translated by Harry Zohn. New York: Schocken Books, 2007.

Berman, Feigue. "Hasidic dance: A Historical and Theological Analysis." PhD Thesis, New York University, 1999.

Biale, David. *Hasidism: A New History*. Princeton, NJ: Princeton University Press, 2018.

Bistritzky, Shmuel. *The Rebbe's Mivtzoyim*, translated by N. Grossman. Kfar Chabad: Sifriat Eshel, 2011-2012. [2 Vols.]

Bowler, Kate. *Blessed: A History of the American Prosperity Gospel*. Oxford: Oxford University Press, 2013.

Branover, Herman; Mond, Michael and Unger, Yeshajahu. *Liquid-metal flows: magneto-hydrodynamics and applications.* Washington D.C.: American Institute of Aeronautics and Astronautics, 1988.

Branover, Herman. "Al mada, madanim veha'idon hatekhnologi." In *Harabi shloshim shenot nesi'ut,* edited by Chanoch Glitzenstein and Adin Steinsaltz, 337-342. Jerusalem: Vaad Hotsa'at Sefer Hayovel, 1980.

———. "Towards Environmental Consciousness: The Need to Educate." *B'or Hatorah* 10 (1997-1998): 11-15.

Brawer, Naftali. "Resistance and Response to Change: The Leadership of Rabbi Shalom DovBer Schneersohn (1860-1920)." PhD Thesis, University College London, 2004.

Buber, Martin. *The Origin and Meaning of Hasidism.* Edited and translated by Maurice Friedman. New York: Harper Torchbooks, 1960.

Cantor, Aviva. *Jewish Women / Jewish Men: The Legacy of Patriarchy in Jewish Life.* New York: HarperCollins, 1995.

Cantor, Harold. "Allen Ginsberg's "Kaddish": A Poem of Exorcism." *Studies in American Jewish Literature* 2, no. 2 (Winter 1976): 10-26.

Chabad.org. "The Farbrengen Series: Chassidic Gatherings with the Rebbe." chabad.org/2143216.

———. "Public Address Archives: Recordings of the Talks of the Lubavitcher Rebbe, of righteous memory." https://www.chabad.org/therebbe/sichoskodesh_cdo/jewish/Sichos-Kodesh.htm.

———. ""Chanukah Live" Celebrations: Live Broadcasts of Chanukah Celebrations and Menorah Lightings Across the Globe." *Chabad.org.* chabad.org/3153123.

———. "Living Torah Archives: An archive of the "Living Torah," the weekly video magazine featuring the Rebbe's application of Torah to timely events and issues." https://www.chabad.org/therebbe/livingtorah/default_cdo/aid/42106/jewish/Archives.htm.

———. "Excerpt from the Lubavitcher Rabbi's א"טילש Letter on the Question of the Regents Prayer." *Chabad.org.* chabad.org/1274011.

———. "Prayer in Public Schools and Separation of Church and State." *Chabad.org.* chabad.org/2051611.

———. "Facts and Statistics." chabad.org/2346206.

Chafe, William. *The American Woman: Her Changing Social, Economic and Political Roles, 1920-1970.* London, Oxford and New York: Oxford University Press, 1972.

Chappell, Marisa. *The War on Welfare: Family, Poverty, and Politics in Modern America.* Philadelphia: University of Pennsylvania Press, 2011.

Charnock, Emily. "Party Polarisation in the United States." *Political Insight* (Sept. 2018): 4-7.

Cohen, Lawrence and Felson, Marcus. "Social Change and Crime Rate Trends: A Routine Activity Approach." *American Sociological Review* 44, no. 4 (Aug., 1979): 588-608.

Cole, Peter. *The Poetry of Kabbalah: Mystical Verse from the Jewish Tradition.* New Haven: Yale University Press, 2011.

Collins, Randall. "The Four M's of Religion: Magic, Membership, Morality and Mysticism." *Review of Religious Research* 50, no. 1 (Sep., 2008): 5-15.

Coplan, Robert and Bowker, Julie. *The Handbook Of Solitude: Psychological Perspectives on Social Isolation, Social Withdrawal, and Being Alone.* Malden, MA: John Wiley and Sons, Ltd., 2014.

Cosoroaba, Eva-Marie. "Multiphysics Simulation, Analysis and Design of a Permanent Magnet Excited Liquid Metal Magnetohydrodynamic Power Generator." PhD Thesis, The University of Texas at Dallas, 2017.

Danzger, Herbert. *Returning to Tradition: The Contemporary Revival of Orthodox Judaism.* New Haven and London: Yale University Press, 1989.

Davie, Grace. "Resacralization." In *The New Blackwell Companion to the Sociology of Religion*, edited by Bryan S. Turner. Chichester, UK: Wiley-Blackwell, 2010.

Davis, Gareth. *See Government Grow: Education Politics from Johnson to Reagan.* Lawrence, KA: University Press of Kansas, 2007.

Dauber, Jonathan. "The Baal Shem Tov and the Messiah: A Reappraisal of the Baal Shem Tov's Letter to R. Gershon of Kutov." *Jewish Studies Quarterly*, 15 (2008): 210-241.

Dolinko, David. "Punishment." In *The Oxford Handbook of Philosophy of Criminal Law*, edited by John Deigh and David Dolinko, 403-440. Oxford, UK: Oxford University Press, 2011.

Douds, Anne; Howard, Daniel; Hummer, Don; Gabbidon, Shaun. "Public opinion on the affluenza defense, race, and sentencing decisions: results from a statewide poll." *Journal of Crime and Justice* 39, no. 1 (2016): 230-242.

Durkheim, Émile. *The Elementary Forms of Religious Life*, translated by Karen E. Fields. New York: The Free Press, 1995.

Dynner, Glenn. *Men of Silk: The Hasidic Conquest of Polish Jewish Society.* Oxford, UK: Oxford University Press, 2006.

Eckenroth, Danielle. "Wealthy "Justice": The Role Wealth Plays in Sentencing and in the Affluenza Defense." *New England Journal on Criminal and Civil Confinement* 41 (2015): 443-461.

Ehrlich, Avrum. *Leadership in the HaBaD Movement: A Critical Evaluation of HaBaD Leadership, History, and Succession.* New Jersey: Jason Aronson Publishers, 2000.

Eiland, Howard. *Walter Benjamin: A Critical Life.* Cambridge, MA: Harvard University Press, 2014.

———. "Walter Benjamin's Jewishness." In *Walter Benjamin and Theology*, edited by Colby Dickinson and Stéphane Symons, 113-143. New York: Fordham University Press, 2016.

Einstein, Albert. *Relativity: The Special and The General Theory - A Popular Exposition*, translated by Robert W. Lawson. London: Methuen & Co., 1920.

Eisenstein, Marie. "Religion and Political Tolerance in the United States: A Review and Evaluation." In *The Oxford Handbook of Religion and American Politics*, edited by James L. Guth, Lyman A. Kellstedt, and Corwin E. Smidt. Oxford University Press,. Retrieved 13 Sep. 2018, from http://www.oxfordhandbooks.com.libproxy.ucl.ac.uk/view/10.1093/oxfordhb/9780195326529.001.0001/oxfordhb-9780195326529-e-15.

Epstein, Nadine and Frankel, Rebecca. "Bob Dylan: The Unauthorized Spiritual Biography." *Moment Magazine*, October 13, 2016. https://www.momentmag.com/bob-dylan-unauthorized-spiritual-biography/.

Ergas, Oren. "The Post-Secular Rhetoric of Contemplative Practice in the Public Curriculum." In Wexler and Hotam, *New Social Foundations for Education: Education in 'Post Secular' Society*, 107-130. New York: Peter Lang, 2015.

Etkes, Immanuel. *The Besht: Magician, Mystic, and Leader.* Waltham, Mas.: Brandeis University Press, 2005.

―――. *Rabbi Shneur Zalman of Liady: The Origins of Chabad Hasidism.* Waltham, Ma.: Brandeis University Press, 2015.

Feldman, Jan. *Lubavitchers as Citizens: A Paradox of Liberal Democracy.* Ithaca and London: Cornell University Press, 2003.

Ferziger, Adam. *Beyond Sectarianism: The Realignment of American Orthodox Judaism.* Detroit, MI: Wayne State University Press, 2015.

Fischer, Shlomo; Hotam, Yotam; Wexler, Philip. "Democracy and Education in Postsecular Society." *Review of Research in Education* 36, no. 1: 261-281.

Fishbane, Michael. "To Jump for Joy." *Journal of Jewish Thought & Philosophy* 6, no. 2 (1997): 371-387.

Fishkoff, Sue. *The Rebbe's Army: Inside The World Of Chabad-Lubavitch.* New York: Schocken Books, 2003.

Ford, Gerald. *Public Papers of the Presidents of the United States: Gerald R. Ford, 1975 - January 1 to July 20, 1975.* Washington D.C.: United States Government Printing Office, 1977.

Franks, Paul. "Inner Anti-Semitism or Kabbalistic Legacy? German Idealism's Relationship to Judaism." In *Yearbook of German Idealism, Volume VII, Faith and Reason*, edited by Fred Rush, Jürgen Stolzenberg and Paul Franks, 254-279. Berlin: Walter de Gruyter, 2010.

Fredman, Stephen. "Allen Ginsberg and Lionel Trilling: The Hasid and the Mitnaged." *Religion & Literature* 30, no. 3 (Autumn, 1998): 67-76.

Freedman, Robert. "Religion, Politics, and the Israeli Elections of 1988." *Middle East Journal* 43, No. 3 (Summer, 1989): 406-422.

Freedman, Samuel. "Brooklyn's Lubavitch Community: A Culture Captured by the Ultimate Outsider." *The New York Times.* Nov 28, 2014. https://www.nytimes.com/2014/11/29/nyregion/brooklyns-lubavitch-community-a-culture-captured-by-the-ultimate-outsider.html.

Freeman, Tzvi. "The Rebbe's Investment: My Thoughts on the Rebbe's Modality of Leadership," *Chabad.org.* chabad.org/402599.

Fuchs, Ilan. *Jewish Women's Torah Study: Orthodox Religious Education and Modernity.* New York: Routledge, 2014.

Gallart, Louis. "The Crossroads of Mental Disorder and Criminal Responsibility." PhD Dissertation, Drew University, 2011.

Gasztold, Brygida. "Self-sacrificing and/or Overbearing: The Jewish Mother in the Cultural Imagination." *Scripta Judaica Cracoviensia* 11 (2013): 161-174.

Garb, Jonathan. *Shamanic Trance in Modern Kabbalah*. Chicago: Chicago University Press, 2011.

———. *Yearnings of the Soul: Psychological Thought in Modern Kabbalah*. University of Chicago Press: Chicago, 2015.

Geltman, Barry and Tal, Rami, *Annual Assessment: The Situation and Dynamics of the Jewish People 2014-2015*. Jerusalem: The Jewish People Policy Institute, 2015. http://jppi.org.il/new/wp-content/uploads/2015/JPPI_AA2015E.pdf.

Gold, Susan. *Engel V. Vitale: Prayer in the Schools*. Tarrytown, NY: Marshall Cavendish Benchmark, 2006.

Grawert, Ames and Lau, Tim. "How the FIRST STEP Act Became Law — and What Happens Next." *BrennanCenter.org*, January 4, 2019. https://www.brennancenter.org/blog/how-first-step-act-became-law-and-what-happens-next.

Green, Arthur. "Wiesel in the Context of Neo-Hasidism." In *Elie Wiesel: Jewish, Literary, and Moral Perspectives*, edited by Steven T. Katz and Alan Rosen, 51-58. Bloomington, IN: Indiana University Press, 2013.

Greenberg, Yosef Yitshak and Zaklikovsky Eliezer. *Yemai beresihit: yoman metekufat kabalat hanesiut*. Brooklyn, NY: Kehot Publication Society, 1993.

Habermas, Jürgen. *Communication and the Evolution of Society*, translated by Thomais McCarthy. London: Heinemann Educational Books, 1979.

———.*Philosophical-Political Profiles*, translated by Frederick G. Lawrence. Cambridge, MA: MIT Press, 1983.

———.*Glauben und Wissen*. Frankfurt: Suhrkamp, 2001.

Hamilton, James. "Historical Oil Shocks." In *Routledge Handbook of Major Events in Economic History*, edited by Randall E. Parker and Robert Whaples, 239-265. New York: Routledge, 2013.

Handelman, Susan. "A Man Apart." *Cross Currents* 45, no. 2 (Summer 1995): 234-240.

Haskins, Anna and Lee, Hedwig. "Reexamining Race When Studying the Consequences of Criminal Justice Contact for Families." *The ANNALS of the American Academy of Political and Social Science* 665, no. 1 (May 2016): 224–230.

Heilman, Samuel. *Who Will Lead Us? The Story of Five Hasidic Dynasties in America*. Oakland, CA: University of California Press, 2017.

———. and Friedman, Menachem. *The Rebbe: The Life and Afterlife of Menachem Mendel Schneerson*. Princeton, NJ: Princeton University Press, 2010.

Hertzberg, Arthur. "American Zionism at an Impasse:A Movement in Search of a Program." *CommentaryMagazine*(OCT.1,1949).https://www.commentarymagazine.com/articles/american-zionism-at-an-impassea-movement-in-search-of-a-program/.

Heschel, Abraham. *The Prophets*. New York, The Jewish Publication Society of America, 1962.

Idel, Moshe. *Hasidism: Between Ecstasy and Magic*. Albany, NY: SUNY Press, 1995.

———. *Vocal Rites and Broken Theologies: Cleaving to Vocables in R. Israel Ba'al Shem Tov's Mysticism*. New York: Herder and Herder, 2019.

Inamura, Kazutaka. *Justice and Reciprocity in Aristotle's Political Philosophy*. Cambridge, UK: Cambridge University Press, 2015.

Jacobs, Louis. "Eating as an Act of Worship in Hasidic Thought." In *Studies in Jewish Religious and Intellectual History Presented to Alexander Altmann on the Occasion of his Seventieth Birthday*, edited by Siegfried Stein and Raphael Loewe, 157-66. Tuscaloosa, AL:University of Alabama Press, 1979.

Jacobson, Eric. *Metaphysics of the Profane: The Political Theology of Walter Benjamin and Gershom Scholem*. New York: Columbia University Press, 2003.

Jaeggi, Rahel. *Alienation*. New York: Columbia University Press, 2014.

Johnston, Barry. "Pitirim A. Sorokin (1889-1968): Pioneer and Pariah." *International Sociology* 11, no. 2: 229-238.

Johnson, Mary Ellen Quinn. "School Prayer and the Constitution: Silence is Golden." *Maryland Law Review* 48, no. 6 (1989): 1018-1044.

Kahanah, Maoz and Mayse, Ariel. "Hasidic Halakhah: Reappraising the Interface of Spirit and Law." *AJS Review* 41(2): 375-408.

Kandiyoti, Rafael. *Powering Europe: Russia, Ukraine, and the Energy Squeeze*. New York: Palgrave Macmillan, 2015.

Kaplan, Mordecai. *A New Zionism*. New York: Herzl Press and the Jewish Reconstruction Press, 1959.

Kauffman, Tsippi. *In All Your Ways Know Him: The Concept of God and Avodah be-Gashmiyut in the Early Stages of Hasidism*. Ramat-Gan: Bar Ilan University Press, 2009. [Hebrew.]

Kaushik, S.C.; Verma, S.S.; and Chandra, A. "Solar-Assisted Liquid Metal MHD Power Generation: A State of the Art Study." *Heat Recovery Systems & CHP* 15, no. 7 (October, 1995): 675-689.

Klein, Meir. "In Search of the Center of the Circle: The Rhetoric of Science and Technology in the Writings of Rabbi Menachem Mendel Schneerson." Masters Thesis, Bar Ilan University, 2014. [Hebrew with English Abstract.]

Kolm, Serge-Christophe. *Reciprocity: An Economics of Social Relations*. Cambridge, UK: Cambridge University Press, 2008.

Koskoff, Ellen. *Music in Lubavitcher Life*. Urbana and Chicago: University of Illinois Press, 2001.

Kurzon, Dennis. "A Pragmatic Analysis of Silence in an American Constitutional Issue." *Lodz Papers in Pragmatics* 6, no. 1 (2010): 49-66.

Kripal, Jeffrey. *Mutants and Mystics: Science Fiction, Superhero Comics, and the Paranormal*. Chicago: University of Chicago Press, 2011.

Lamm, Norman. *The Religious Thought of Hasidism: Text and Commentary*. Yeshiva University Press, 1999.

Lerner, Daniel. *The Passing of Traditional Society*. New York: Free Press of Glencoe, 1964.

Levin, Faitel. *Heaven on Earth: Reflections on the Theology of Rabbi Menachem M. Schneerson, the Lubavitcher Rebbe*. Brooklyn, NY: Kehot Publication Society, 2002.

Levine, Shalom DovBer. *Toldot chabad be'artsot habrit*. Brooklyn, NY: Kehot Publication Society, 1988.

———. *Toldot chabad bepolin, lita, velatviya*. Brooklyn, NY: Kehot Publication Society, 2011.,

———. and Mondshine, Yehoshua. *Igrot kodesh admor hazaken*. New York: Kehot Publication Society, 2012.

Lightstone, Mordechai. "How 1970s Chassidic Hackers Created a Worldwide Broadcast Network: The backroom of a Brooklyn landmark building served as the global hub for Jewish connectivity." *Chabad.org.* chabad.org/3422879.

Lipsker, Shalom. "A Little Light Dispels a Lot of Darkness." *American Jails* 32, no. 6 (Jan/Feb, 2019): 77-79.

Little, Douglas. "The Cold War in the Middle East: Suez crisis to Camp David Accords." In *The Cambridge History of the Cold War,* edited by Melvyn P. Leffler and Odd Arne Westad, 319-322. Cambridge, UK: Cambridge University Press, 2010.

Loewenthal, Naftali. *Communicating the Infinite: The Emergence of the Habad School.* Chicago: Chicago University Press, 1990.

———. "The Ethics of Joy: Chabad Perspectives on Happiness." *Chabad.org.* chabad.org/2219688.

———. "Hasidism and Modernity: The Case of Habad," Proceedings of the World Congress of Jewish Studies 11C(2) (1993): 109-116.

———. "The Baal Shem Tov's "Iggeret ha-Kodesh" and Contemporary Habad "Outreach." In *"Let the Old Make Way for the New," Vol. 1,* edited by David Assaf and Ada Rapoport-Albert, 69-101. Jerusalem: The Zalman Shazar Center for Jewish History, 2009.

———. "Is Socialism Kosher? Proto-Socialist Resonances in Chassidic Thought." *Chabad.org.* chabad.org/2703778.

———. "The Hasidic Ethos and the Schisms of Jewish Society." *Jewish History* 27(2): 377-398.

———. ""The Thickening of the Light": The Kabbalistic-Hasidic Teachings of Rabbi Shalom Dovber Schneersohn in Their Social Context." In Jonatan Meir and Gadi Sagiv, *Habad Hasidism: History, Thought, Image,* 7*-43*. The Zalman Shazar Center: Jerusalem, 2016.

———. "Chassidic Prayer and Society." In *Jewish Spirituality and Social Transformation,* edited by Philip Wexler, 81-98. New York: Herder and Herder, 2019.

Löwy, Michael. "Weber Against Marx? The Polemic with Historical Materialism in the Protestant Ethic." *Science & Society* 53, no. 1 (Spring, 1989): 71-83.

———. *Fire Alarm: Reading Walter Benjamin's "On the Concept of History"* translated by Chris Turner. London and New York: Verso, 2016.

Luban, David. "Heroic Judging in an Antiheroic Age," *Columbia Law Review* 97, no. 7 ("A Special Issue Dedicated to Judge Jack B. Weinstein," Nov., 1997): 2064-2090.

Lurie, Ilia. *Edah umedinah: hasidut habad be'impariyah harusit 5588-5643.* Jerusalem: Magnes Press, 2006.

Luthar, Suniya; Barkin, Samuel; Crossman, Elizabeth. ""I can, therefore I must": Fragility in the upper-middle classes." *Development and Psychopathology* 25 (2013): 1529–1549.

———. and Karen D'Avanzo, "Contextual factors in substance use: A study of suburban and inner-city adolescents," *Development and Psychopathology,* 11 (1999): 845–867.

————. and Latendresse, Shawn. "Adolescent risk: The costs of affluence." *New Directions for Student Leadership* Vol. 2002, Issue 95, *Special Issue: Pathways to Positive Development Among Diverse Youth* (Autumn, 2002): 101-122.

Macauley, David. *Elemental Philosophy: Earth, Air, Fire, and Water as Environmental Ideas.* Albany, NY: SUNY Press, 2010.

Madero-Hernandez, Arelys and Fisher, Bonnie. "Routine Activity Theory." In *The Oxford Handbook of Criminological Theory*, edited by Francis T. Cullen and Pamela Wilcox, 513-530. Oxford, UK: Oxford University Press, 2013.

Magid, Shaul. *American Post-Judaism: Identity and Renewal in a Postethnic Society.* Bloomington, IN: Indiana University Press, 2013.

————. "When Will the Wedding Take Place? A Little Known Discourse of the Seventh Lubavitcher Rebbe." In *One God, Many Worlds: A Festschrift in Honor of Rabbi Zalman Schachter-Shalomi, z"l*, edited by Netanel Miles-Yepez, 95-106. Boulder, CO: Albion Andalus, 2015.

Margolin, Dovid. "The Backstory of the Chassidim Who Got Criminal Justice Reform Done." *Chabad.org/News.* December 27, 2018. chabad.org/4246392.

————."30 Years Since Chernobyl: How 3,000 Children Were Airlifted Out of Nuclear Disaster." *Chabad.org.* chabad.org/3377542.

————. "The Roots of Today's Revival of Russian Judaism Lies Deep in the Soviet Past." *Mosaic Magazine.* <https://mosaicmagazine.com/response/2017/03/the-roots-of-todays-revival-of-russian-judaism-lie-deep-in-the-soviet-past/.

Martens, Emily. "The Discourses of Energy and Environmental Security in the Debate Over Offshore Oil Drilling Policy in Florida." MA Thesis, The University of Miami, 2011.

Mason, Lilliana. "Losing Common Ground: Social Sorting and Polarization." *The Forum* 16, no. 1 (June 2018): 47–66.

Mayse, Ariel Evan. "Beyond the Letters: The Question of Language in the Teachings of Rabbi Dov Baer of Mezritch." PhD Thesis, Harvard University, 2015.

————."The Development of Neo-Hasidism: Echoes and Repercussions." *The Lehrhaus.* https://www.thelehrhaus.com/scholarship/the-development-of-neo-hasidism-echoes-and-repercussions-part-i-introduction-hillel-zeitlin-and-martin-buber/. [In four parts.]

Meir, Jonatan. "Reform Hasidism: The Image of Habad in Haskalah Literature." *Modern Judaism* 37, no. 3 (October, 2017): 297-315.

Melamed, Yitzhak. "Spinozism, Acosmism, and Hassidism: A Closed Circle." In *The Concept of Judaism in German Idealism*, edited by Amit Kravitz and Jörg Noller, 75-85. Berlin: Suhrkamp Verlag, 2018.

Melissaris, Emmanuel. "Theories of Crime and Punishment." In *The Oxford Handbook of Criminal Law*, edited by Markus D. Dubber and Tatjana Hörnle, 355-378. Oxford, UK: Oxford University Press, 2014.

Merkos L'Inyonei Chinuch. "Education Day—U.S.A." Legislation. Brooklyn, NY: Merkos L'Inyonei Chinuch, 1979.

Milner, Allison. "Globalization and Suicide: An Ecological Study Across Five Regions of the World." *Archives of Suicide Research* 16, no. 3 (2012): 238–249.

Morgenstern, Arie. *Hastening Redemption: Messianism and the Resettlement of the Land of Israel.* Oxford, UK: Oxford University Press, 2006.

Morris, Jeffrey. *Leadership on the Federal Bench: The Craft and Activism of Jack Weinstein.* Oxford, UK: Oxford University Press, 2011.

———. "Jack B. Weinstein: Judicial Entrepreneur." *University of Miami Law Review* 69, no. 2 (Winter, 2015): 393–428.

Moseson, Chaim Elly. "From Spoken Word to the Discourse of the Academy: Reading the Sources for the Teachings of the Besht." PhD Thesis, Boston University, 2017.

Nichols, Lawrence. "Deviance and Social Science: The Instructive Historical Case of Pitirim Sorokin." *Journal of the History of the Social Sciences* 25 (October 1989): 335–355.

Oberlander, Boruch and Shmotkin, Elkanah. *Early Years: The formative years of the Rebbe. Rabbi Menachem M. Schneerson, as told by documents and archival data 1902-1921.* Brooklyn, NY: Kehot Publication Society, 2016.

Ollman, Bertell. *Alienation: Marx's Conception of Man in a Capitalist Society.* Cambridge, UK: Cambridge University Press, 1976.

Orent, Leah. "Religious Experience and the National Community - The Version of R. Shneur Zalman of Liadi." *Studies in Spirituality* 13 (2003): 99–117.

Parsons, William. *Being Spiritual but Not Religious: Past, Present, Future(s).* New York: Routledge, 2018.

Pedaya, Haviva. "Lehitpathuto shel ha-degem ha-hevrati-dati-kalkali behasidut: hapidion, hahavurah veha-aliyah leregel." In *Dat ve-kalkalah: yahasei gomelin, shay le-Ya'akov Kats bi-melot lo tish'im shanah: kovets ma'amarim,* 311–73. Jerusalem, 1995.

Penn, Ascher. *Iydishkeit in amerike, Vol. 1.* New York, 1958.

Perkin, Harold. "The Tyranny of the Moral Majority: American Religion and Politics Since the Pilgrim Fathers." *Cultural Values* 3, no. 2 (1999): 182–195.

Polen, Nehemia. "Miriam's Dance: Radical Egalitarianism in Hasidic Thought." *Modern Judaism* 12, no. 1 (Feb., 1992): 1-21.

———. "Charismatic Leader, Charismatic Book: Rabbi Schneur Zalman's Tanya and His Leadership." In Suzanne Last Stone, *Rabbinic and Lay Communal Authority,* 53-64. New York: Yeshiva University Press, 2006.

———. Review of *The Rebbe: The Life and Afterlife of Menachem Mendel Schneerson,* by Samuel C. Heilman and Menachem M. Friedman. *Modern Judaism* 34, no. 1, (February, 2014): 123–134.

Priest, Tyler. "The Dilemmas of Oil Empire." *Journal of American History* 99, no. 1 (June 2012): 236–251.

Prothero, Stephen. "On the Holy Road: The Beat Movement as Spiritual Protest." *The Harvard Theological Review* 84, no. 2 (Apr., 1991): 205-222.

Radin, Beryl and Hawley, Willis. *The Politics of Federal Reorganization: Creating the U.S. Department of Education.* New York: Pergamon Press, 1988.

Raines, John. *Marx on Religion.* Philadelphia: Temple University Press, 2002.

Rakove, Jack. *Interpreting the Constitution: the Debate over Original Intent.* Boston: Northeastern University Press, 1990.

Rapoport, Chaim. *The Afterlife of Scholarship.* Oporto Press, 2011.

Rapoport-Albert, Ada. *Hasidism Reappraised.* Oxford: The Littman Library of Jewish Civilization, 1996.

———.*Hasidic Studies: Essays in History and Gender.* Liverpool: The Littman Library of Jewish Civilization, 2018.

———."The Problem of Succession in the Hasidic Leadership with Special Reference to the Circle of R. Nachman of Braslav." PhD Thesis, University of London, 1974.

Rosen, Avraham. ""Today is the Day": Reading Between the Lines of the Lubavitcher Rebbe's Holocaust Era Calendar." *Chabad.org.* chabad.org/1902777.

———. ""A Calendar For all Occasions": How Hayom Yom Became a Jewish Classic." *Chabad.org.* chabad.org/3772406.

Rosman, Moshe. *Founder of Hasidism: The Quest for the Historical Ba'al Shem Tov.* Liverpool: The Littman Library of Jewish Civilization, 2013.

Rubin, Eli. "Divine Zeitgeist—The Rebbe's Appreciative Critique of Modernity," *Chabad.org,* Chabad.org/2973252.

———."Traveling and Traversing Chabad's Literary Paths: From Likutei torah to Khayim gravitser and Beyond." *In Geveb: A Journal of Yiddish Studies,* October 2018. https://ingeveb.org/articles/traveling-and-traversing-chabads-literary-paths-from-likutei-torah-to-khayim-gravitser-and-beyond.

———. "A Linguistic Bridge Between Alienation and Intimacy: Habad's Theorization of Yiddish in Historical and Cultural Perspective." *In geveb: a journal of Yiddish studies,* January, 2019. https://ingeveb.org/articles/a-linguistic-bridge-between-alienation-and-intimacy.

———. "Habad Hasidism and the Mystical Reconstruction of Society." In *Jewish Spirituality and Social Transformation,* edited by Philip Wexler, 59-78. Herder and Herder, 2019.

———. "'The Pen Shall Be Your Friend': Intertextuality, Intersociality, and the Cosmos - Examples of the Tzemach Tzedek's Way in the Development of Chabad Chassidic Thought." *Chabad.org.* chabad.org/3286179.

———. "Purging Divisiveness, Embracing Difference: Rabbi Shalom DovBer Schneersohn's manifesto against self-righteousness in interpersonal discourse." *Chabad.org.* chabad.org/3800391.

———. "The Idealistic Realism of Jewish Messianism." *Chabad.org.* chabad.org/2766417.

———. "The Rebbe: An In-Depth Biography of a Scholar, Visionary and Leader." *Chabad.org.* chabad.org/2619397.

Ruby, Daniel. "Rooftop MHD: on site electricity from low-grade heat." *Popular Science.* November 1982, 64-66.

Sabin, Paul. "Crisis and Continuity in U.S. Oil Politics, 1965–1980." *Journal of American History* 99, no. 1 (June 2012): 177–186.

Schatz-Uffenheimer, Rivka. *Hasidism as Mysticism: Quietistic Elements in Eighteenth Century Hasidic Thought.* Princeton, NJ: Princeton University Press, 1993.

Scher, Abby. "Cold War on the Home Front: Middle Class Women's Politics in the 1950s." PhD Thesis, The New School for Social Research, 1995.

Schneersohn, Shalom DovBer. *Igrot kodesh Vol. 1.* Brooklyn, NY: Kehot Publication Society, 1982.

———. *Yom tov shel rosh hashanah 5666.* Brooklyn, NY: Kehot Publication Society, 1991.

———. *Kuntras hicholtsu.* Kehot Publication Society: New York, 1948.

———. *Kuntras ets hachayim.* Brooklyn, NY: Kehot Publication Society, 1946.

———. *Torat shalom.* Brooklyn, NY: Kehot Publication Society, 1983.

Schneersohn, Shmuel. *Likutei torah—torat shmuel, shaar revi'ei, ve'kakhah—5637.* Brooklyn, NY: Kehot Publication Society, 1945.

Schneersohn, Yosef Yitschak. *Sefer hasichot 5703.* Brooklyn, NY: Kehot Publication Society, 2010.

———. *Sefer hasichot kayitz 5700.* Brooklyn, NY: Kehot Publication Society, 1986.

———. *Sefer hasichot 5703.* Brooklyn, NY: Kehot Publication Society, 1986.

———. *Igrot kodesh, Vol. 15.* Brooklyn, NY: Kehot Publication Society, 2011.

———. *Igrot kodesh Vol. 2.* Brooklyn, NY: Kehot Publication Society, 2016.

———. *Sefer hamamarim 5708-5709.* Brooklyn, NY: Kehot Publication Society, 1986.

———. *Sefer hamamarim 5710.* Brooklyn, NY: Kehot Publication Society, 1986.

Schneerson, Levi Yitschak. *Likutei levi yitschak - igrot kodesh.* Brooklyn, NY: Kehot Publication Society, 1985.

Schneerson, Menachem Mendel. *Sichot kodesh.* Brooklyn: Vaad Hanachot Hatemimim, 1986. [51 Vols.]

———. *Torat menachem - hitvaduyot.* Brooklyn, NY: Kehot Publication Society, 1991-2019. [109 Vols.]

———. *Likutei sichot.* Brooklyn, NY: Kehot Publication Society, 2000. [39 Vols.]

———. *Igrot kodesh.* Brooklyn, NY: Kehot Publication Society, 1988-2017. [32 Vols.]

———. *Kuntras binyan mikdash me'at.* Brooklyn, NY: Kehot Publication Society, 1992.

———. *Sefer hasichot.* Brooklyn, NY: Kehot Publication Society, 1998. [11 Vols.]

———. *Reshimot.* Brooklyn, NY: Kehot Publication Society, 2012. [3 Vols.]

———. *Torat menachem sefer hamamarim melukat.* Brooklyn, NY: Kehot Publication Society, 2012. [4 Vols.]

———. *Hayom yom.* Brooklyn, NY: Kehot Publication Society, 1943.

———. *Seder birchat hachamah al pi minhag chabad .* Brooklyn, NY: 1981.

Schneur Zalman of Liadi. *Likutei amarim tanya.* Vilna: The Widow and Brothers Romm, 1900 / New York: Kehot Publication Society, 1985.

———. *Mamarei admor hazaken 5562.* Brooklyn, NY: Kehot Publication Society, 2012. [2 Vols.]

———. *Torah or.* Brooklyn, NY: Kehot Publication Society, 2001.

———. *Likutei torah.* Brooklyn, NY: Kehot Publication Society, 2002.

———. *Seder tefilot mikol hashanah im pirush hamilot al pi dach.* Brooklyn, NY: Kehot Publication Society, 1965.

Scisco, Logan Michael. *Vanguard of the Right: The Department of Education Battle, 1978-1979.* Master Thesis, Western Kentucky University, 2014.

Schochet, Immanuel. *Keter shem tov hashalom.* Brooklyn, NY: Kehot Publication Society, 2016.

Scholem, Gershom. *Major Trends in Jewish Mysticism.* New York: Schocken Books, 1941.

Schwarz, Alan. "No Imposition of Religion: The Establishment Clause Value." *The Yale Law Journal* 77, no. 4 (1968): 692-737.

Setton, Damián. "The consumption of alcohol in the Lubavitch Movement in Buenos Aires. Diversity of meanings." *Revista de Antropología Iberoamericana* 8(3) (September - December 2013): 345 - 366.

Shandler, Jeffrey. *Jews, God, and Videotape: Religion and Media in America.* New York: New York University Press, 2009.

Sharkey, Patrick; Besbris, Max; and Friedson, Michael. "Poverty and Crime." In *The Oxford Handbook of the Social Science of Poverty,* edited by David Brady and Linda M. Burton, 623-633. Oxford, UK: Oxford University Press, 2016.

Slater, Mariam. "My Son the Doctor: Aspects of Mobility Among American Jews." *American Sociological Review* 34, no. 3 (Jun., 1969): 359-373.

Slater, Philip. *The Chrysalis Effect: The Metamorphosis of Global Culture.* Eastborne, UK: Sussex University Press, 2009.

———. *The Pursuit of Loneliness: American Culture at the Breaking Point.* Boston: Beacon Press, 1990.

Slonim, Rivkah. "Education as Life: Reflections from the Field by a Chabad Shlucha on a College Campus." In *Jewish Spirituality and Social Transformation,* edited by Philip Wexler, 113-124. New York: Herder and Herder, 2019.

Solomon, Aryeh. *Spiritual Education: The Educational Theory and Practice of the Lubavitcher Rebbe Rabbi Menachem M. Schneerson.* New York: Herder and Herder, 2019.

Sorkin, David. "Between Messianism and Survival: Secularization and Sacralization in Modern Judaism." *Journal of Modern Jewish Studies,* 3:1 (2004): 73-86.

Sorokin, Pitirim. *Social and Cultural Dynamics, Vol. I.* London: George Allen & Unwin Ltd., 1937.

———. *The Crisis of Our Age: The Social and Cultural Outlook.* New York: E.P. Dutton & Co. Inc., 1941.

Spezio, Teresa Sabol. "Rising Tide: The Santa Barbara Oil Spill and Its Aftermath." Ph.D. diss., University of California, Davis, 2011.

Stanislawski, Michael. "Gordon, Yehudah Leib." In *YIVO Encyclopedia of Jews in Eastern Europe* (9 August 2010), accessed 19 October 2018. http://www.yivoencyclopedia.org/article.aspx/Gordon_Yehudah_Leib.

Steinbock, Anthony. *Phenomenology and Mysticism: The Verticality of Religious Experience.* Bloomington: Indiana University Press, 2009.

———. *Moral Emotions: Reclaiming the Evidence of the Heart.* Evanston, IL: Northwestern University Press, 2014.

Strum, Harvey and Strum, Fred. "Solar Energy Policy, 1952-1982." *Environmental Review* 7, no. 2 (Summer, 1983): 135-154.

Summers-Effler, Erika and Kwak, Hyunjin Deborah. "Weber's missing mystics: inner-worldly mystical practices and the micro potential for social change." *Theory and Society* 44 (May, 2015): 251-282.

Symons, Stéphane. *Walter Benjamin: Presence of Mind, Failure to Comprehend.* Leiden and Boston: Brill, 2013.

Tauber, Yanki. "The Fluidity of Life: Based on the Notebooks of Rabbi Menahem Mendel Schneerson." *B'or Hatorah* 10 (1997-1998): 59-67.

Taubes, Jacob. "Seminar Notes on Walter Benjamin's "Theses on the Philosophy of History"." In *Walter Benjamin and Theology*, edited by Colby Dickinson and Stéphane Symons, 179-214. New York: Fordham University Press, 2016.

Teicher, Jordan. "A Glimpse Inside Crown Heights' Hasidic Community in the '90s." *Slate. com.* Nov 18, 2014. https://slate.com/culture/2014/11/the-brooklyn-public-library-presents-chie-nishios-photographs-of-crown-heights-hasidic-community.html.

Tidhar, David. *Entsiklopedyah lehalutse hayishuv uvonav.* http://www.tidhar.tourolib.org/.

Troy, Gil. *Morning in America: How Ronald Reagan Invented the 1980's.* Princeton: Princeton University Press, 2005.

Vietor, Richard. *Energy Policy in America since 1945: A Study of Business-Government Relations.* New York: Cambridge University Press, 1984.

Weber, Max. *The Protestant Ethic and the Spirit of Capitalism.* Translated by Talcott Parsons. New York and London: Charles Scribner's Sons / George Allen & Unwin Ltd., 1950.

———. Science as a Vocation." In *From Max Weber: Essays in Sociology.* Trans. H.H. Gerth and C. Wright Mills. New York: Oxford University Press, 1946.

———. *The Sociology of Religion.* Translated by Talcott Parsons. London: Mathuen & Co Ltd, 1965.

———. *Economy and Society*, edited by Guenther Roth and Claus Wittich. Berkley, CA: University of California Press, 1978.

Weinstein, Jack B., Ilene H. Nagel, and J. Michael Quinlan. "Symposium: Alternative Punishments under the New Federal Sentencing Guidelines." *Federal Sentencing Reporter* 1, no. 2 (1988): 96-110.

Werczberger, Rachel. "Feminine Messianism and Messianic Femininity: An Ethnography of Women's Shiur in Chabad." M.A. Thesis, Hebrew University 2003. [Hebrew.]

———. *Jews in the Age of Authenticity: Jewish Spiritual Renewal in Israel.* New York: Peter Lang, 2017.

Wexler, Philip, with Crichlow, Warren; Kern, June; Martusewicz, Rebecca, *Becoming Somebody: Toward a Social Psychology of School.* London and Washington D.C.: The Falmer Press, 1992.

———. *Holy Sparks: Social Theory, Education and Religion.* New York: St. Martin's Press, 1996.

———. *The Mystical Society: An Emerging Social Vision.* Boulder, CO: Westview Press, 2000.

————. *Mystical Interactions: Sociology, Jewish Mysticism and Education.* Los Angeles, CA: Cherub Press, 2007.

————. "Social Psychology, the Hasidic Ethos and the Spirit of the New Age." *Kabbalah: Journal for the Study of Jewish Mystical Texts* 7 (2002): 11-36.

————. and Garb, Jonathan. After Spirituality: Studies in Jewish Mystical Traditions (New York: Peter Lang, 2012)

————. *Mystical Sociology: Toward Cosmic Social Theory.* New York: Peter Lang, 2013.

————. and Hotam, Yotam. *New Social Foundations for Education: Education in 'Post Secular' Society.* New York: Peter Lang, 2015.

————. *Jewish Spirituality and Social Transformation: Hasidism and Society.* New York: Herder and Herder, 2019.

White House Conference on Children and Youth. *Conference Proceedings: Golden Anniversary White House Conference on Children and Youth March, 27 — April 2, 1960, Washington D.C.* Golden Anniversary White House Conference on Children and Youth, Inc., 1960.

Wilkinson, Deanna and Fagan, Jeffrey. "What We Know About Gun Use Among Adolescents." *Clinical Child and Family Psychology Review* 4, no. 2 (June, 2001): 109–132.

Wodziński, Marcin. *Haskalah and Hasidism in the Kingdom of Poland: A History of Conflict.* Oxford, UK: Littman Library of Jewish Civilization, 2005.

————. "The Socio-Economic Profile of a Religious Movement: The Case of Hasidism." *European History Quarterly* 46(4): 668-701.

————. *Historical Atlas of Hasidism.* Princeton, NJ: Princeton University Press, 2018.

————. *Hasidism: Key Questions.* Oxford: Oxford University Press, 2018.

Wolf, Zushe. *Hotsa'at seforim kehot: toldot hotsa'at hasefarim hachabadit.* Brooklyn, NY: Kehot Publication Society, 2013.

Wolff, K. H. *Émile Durkheim (1858-1917): A Collection of Essays, with Translations and a Bibliography.* Columbus, Ohio: Ohio State University Press, 1960.

Wolfson, Elliot. *Open Secret: Postmessianic Messianism and the Mystical Revision of Menachem Mendel Schneerson.* New York: Columbia University Press, 2009.

————. "Walking as a Sacred Duty: Theological Dimensions of Social Reality in Early Hasidism." In Hasidism Reappraised, edited by Ada Rapoport-Albert, 180-207. Oxford: The Littman Library of Jewish Civilization, 1996.

————. *Venturing Beyond: Law and Morality in Kabbalistic Mysticism.* Oxford and New York: Oxford University Press, 2006.

Yakov Yosef hakohen of Polonnoye. *Ben porat yosef.* Koretz, 1781 / New York, 1954.

Zaklikowski, David. "Northeastern Matriarch of Jewish Education Passes Away at 91." *Chabad.org.* chabad.org/1251764.

————. "The Rebbe and President Ford." *Chabad.org.* chabad.org/461848.

————. "Recovering Reagan Writes to the Rebbe." *Chabad.org.* chabad.org/979502.

Zaltzman, Hillel. *Samarkand: The Underground With A Far-Reaching Impact.* New York: Chamah, 2015.

INDEX

ABOUT THE AUTHORS

PHILIP WEXLER is Executive Director of the Institute of Jewish Spirituality and Society, and emeritus Professor of Sociology of Education and Unterberg Chair in Jewish Social and Educational History at the Hebrew University of Jerusalem. He was formerly at the University of Rochester as the Scandling Professor of Education and Sociology, where he was also Founding Dean of the Warner Graduate School (1989–2000). He later served as Director of the School of Education at the Hebrew University of Jerusalem (2002–2010), Visiting Bronfman Professor at Brandeis University (2010–2012), and Professor of Social Pedagogy and Social Policy at the Bergische University, Wuppertal, Germany (2012–2014). He received his Ph.D. in Sociology and Anthropology from Princeton University, where he was a Woodrow Wilson Fellow and Woodrow Wilson Dissertation Fellow. He has published eighteen books on sociology, education, postmodernism and religion.

ELI RUBIN is an editor and research writer at Chabad.org, and a graduate research student in the Department of Hebrew and Jewish Studies, University College London. He has studied Hasidic literature and Jewish Law at the Rabbinical College of America, and at yeshivot in the UK, the US and Australia.

MICHAEL WEXLER is a Princeton University graduate with a degree in English Literature and a master's of fine arts (MFA) in creative writing. He has published six books of both fiction and non-fiction, including the acclaimed young-adult fantasy series *The Seems*. He has served as an Adjunct Professor of writing at The University of Missouri-Kansas City and is the creator of projects for Fox, ABC, Microsoft, AFLAC, SiriusXM Radio, and more.